The Partition of India

The British divided and quit India in 1947. The Partition of India and the creation of Pakistan uprooted entire communities and left unspeakable violence in its trail. This volume – by two highly regarded scholars in this field – tells the story of Partition through the events that led up to it and the terrors that accompanied it, to migration and resettlement. In a new shift in the understanding of this seminal moment, the book also explores the legacies of Partition which continue to resonate today in the fractured lives of individuals and communities, and more broadly in the relationship between India and Pakistan and the ongoing conflict over contested sites such as Jammu and Kashmir. In conclusion, the book reflects on the general implications of partition as a political solution to ethnic and religious conflict. The book, which is accompanied by photographs, maps and a chronology of major events, is intended for students as a portal into the history and politics of the Asian region.

Ian Talbot is Professor of History at the University of Southampton. His recent publications include *The Deadly Embrace: Religion, Politics and Violence in India and Pakistan 1947–2002* (ed., 2007) and *Divided Cities: Partition and its Aftermath in Lahore and Amritsar 1947–1957* (2006).

Gurharpal Singh is Nadir Dinshaw Professor of Inter-Religious Relations in the Department of Theology and Religion at the University of Birmingham. His recent publications include *Governance in Multicultural Societies* (ed. with John Rex, 2004) and *Culture and Economy in the Indian Diaspora* (ed. with Bhikhu Parekh and Steven Vertovec, 2003).

New Approaches to Asian History

This dynamic new series will publish books on the milestones in Asian history, those that have come to define particular periods or mark turning-points in the political, cultural and social evolution of the region. Books are intended as introductions for students to be used in the classroom. They are written by scholars, whose credentials are well established in their particular fields and who have, in many cases, taught the subject across a number of years.

Books in the series
Judith M. Brown, *Global South Asians: Introducing the Modern Diaspora*
Diana Lary, *China's Republic*
Peter A. Lorge, *The Asian Military Revolution: From Gunpowder to the Bomb*
Ian Talbot and Gurharpal Singh, *The Partition of India*

The Partition of India

Ian Talbot
University of Southampton

and

Gurharpal Singh
University of Birmingham

CAMBRIDGE
UNIVERSITY PRESS

CAMBRIDGE UNIVERSITY PRESS
Cambridge, New York, Melbourne, Madrid, Cape Town, Singapore,
São Paulo, Delhi

Cambridge University Press
The Edinburgh Building, Cambridge CB2 8RU, UK

Published in the United States of America by Cambridge University Press,
New York

www.cambridge.org
Information on this title: www.cambridge.org/9780521672566

First published 2009

Printed in the United Kingdom at the University Press, Cambridge

A catalogue record for this publication is available from the British Library

ISBN 978-0-521-85661-4 hardback
ISBN 978-0-521-67256-6 paperback

Contents

Maps

Plates

Figures

Acknowledgements

Our major debt is to all those who, over the years, have nurtured and sustained our interest in the study of the Partition of India, first as research students, and then as colleagues within the Punjab Studies network. Foremost among these are Professor Judith Brown, Professor Paul R. Brass, Professor Francis Robinson and Professor Uday S. Mehta. No less significant have been our colleagues and friends, of whom the following deserve a special mention: Professor Mohammad Waseem, Dr Yunas Samad, Dr Sarah Ansari, Dr Joya Chatterji, Professor Iftikhar H. Malik, Professor Imran Ali, Professor Tan Tai Yong, Dr Gyanesh Kudaisya, Professor David Gilmartin and Dr Darshan S. Tatla. We have also drawn much encouragement from a younger generation of scholars whose work on partition we have seen develop over the past decade. They include Dr Yasmin Khan, Dr Pippa Virdee and Dr Ravinder Kaur.

We would like to record our thanks to all those who participated in the 'Partition Conference' to commemorate the sixtieth anniversary of the independence of India and Pakistan, held at the University of Southampton between 17 and 20 July 2007. The ideas that flowed from that gathering have fed into this publication in a number of ways. The sterling organisation of Professor Chris Woolgar, Head of the Special Collections, should be acknowledged, as should the financial contribution of the Hansard Trust to making the occasion such a memorable event.

Marigold Acland deserves special praise for her encouragement during all stages of the work. We thank her for persevering with us even when, at times, it appeared that the book would not see the light of day. The task of writing on such a sensitive area with its contested and complex scholarship was both immensely challenging and infinitely rewarding.

We also record here our thanks to our respective institutions, University of Southampton and the University of Birmingham, for making research leave available to complete this work.

Finally, our major debt is to our families. This work has been long in the making and they have suffered inordinately as a result. We dedicate this work to Lois and Martin, and Raghu, Sukhmani and Harman for their patience and good humour during the years of commuting and incessant change.

March 2009
Ian Talbot University of Southampton
Gurharpal Singh University of Birmingham

Glossary

akhara	wrestling pit
anjuman	association
ansars	helpers; refers back to the inhabitants of Medina who assisted the Prophet and his followers after their flight from Medina
antahpur	inner household rooms
bait-ul-maal	Islamic treasury
Bangaals	Bengali refugees from East Bengal
bania	Hindu trading caste; the term was often used pejoratively to mean moneylender
batai	rent in kind
bhadralok	gentlefolk, respectable folk
bhadramahila	gentlewoman
biraderi	brotherhood, patrilineal kinship group
chak	village
chowk	crossroads, junction
crore	ten million
dacoit	criminal; *dacoities*: criminal actions, robberies
dargah	tomb, shrine of a Sufi saint
desh	native place; could refer to nation, province or village
doab	region lying between two rivers
dupatta	long scarf
ghallughara	massacre
goondas	thugs
gurdwara	Sikh temple
hakim	practitioner of Unani medicine
Harijan	member of Untouchable caste
hartal	strike, political protest
izzat	prestige, honour, reputation
jatha	band, armed group
jathedar	Sikh leader

jihad	striving, collective war against unbelief, or individual moral endeavour
jotedar	peasant farmer, usually one with large holdings
kafla	caravan, convoy of people
kanal	measurement of land, one twentieth of an acre
katra	originally fortified market, a residential locality
kothi	residential plot
kotwali	headquarters of city police
kucha	neighbourhood, residential quarters
lakh	one hundred thousand
langar	public kitchen in which free food is served at a Sufi shrine or gurdwara
lathi	wooden club
mali	gardener
mandir	Hindu temple
maulvi	learned Muslim
mela	a fair
mirasi	musician
misl	Sikh territorial unit; *misldar*: military chief
mohajir	refugee, Muslim who has fled for religious reasons
mohalla	neighbourhood
pir	Sufi spiritual guide
pukka	superior, often referring to a brick- or stone-built dwelling
pursharti	term used for Hindu refugee
qurbani	sacrifice
rais	an important, or honourable man
roti	bread, food
sahukar	moneylender
samadh	tomb associated with Sikh and Hindu holy men
Sant	saint or holy man; one who realises Truth (*sat*)
sardar	leader, chief
satyagraha	truth force, often referring to Gandhian non-violent struggle
sewa	Sikh community service, religious service
shuddhi	Hindu re-purification right, adopted by the Arya Samaj for conversion purposes
Sufi	Muslim mystic
swadeshi	home-produced goods
tehsil	major administrative sub-division of a district
udvastu	uprooted out of place, out of home

ulama	(pl. of *alim*) Muslims learned in Islamic religion
unani	medical system practised in some parts of the subcontinent
Zamindar	landholder
zila	revenue sub-division, district

Chronology

Main events leading to Independence and Partition, 1937–1947

1937	February	Provincial elections held under the terms of the 1935 Government of India Act. Congress wins 716 out of the 1,161 seats it contested. Muslim League, with the exception of Bengal, fares dismally in the Muslim-majority provinces.
	July	Congress forms ministries in seven Indian provinces. Failure to create coalition ministry with Muslim League in United Provinces (UP).
	October	Reorganisation of Muslim League at its Lucknow session. Muslim prime ministers of Assam, Bengal and Punjab advise their followers to join All-India Muslim League.
1938	December	Jinnah at Patna League session raises the spectre of 'Congress Fascism'. Pirpur Report published into Muslim grievances in Congress-ruled provinces.
1939	March	Shareef Report into the grievances of Muslims in Bihar.
	September	Outbreak of Second World War.
	October	Tenancy Act passed in UP. Sind Muslim League Conference calls for examination of future constitutional proposals designed to safeguard the Muslim national interest. Resignation of Congress Provincial Ministries.
	December	Muslim League celebrates 'Deliverance Day' from Congress rule.
1940	March	Lahore Resolution for a Pakistan state raised at Muslim League Annual Session.
	August	Viceroy Lord Linlithgow sets out in his 'August Offer' plans for an expanded Executive Council and new War Advisory Council. Assurance given

		that power will not be transferred to any government whose authority is denied by important elements in India.
	October	Congress launches individual civil disobedience.
1941	May	By this date over 25,000 *satyagrahis* had been convicted for offering individual civil disobedience.
	July	Viceroy enlarges his Executive Council and creates National Defence Council. Jinnah successfully gets Muslim prime ministers of Assam, Punjab and Bengal to resign from the latter body in a demonstration of his authority in All-India Muslim politics.
	December	USA enters the war after the Japanese attack on Pearl Harbor on 7th.
1942	February	Fall of Singapore to the Japanese on 15th.
	March	Mission of Sir Stafford Cripps to India. Key promise of Dominion Status at the end of the war, with the proviso that provinces would have the right to opt out. Cripps Mission widens gulf between British and Congress.
	April	Congress launches Quit India movement. This becomes the gravest challenge to British authority since 1857. Congress is declared an unlawful organisation and most of its leaders spend the remainder of the war years in jail.
1943	October	Wavell replaces Linlithgow as Viceroy. One of his first acts is to fly to Calcutta to see the effects of the devastating famine in Bengal.
1944	April	Gandhi is released from custody on medical grounds.
	September	Gandhi–Jinnah talks fail but Jinnah's prestige is further enhanced.
1945	March–June	Wavell in London for discussions over India's future.
	June	Simla Conference to discuss the formation of a new Executive Council convenes on 25th.
	July	Clement Attlee becomes prime minister after Labour Party general election victory. Simla Conference fails over Jinnah's insistence that all

		Muslim members of the Executive Council must be Muslim League nominees.
	August	Surrender of Japan on 14th ends Second World War.
1946	January	Provincial elections in India see a Muslim League triumph in the Majority 'Pakistan' provinces.
	March–June	Cabinet Mission to India. Proposal for a three-tiered Indian Union initially accepted by Congress and Muslim League, but then rejected when Nehru questions the grouping arrangements of the provinces.
	August	Muslim League observes 'Direct Action Day' on 16th. The 'Great Calcutta Killing' on 16th–18th. Around 4,000 victims and 100,000 people made homeless.
	October	Communal killing spreads to Noakhali in East Bengal. Gandhi undertakes foot-pilgrimage for peace. Muslim League joins the Interim Government, but is accused by Congress of attempting to wreck it.
	November	Muslims massacred in Bihar. Wavell estimates the death toll at between 5,000 and 10,000. Over 120,000 Muslims made homeless.
	December	Failed meeting of Jinnah, Nehru and Baldev Singh in London. Constituent Assembly meets on 9th without Muslim League members. Attlee offers the Viceroyalty to Mountbatten.
1947	February	Attlee announces on 20th that the British will leave India by June 1948, and that Mountbatten is to succeed Wavell as Viceroy.
	March	Resignation of Khizr Tiwana Coalition Government in Punjab sparks off widespread communal violence. Mountbatten arrives in India on 22nd.
	April	Mountbatten has meetings with Indian political leaders to the backdrop of endemic violence in the Punjab which is now under direct Governor's rule.
	May	Work begins on the plan for Partition. When Nehru is confidentially made aware of it, he sees it as a threat of Balkanisation and the plan has to be

redrafted. Dominion Status enables the plan to be accelerated.

June — The Indian leaders accept the 3 June Partition plan. The machinery for Partition is established including a Partition Council and Boundary Commission. Mountbatten announces that the date for Independence is to be brought forward from June 1948 to 15 August 1947. The States Department is created to oversee relations between the States and the successor governments.

July — Sir Cyril Radcliffe, the Chairman of the Punjab and Bengal Boundary Commissions, arrives in India on 8th. Draft Standstill Agreement and Draft Instrument of Accession created for the States between 26 and 31 July.

August — Jinnah and Mountbatten attend the Independence celebrations in Karachi on 14 August and address the Pakistan Constituent Assembly.

Celebration of Indian Independence in New Delhi on 15th. Massacres and migrations on a large scale in Punjab. The Boundary Awards are announced on 17th August.

Introduction

Increased ethnic and religious violence in post-Cold War Europe, the Horn of Africa and the Middle East has rekindled academic and policy interest in partitions. Until recently, territorial divisions, either in the context of war or to regulate ethnic and communal conflict, were considered a mid-century relic of decolonisation. By the 1990s, however, there was renewed interest in the phenomenon, though some have argued that the late-twentieth-century 'partitions' affecting Yugoslavia, the USSR, Czechoslovakia and Ethiopia are best understood as 'secessions' because they did not involve 'fresh border cuts across a national homeland'.[1] Partitions, it has been persuasively argued, have traditionally involved imperial or external organisations (such as the UN) along with collaborationist insiders, and are distinguished from other kinds of territorial change by the fact that they involve the modification and transformation of borders rather than just their adjustment. Strictly speaking, modern incidences of 'pure' partitions are few and far between.[2]

In this volume we examine one of the leading twentieth-century examples of partition. Indeed, for many the Indian subcontinent's division in August 1947 is seen as a unique event which defies comparative historical and conceptual analysis. It is thus like the Holocaust, similarly capitalised in its rendering. The British transfer of power to the two dominions of India and Pakistan, like the earlier division of Ireland, was a response of imperial statecraft to intractable religious conflict. The carving of a Muslim homeland out of India also involved the partition of the provinces of Punjab and Bengal along Muslim and non-Muslim lines. In addition, Pakistan also received the undivided, Muslim-majority provinces of Sindh, Balochistan and the North West Frontier Province.

---

[1] Brendan O'Leary, 'Analysing Partition: Definition, Classification and Explanation', *Political Geography* 26, 8 (2007), pp. 886–908.
[2] O'Leary gives the following six examples which fit his definition: Ireland (1920); Hungary (1920); Kurdistan (1920–1923); India (1947); Palestine (1948); Cyprus (1974).

1

Although this strategy appears to have been followed contemporaneously in Palestine, leading some to argue that it was a peculiarly British practice at the time of imperial withdrawal,[3] documentary evidence overwhelmingly suggests an official reluctance to divide and quit India. Given that the British were 'reluctant partitionists', what impelled them to pursue this course of action? Was it because they not only had begun the democratisation of India from the early twentieth century onwards, but had also ruled indirectly and thereby, unintentionally, strengthened ethnic and communal cleavages? Was democratisation in a plural ethnic and communal setting a cause of Indian and later post-Cold War European 'partitions'? This volume through its detailed case study of the background to the causes and consequences of the 1947 division of the subcontinent aims to shed more light on these questions than hitherto.

Partitions in the name of conflict resolution have often been accompanied by heightened levels of violence that they sought to eliminate. As well as the social dislocation attendant on partition-related ethnic cleansing,[4] the divided states, as in the case of North and South Korea and India and Pakistan, can be locked into unremitting enmity or 'enduring conflicts' as they translate their internal differences into inter-state rivalries. Significantly, at the dawn of the twenty-first century, the fears of nuclear conflict are most pronounced in two regions: Korea and the Indian subcontinent. This study with its focus on India and Pakistan provides opportunities for appraising the aftermath of partition as a policy option in situations of ethnic and communal conflict. The sheer magnitude of the territorial division and the accompanying demographic transformation that took place dwarfs all other historical precedents.

Clearly the British had reluctantly conceded India's Partition to avoid civil war. Yet Pakistan's birth coincided with the intensification of the violence which had wracked north India during the final year of colonial rule. Its epicentre lay in the Punjab, but the shock waves were felt across the subcontinent. Communal massacres sparked a chaotic two-way flight of Hindus and Sikhs from Pakistan and Muslims from India. In all an estimated 15 million people were displaced in what became the largest forced migration in the twentieth century. The death toll remains disputed to this day, with figures ranging from 200,000 to 2 million. Families were separated and nearly 100,000 women were kidnapped on both sides

---

[3] C. Hitchens, 'The Perils of Partition', *Atlantic Monthly* (March 2003), pp. 99–107.

[4] Partitions are regularly accompanied by exchange of populations. This often involves: (i) voluntary (anticipatory) migration; (ii) forced migration; (iii) ethnic cleansing; or (iv) genocide. In the Indian case, as we shall see in chapters three and four, the historiography often uses these terms interchangeably.

of the border. Women were especially victimised because they symbolised community 'honour'.

Over sixty years on, the effects of 1947 continue to impact on both state and society. India and Pakistan, two nuclear-armed states, remain in uneasy dialogue, and the 'unfinished businesses of partition', the Jammu and Kashmir dispute, still makes them 'distant neighbours'. Millions of families still carry the psychological and physical scars of uprooting. All major cities in the north of the subcontinent still possess their clearly demarcated refugee quarters. The volume will explore the political geographies arising from this refugee population and the extent to which refugees and their descendents have retained a distinctive cultural and political presence.

Partitions have seldom been reversed, whatever new difficulties they have brought in their wake. Of course, in the post-Cold War world, Germany was reunited in 1989, and Korea and Ireland may also go the same way as a 'hard' partition gives way increasingly to a 'soft' association. Nonetheless statecraft, geopolitics and demography all provide high thresholds to the reversal of partition. We will consider how significant these factors have been in the context of the subcontinent and the extent to which India and Pakistan have moved further apart from each other in the years since Independence.

Importantly both states have been internally shaped more by the division of 1947 than is publicly acknowledged. As Paul Brass has shown, a legacy of partition was the unwritten 'informal rule' that political demands based on religion were impermissible for the Indian state.[5] Within Pakistan, any pretensions to provincial autonomy were abandoned almost on the achievement of independence. Centralisation was accompanied by a homogenising response to national identity which regarded pluralism as a threat. Pakistan's national ideology was constructed around Urdu as the official language and an increasing attachment to Islam. Yet neither provided the necessary cohesion. The growing identification of Punjab with the interests of the Army further alienated the smaller 'nationalities'. There has been a tendency in both India and Pakistan to de-legitimise demands for greater autonomy and treat them as a law-and-order issue. Both states have thus used heavy-handed repression especially when subnationalist demands have been raised in the sensitive border areas. Some writers have gone so far as to speak of a 'fearful state' in South Asia.[6]

---

[5] See P. Brass, *Language, Religion and Politics in North India* (Cambridge University Press, 1974).

[6] S. Mahmud Ali, *The Fearful State: Power, People and Internal Wars in South Asia* (London: Zed Books, 1993).

This volume also examines how ideas as well as policies have flowed from the effects of the 1947 division. It seeks to assess the extent to which the partition experience strengthened the ideologies of secularism and the two-nation theory on which the two states had been founded. The 1947 disturbances revealed the dangers of communalism and thereby strengthened the claims of secularism within the Congress. At the same time, the violence reinforced the claims of the two-nation theory that there were irreconcilable differences between Hindus and Muslims. As Partition replaced the abstract imagery of an Indian Muslim nation with the harsh reality of a territorially limited state of Pakistan, it created the paradox that a homeland made in the name of all Indian Muslims was incapable of accommodating all those who wanted to migrate to the new state. Ironically, this state could only fulfil its 'duty' to Muslims in India if it treated its own minorities well.[7] Hence repeated appeals were made in the early months of Independence for the Hindu and Sikh population of Sindh to continue living in the new Muslim state.[8]

So rich is partition as an ideological resource that its possibilities are continuously reconstructed at both state and community level. For the Sikh community, for example, it has become a source of reaffirmation of its self-identity in which violence, valour and martyrdom take a central place with episodes of female suicide to protect family and community *izzat* (honour) valorised as the ultimate sacrifice. For post-Independence states, the project of 'rehabilitating' the millions of refugees became inextricably bound up with cultivating new sources of legitimacy when the very premises of new nation-statehood stood on extremely insecure foundations. Both the Indian and Pakistan states went into overdrive to highlight the heroic and improvised efforts to feed, clothe and house the unintended victims of independence. Subsequently, notwithstanding the generally unfavourable assessment of these efforts by their recipients, the post-colonial nation-state in India and Pakistan was to invest a great deal of energy into carefully reconstructing the official record and embedding it in the conscious design of nation- and state-building.

One of the major shortcomings of existing research on partition is that it is overwhelmingly Indian Punjab-centric. This pattern was first established in the 1950s with official and semi-official publications that had

[7] This was the so-called hostage theory. It was initially undermined by the mass exchange of population in Punjab. The exodus of Hindus and Sikhs from Sindh from January 1948 onwards dealt it a further blow. A large Hindu population remained in East Pakistan.

[8] There were also good economic reasons for encouraging this population to remain. In addition Sindhi Muslim politicians such as M. A. Khuhro saw the retention of Sindhi Hindus as important for the cultural life of the province which was endangered by the influx of Urdu- or Punjabi-speaking Muslim refugees.

their own particular motives. Although the state was undoubtedly a key player in the resettlement process, the same however cannot be said in West Bengal. In this book we will consider why the Bengal experience did not lend itself to official construction in the same way as that of Punjab. Central to this understanding is the fact that migration in Bengal came in waves after 1947 right until the mid-1950s. Thereafter migrants continued to be uprooted whenever there were serious communal riots elsewhere in India or when the cold war between India and Pakistan threatened to heat up. We also, where possible, aim to evaluate the contribution of West and East Pakistan authorities in dealing with equally, if not more, onerous tasks of rehabilitating refugees in what were near-chaotic conditions for the then-fledgling state.

This study will thus attempt to broaden the understanding of the subcontinent's division by looking *beyond* Indian Punjab by drawing on literature on regional developments in West Punjab, East and West Bengal, Jammu and Kashmir, Sindh, the princely states, and the north-eastern states of India. As well as broadening the regional coverage, we will examine how the experiences of violence, migration and resettlement were mediated by gender, existing structures of power and accepted norms and conventions about caste and community. These mediations, as we shall see in subsequent chapters, were to be crucial in shaping the development of resettled communities.

Central to our approach is to recognise the seismic shift that has taken place in the historiography of the Partition in the last three decades from 'high politics', with its emphasis on the causes of the division, to its 'human consequences' in which there is a greater reliance on subjective individual and collective experiences drawn from oral testimonies and personal memories. In many ways this new emphasis has been a necessary corrective to the fixation with power politics, and brings into sharp focus previously neglected and unproblematised groups and perspectives – gender, subaltern groups, marginalised regions and the need for greater reflectivity of the sources and their reading. Yet these innovations, we contend, only become meaningful if they retain some measure of understanding of the broader developments that have framed the Partition and the post-Partition processes. Such recognition, we believe, will enable a more comprehensive evaluation of the Partition as an historical event as well as a living reality for the contemporary subcontinent.

Accordingly, the structure of the volume reflects these concerns. The opening chapter reviews the partition historiography and outlines the major developments that have taken place in scholarship since the early 1980s in changing our understanding of the reading of 1947 of its causes and consequences, as well as the new approaches for re-examining the human consequences that centre on gender and subaltern studies. In chapter two we return to the historical background to the emergence of Pakistan and the partition of Punjab and Bengal, evaluating critically the 'inevitability' of division and the contribution of Indian as well as British actors in the *dénouement* of the Raj. The violence and the turmoil which accompanied 1947 is the subject of the next chapter. Here we explore the arguments as to whether the violence was spontaneous or planned, and in particular the utility of such concepts as 'genocide' and 'ethnic cleansing' to understand what happened. The chapter also brings to our attention the contemporaneous nature of partition violence by drawing out the remarkable similarities in the post-1947 Indian experience of managing communal riots. Large-scale violence was, of course, followed by the mass transfers of Hindu, Sikh and Muslim populations. Chapter four explores in detail the different patterns of migration histories of refugee resettlement and rehabilitation, examining the contrast between East Punjab and West Bengal. But the impact of migration and violence was more enduring than in 1947: it was to leave a lasting imprint on post-1947 nation- and state-building projects in India and Pakistan, and create new forms of ethnic consolidation among the migrants, as well as to reinvent old religious nationalism among the heartlands. These processes are assessed in chapter five where we examine why the Partition created centralised states against further partitions, especially in the border provinces that were often reluctant or hostile bedfellows of Indian and Pakistani nationalisms. Finally, chapter six examines the legacy of 1947 for Indo-Pakistan relations. It looks both at the central Jammu and Kashmir dispute and at a wider range of influences which have determined the relations between the two successor states to the Raj and the prospects for overcoming the troubled legacy since decolonisation. The volume concludes by reflecting on the broader partition literature and the implications of the Indian case-study for the wider understanding of partitions and their aftermath in situations of intense ethnic and communal conflict.

1   Understanding the Partition historiography

The final period of colonial rule in India from 1945 onwards was dominated by one consideration: the manner and the timing of the British
departure. A key thought for imperial statecraft was to protect economic
and strategic interests in the transition to independence while negotiating a
settlement with the Congress and Muslim League leaders. In some measure the dangers of a disorderly British withdrawal were mitigated by the
success of the Labour Party, which possessed good lines of communication
with the Congress leadership. At the same time, there was a pressing need
to politically accommodate the growing influence of the Muslim League
that posed a basic threat to the idea of a united, post-colonial India with its
demand for a separate Muslim homeland of Pakistan. In the event, the
endgame of the empire was conducted against a crescendo of violence that
began with the Great Calcutta Killing of August 1946 and climaxed in the
genocidal violence after 15 August 1947. This violence was orchestrated
with political purpose and organisation resulting in near civil war conditions
in north India where religion alone defined the basis of political identity.
And in these circumstances, partition emerged as a practical solution which
the Indian political elites accepted reluctantly with the 3 June 1947 Plan
that agreed to transfer power to two dominions: India and the Muslim-
majority provinces (Punjab, Sindh, Bengal, Baluchistan and North West
Frontier Province). The glow of freedom arrived but at the cost of division.
The partition of India was accompanied by the partition of Bengal and
Punjab into their Muslim and non-Muslim majority areas. Muslims
established a territorial homeland, but it was a truncated, 'moth-eaten'
Pakistan. Indeed, the conflicting claims surrounding the demarcation of
the new international boundary in Bengal and Punjab, along with tussles
over the division of assets between the two states, meant that the 3 June
Plan ushered in a new period of uncertainty and hostility, rather than a
dampening of the embers of religious hatred. Thus when the British finally
'divided and quit' after 15 August 1947, their departure was accompanied
by large-scale disturbances in the Punjab for which the newly independent
Indian and Pakistan states were totally unprepared – violence that resulted

in mass migrations and a total exchange of population along religious lines in the Punjab region. Partition produced the largest migration in the twentieth century that continued unabated in Bengal well into the mid-1950s and beyond. It was to leave a legacy of bitter hatred and resentment among the people and states of India and Pakistan alike.

Naturally, given the foundational nature of 1947 for the states of India and Pakistan and its immediate and long-term consequences, the events culminating in the division have produced a highly contested scholarship in which heroes and villains are all too obvious. In this study our aim is to bring together much of the recent literature on the background to Partition, its accompanying violence and the implications of the mass migrations for both individuals and the governance of post-Independence India and Pakistan. We argue that Partition was not the 'parting gift' of an outgoing imperial rule: rather the Congress and Muslim League leaders, both nationally and regionally, were heavily implicated in the outcome, especially in Bengal and Punjab. It is important when addressing the growing and bewildering body of work on the subject to keep in mind that compulsions of nation-building or community assertion have shaped historical writings, thereby producing selective histories and fragmented memories. Partition was more than a mere territorial division; it was foremost accompanied by a division of minds.

In this chapter, we assess the conflicting historical interpretations surrounding the British transfer of power and argue that no single interpretation can fully explain the complex developments surrounding Independence. We then move on to examine the increasing attention devoted to the 'human dimension' of partition – the new research arising from the turn to feminist history, psychologies of violence and the use of deconstructionist methodologies that have placed subjective experiences at the centre of their analysis. These approaches, as we shall note, have provided fascinating new departures from which to re-examine the event of 1947, but at the expense of encouraging fragmentation, particularism and localism that eschews the overarching reading of events. Our approach, in contrast, recognises these developments, but aims to synthesise the evidence from the new research into a broader understanding of the narrative around Partition.[1]

The historiography of the 'high politics' of Partition

The phrase the 'high politics' of Partition has become shorthand for the constitutional negotiations between the British and Indian leaders during

---

[1] For a recent example of a return to the narrative approach, see Yasmin Khan, *The Great Partition: The Making of India and Pakistan* (New Haven, CT: Yale University Press, 2007).

the 1940s, and is normally contrasted with the term 'history from below' which reflects a focus on the human consequences of partition. Students of high politics, in contrast, are especially distinguished by their efforts to 'blame' individuals, parties and states. Take Bahadur's volume on the subject, for instance. It has as its subtitle the 'Tragedy of the Triumph of Muslim Communalism in India, 1906–1947'.[2] From the 1940s onwards, Congress authors maintained that Muslim communalism – a form of identity politics based on religion[3] – was a British creation designed to weaken nationalist struggle against imperial rule.[4] The road to 1947, they insist, was laid in 1909 when the colonial state succumbed to the Muslim League's lobbying for separate electorates based on religious lines to the newly introduced representative institutions.

The thesis that the Muslim League's intransigence forced the Congress to accept the division of the country in 1947 was restated in 2000 in Sucheta Mahajan's *Independence and Partition*[5] in which she boldly claims that

Congress had regretfully accepted Partition as unavoidable [this] was only the final act of a process of step-by-step concession of the League's intransigent championing of a sovereign Muslim state … If Partition was the most traumatic event of the century, then independence was surely the most significant turning point.[6]

Mahajan replays the nationalist lament of Muslim League stubbornness, the regrettable character of partition and the need to emphasise the greater

---

[2] See Lal Bahadur, *Struggle for Pakistan: Tragedy of the Triumph of Muslim Communalism in India, 1906–1947* (New Delhi: Sterling, 1988).

[3] There is a vast literature on communalism. This is variously seen as a creation of deliberate British 'divide and rule' strategies, or of the unintentional consequences of a modernising state that organised political representation from 1909 onwards around notions of a distinctive religious identity as enumerated in the census surveys. Officials argued that, as representation was extended, the 'backward' Muslim community needed separate electorates to safeguard its interests. While it is facile to argue that the introduction of separate electorates made Pakistan inevitable, it lent credence to the premise that people following a particular religion naturally shared common interests from which 'others' were excluded. The other side of the coin of separate electorates is the idea that the British not only created new political arenas for competition along religious lines, but by withdrawing patronage from public religious ceremonial in an attempt to demonstrate religious neutrality, created a space for competing groups drawn from the rising Hindu merchant classes to sponsor public ritual to enhance their 'social dignity'. Public ritual not only helped create a supra-local Hindu community identity but was a factor in rising tension between 'Hindus' and 'Muslims'.

[4] See Rajendra Prasad, *India Divided*, 3rd edn (Bombay: Hind Kitabs, 1947); Humayn Kabir, *Muslim Politics, 1906–1942* (Calcutta: Gupta, Rahman, Gupta, 1943); Asoka Mehta and Achut Patwardhan, *The Communal Triangle in India* (Allahabad: Kitabistan, 1942).

[5] Sucheta Mahajan, *Independence and Partition: The Erosion of Colonial Power in India* (New Delhi: Sage, 2000).

[6] Mahajan, *Independence and Partition*, pp. 393 and 391.

achievement of Indian independence – all familiar themes in Indian nationalist accounts.[7]

In contrast, the traditional Pakistani approach to the 'high politics' of Independence is to eschew the term 'partition' because it is viewed as a politically loaded concept which echoes the Hindu Right's preoccupation with the 'loss' of national unity. Moreover to say that India was partitioned is to acknowledge the fact that Pakistan was a *seceding* power from an Indian state that had inherited sovereignty from British India. Official histories therefore focus on the achievement of Pakistan in which its birth is thus generally explained in terms of the Muslim League's historic creed of the two-nation theory that maintained that the Indian Muslims' identity was defined by religion rather than language or ethnicity. Islam, these accounts always insist, had given birth to a distinctive social order that was fundamentally at odds with Hindu society. The demand for a separate state was thus a 'natural' expression of this reality.[8] The doyen of this understanding was Ishtiaq Hussain Qureshi of Karachi University,[9] though more sophisticated works within this genre have emerged among Pakistani scholars resident in the west.[10] K. bin Sayeed has perhaps provided the clearest exposition of this thesis. 'There has never taken place', according to him,

[a] confluence of the two civilisations in India – the Hindu and the Muslim. They may have meandered towards each other here and there, but on the whole the two have flowed their separate courses – sometimes parallel and sometimes contrary to one another.[11]

Beyond stating the inevitability of Pakistan as the realisation of Muslim destiny, many studies find it sufficient merely to list the documents around the Pakistan idea, or to provide potted biographies of eminent nationalist leaders[12] that chronicle the struggle to achieve a separate state against overwhelming odds in which Muslim League leaders were

[7] See for example, Bimal Prasad, 'Jawaharlal Nehru and Partition', in Amrik Singh (ed.), *The Partition in Retrospect* (New Delhi: Animika Publishers, 2000) pp. 27–47.

[8] For an understanding of how this 'communal' historical consciousness was constructed see the following works: S. Rahman, *Why Pakistan?* (Lahore: Islamic Book Service, 1946); F. K. Durrani, *The Meaning of Pakistan* (Lahore: Muhammad Ashraf, 1944).

[9] See for example his book, *The Muslim Community of the Indo-Pakistan Subcontinent (610–1947): A Brief Historical Analysis*, 2nd edn (Karachi: Ma'aref, 1977)

[10] See Hafeez Malik, *Moslem Nationalism in India and Pakistan* (Washington, DC: Public Affairs Press, 1963); Khalid bin Sayeed, *Pakistan: The Formative Phase, 1857–1948* (Oxford University Press, 1968)

[11] Sayeed, *The Formative Phase*, p. 12.

[12] Typical of this approach is A. H. Albiruni, *Makers of Pakistan and Modern Muslim India* (Lahore: Muhammad Ashraf, 1950).

constantly check-mated by Gandhi, Nehru and Mountbatten.[13] Yet one crucial element that differentiates Pakistan nationalist historiography from its Indian counterpart is bitterness about the alleged British 'unfair' treatment of Muslim League interests.

A less partisan group of scholars who have utilised the 'high politics' approach have concentrated their studies on the impact of developments in South Asia flowing from the Second World War. For them the major concern has been to identify the influences from the war experience that undermined the long-term colonial capacity for governance – ground-level mobilisation by the Congress, wartime international relations, especially the alliance with the anti-imperialist US, and the exigencies of the war effort in South Asia which was in the frontline of the Japanese advance.[14] Writers such as Rizvi, Moore and Singh maintain that the short-term policy of marginalising the non-cooperating Congress (which was anti-war and led a national 'Quit India' agitation from 1942) during the war years, by bolstering the position of the Muslim League and Jinnah from 1940 onwards, ultimately jeopardised the long-term British commitment to a united India.[15] These were undoubtedly seismic developments that transformed the pre-war equipoise between the colonial state and Congress and the Muslim League, but in these readings there is also a danger of over-reading British intentionality as the final arbiter. After all, the logic of outcomes in 1947, arguably, was defined equally by the drive for national power by the Congress and the Muslim League from the 1946 elections onwards.

---

[13] Latif Ahmed Sherwani, *The Partition of India and Mountbatten* (Karachi: Council for Pakistan Studies, 1986).

[14] On the war and administrative decline see: D. C. Potter, 'Manpower Shortage and the End of Colonialism: The Case of the Indian Civil Service', *Modern Asian Studies* 7 (1973), pp. 47–73; Simon Epstein, 'District Officers in Decline: The Erosion of British Authority in the Bombay Countryside, 1919 to 1947', *Modern Asian Studies* 16 (1982), pp. 493–518. On the growing challenges arising from popular agitation see: F. G. Hutchins, *India's Revolution: Gandhi and the Quit India Movement* (Cambridge, MA: Harvard University Press, 1973); Sucheta Mahajan, 'British Policy, Nationalist Strategy and Popular National Upsurge, 1945–1946', in Amit Kumar Gupta (ed.), *Myth and Reality: The Struggle for Freedom in India, 1945–47* (New Delhi: Manohar, 1987), pp. 54–98; Sumit Sarkar, *Modern India, 1885–1947* (New Delhi: Macmillan, 1983). On India's declining value to Britain, see B. R. Tomlinson, *The Political Economy of the Raj, 1914–47: The Economics of Decolonisation in India* (London: Macmillan, 1979); on international pressures for decolonisation, see Wm. Roger Louis, *The British Empire in the Middle East, 1945–51: Arab Nationalism, the United States and Postwar Imperialism* (Oxford: Clarendon, 1984); Alan Bullock, *Ernest Bevin: Foreign Secretary, 1945–1951*, 3 vols (London: Heinemann, 1983).

[15] Gowher Rizvi, *Linlithgow and India: A Study of British Policy and the Political Impasse in India, 1936–43* (London: Royal Historical Society, 1978); R. J. Moore, *Churchill, Cripps and India, 1939–1945* (Oxford: Clarendon Press, 1979); Anita Inder Singh, *The Origins of the Partition of India, 1936–1947* (New Delhi: Oxford University Press, 1987).

Many of the traditional assumptions shared by the above scholars have been questioned by Ayesha Jalal in a strikingly original contribution that claims that Jinnah's real political objective from 1940 (when the Muslim League passed the resolution calling for Pakistan) was for an equal parity for Muslims in an All-India polity.[16] In this strategy the demand for Pakistan was primarily a bargaining counter to achieve this end. However Jinnah was finally forced to accept the 'moth-eaten' Pakistan offered by the 3 June Plan because it was the only realistic offer available to him by 1947 in a context where his political leverage had diminished significantly after the Second World War and where the British had announced the intention to leave India.

Jalal's bold reinterpretation of Jinnah's role has inevitably evoked strong criticism in India as well as in Pakistan.[17] A major difficulty with this interpretation, Jalal's critics argue, is its disregard for the power of cultural and religious ideals in the Pakistan movement.[18] For many Muslims, it is suggested, support for the Pakistan ideal was instinctive rather than a matter of political choice and calculation. Yet these criticisms notwithstanding, Jalal's revisionism has exerted a lasting impact on scholarship with some praising her critique of the orthodox view that Jinnah saw Partition as the only solution to India's communal question from March 1940 onwards.[19]

Similarly, Moore has argued that if the Conservatives – instead of Labour – had won the 1945 British general election then Jinnah might have achieved what Jalal believes he wanted – 'A full six-province Pakistan with subordinate Dominion Status, under a limited central authority reflecting the principle of parity and secured by British-commanded forces.'[20] That Attlee's administration replaced the Conservative-led coalition instead led to a historic tilt towards Indian nationalism rooted in Labour's traditional sympathy for the Congress;[21] it also, on *realpolitik*

---

[16] See A. Jalal, *The Sole Spokesman: Jinnah, the Muslim League and the Demand for Pakistan* (Cambridge University Press, 1985).

[17] See V. N. Datta, 'Interpreting Partition', in Amrik Singh (ed.), *The Partition in Retrospect* (New Delhi: Anamika Publishers, 2000), pp. 274–87.

[18] Akbar S. Ahmed, *Jinnah, Pakistan and Islamic Identity: The Search for Saladin* (London: Routledge, 1997), p. 30.

[19] Asim Roy, 'The High Politics of India's Partition: The Revisionist Perspective', in Mushirul Hasan (ed.), *India's Partition: Process, Strategy and Mobilization* (Delhi: Oxford University Press, 1994), pp. 101–31.

[20] Robin J. Moore, 'India in the 1940s', in Robin W. Winks (ed.), *Historiography*, vol. 5, *The Oxford History of the British Empire* (Oxford University Press, 2001), p. 239.

[21] In addition to Cripps's well-documented interest in India, it should be noted that Attlee had been a member of the Indian Statutory Commission (1927–1930) chaired by Sir John Simon. The Labour members of the wartime Coalition Government had been active in attempting to secure Congress participation in a reformed central executive.

grounds, ensured that Britain would not impose a settlement that Congress opposed. Indeed, pressing domestic political considerations and imperial commitments, according to Moore, necessitated that London would do all in its power to achieve an orderly withdrawal,[22] and as the endgame of empire approached, British and Congress interests intersected in the need for a speedy handover to a strong Indian centre. Partition, with a considerably reduced Pakistan, by the early months of 1947 seemed to offer a means to achieve these goals.

Revisionist historians of high politics have also sought to reassess the controversial role of the last Viceroy of India, the flamboyant Louis Mountbatten, who is 'blamed' for accelerating the British departure and thereby creating the circumstances for the massacres and mass migrations which accompanied it. As we have already noted, he is also regarded as a partisan figure by Pakistani scholars because of his close ties with Nehru which, it is alleged, led him to influence the process of boundary demarcation in Punjab, thereby giving New Delhi all-year road access to the princely state of Jammu and Kashmir (see p. 48). Pakistani criticisms of Mountbatten have found favour with western scholars such as Andrew Roberts and Stanley Wolpert,[23] both of whom are trenchant in their criticism of Mountbatten's failings as Viceroy that they see rooted in his personality which was marked by impetuosity and vanity. Mountbatten's position has received weighty support from his official biographer Philip Ziegler, as well as from the commissioned work of H. V. Hodson[24] and the diary of Alan Campbell-Johnson.[25] Despite the lively and intemperate debates about the final Viceroyalty, it needs to be remembered that emphasis on Mountbatten's personality obscures the extent to which he was carrying out policy, rather than making it. It also occludes the pressures from below with the rising tide of religious violence which limited his room for manoeuvre.

The historiography of provincial politics and Partition

Whereas the high politics approach has focused on national and international developments which culminated in Partition, provincial-level

---

[22] R. J. Moore, *Escape from Empire: The Attlee Government and the Indian Problem* (Oxford: Clarendon, 1983); Singh, *The Origins of the Partition of India*.

[23] Andrew Roberts, *Eminent Churchillians* (London: Weidenfeld and Nicolson, 1994), pp. 55–137; Stanley Wolpert, *Shameful Flight: The Last Years of the British Empire in India* (New York: Oxford University Press, 2006).

[24] P. Ziegler, *Mountbatten: The Official Biography* (London: Collins, 1985); H. V. Hodson, *The Great Divide: Britain–India–Pakistan* (London: Hutchinson, 1969).

[25] A. Campbell-Johnson, *Mission with Mountbatten* (London: Hamilton, 1985).

studies have sought to explain how the Muslim League was able to secure credibility for its demands for a homeland in the main centres of Muslim population (Punjab, Bengal and Sindh) where it had been politically marginalised from the 1937 elections onwards. The earliest provincial-level studies, however, focused on United Provinces (UP) which was the birthplace of Muslim separatism. Provincial studies emerged in the early 1970s as a result of increasing access to official, private and party records,[26] and the simultaneous development of what became known as the Cambridge School of Indian history that was signalled by the now-seminal collection by John Gallagher, Gordon Johnson and Anil Seal, *Locality, Province and Nation.*[27] The Cambridge School, in its own modified version of 'high politics', saw elite self-interest, rather than ideas, as driving Indian nationalism, and refocused attention on intra-elite factional conflicts and the colonial state's role in framing provincial politics.[28] This new departure for studying the growth of Muslim separatism was explored in detail by Francis Robinson.[29]

Robinson was the first scholar to undertake a major study of the emergence of the Muslim separatist movement in UP, a minority-Muslim province but one in which the movement would provide leadership for the idea of Pakistan. According to him, this movement arose out of the interplay of a 'dynamic relationship' between 'visions of the ideal Muslim life' and political activity and both were inextricably entwined in the articulation of

---

[26] Scholars were not only able to access Provincial Governors' Fortnightly Reports but the twelve-volume series on the British Transfer of Power which appeared between 1970 and 1983 (Nicholas Mansergh, E. W. R. Lumby and Penderel Moon (eds), *Constitutional Relations Between Britain and India: The Transfer of Power 1942–7* (London: HMSO, 1970–83)). The first four volumes were edited by Nicholas Mansergh and E. W. R. Lumby, the remainder by Mansergh and Penderel Moon: vol. 1, *The Cripps Mission, Jan.–April 1942* (London: HMSO, 1970); vol. 2, *'Quit India', 30 April – 21 Sept. 1942* (London: HMSO, 1971); vol. 3, *Reassertion of Authority, Gandhi's Fast and the Succession to the Viceroyalty, 21 Sept. 1942 – 12 June 1942* (London: HMSO, 1971); vol. 4, *The Bengal Famine and the New Viceroyalty, 15 June 1943 – 31 Aug. 1944* (London: HMSO, 1973); vol. 5, *The Simla Conference, Background and Proceedings, 1 Sept. 1944 – 28 July 1945* (London: HMSO, 1974); vol. 6, *The Post-war Phase: New Moves by the Labour Government, 1 Aug. 1945 – 22 March 1946* (London: HMSO, 1976); vol. 7, *The Cabinet Mission, 23 March – 29 June 1946* (London: HMSO, 1977); vol. 8, *The Interim Government, 3 July – 1 Nov. 1946* (London: HMSO, 1979); vol. 9, *The Fixing of a Time Limit, 4 Nov. 1946 – 22 March 1947* (London: HMSO, 1980); vol. 10, *The Mountbatten Viceroyalty, Formulation of a Plan, 22 March – 30 May 1947* (London: HMSO, 1981); vol. 11, *The Mountbatten Viceroyalty, Announcement and Reception of the 3 June Plan, 31 May – 7 July 1947* (London: HMSO, 1982); vol. 12, *The Mountbatten Viceroyalty: Princes, Partition and Independence, 8 July – 15 Aug. 1947* (London: HMSO, 1983).

[27] John Gallagher, Gordon Johnson, Anil Seal (eds), *Locality, Province and Nation: Essays on Indian Politics, 1870–1940* (Cambridge University Press, 1973).

[28] For a sustained critique of the School, see Tapan Raychaudhuri, 'Indian Nationalism as Animal Politics', *Historical Journal* 22 (1979), pp. 747–63.

[29] Francis Robinson, *Separatism among Indian Muslims: The Politics of the United Provinces' Muslims 1860–1923* (Cambridge University Press, 1974).

Muslim political identity in the province. Robinson's thesis has also been supported by Farzana Shaikh who further elaborated this idea by arguing that the separatist platform was not primarily encouraged by colonial definitions of Indian society, or by a bid for power, but was inspired by Islamically derived values of political consensus and legitimacy that increasingly conflicted with liberal-democratic approaches to political representation.[30] Both these writers come close to a primordialist reading of ethnicity, one in which the political identity of being a Muslim is deemed immutable, unchanging and constant. Critics of this view, notably Paul Brass, who has also worked on identity politics among UP Muslims, insist that Muslim elites in the province self-consciously chose divisive historical symbols in order to mobilise popular support in their struggle for power with their Hindu counterparts.[31]

From UP, academic attention turned to the Muslim majority areas of north-west India (Punjab, NWFP and Sindh) that were the main battleground in the struggle for Pakistan. The work of David Gilmartin and Ian Talbot has sought to explain the ways in which the Muslim League – which was essentially a national organisation with little following in the provinces – finally overcame the entrenched power of the Unionist Party in the key Punjab province. Gilmartin has subtly revealed the underlying tensions during the Pakistan movement arising from the construction of a new ideological identity within the colonial state's structure of mediatory politics that were designed to deflect identity in favour of interest, especially of the cross-community alliance of Hindu, Muslim and Sikh landowners.[32] Similarly, Talbot has focused on the importance of elite factional realignment and the ways in which these and the Second World War undermined the structures that sustained the Unionists' basis of power.[33]

As well as UP and Punjab, recent scholarship has also provided important insights into how the Muslim League increased its influence in Sindh and the NWFP. In the latter, Erland Jansson has echoed the Punjab findings that its advance was linked to factional divisions.[34] He has shown that the Congress government of the Khan brothers was ultimately

---

[30] Farzana Shaikh, *Community and Consensus in Islam: Muslim Representation in Colonial India, 1860–1947* (Cambridge University Press, 1989).

[31] See Paul Brass, 'Elite Groups, Symbol Manipulation and Ethnic Identity among the Muslims of South Asia', in David Taylor and Malcolm Yapp (eds), *Political Identity in South Asia* (London: Curzon Press, 1979), pp. 35–77; Francis Robinson, 'Islam and Muslim Separatism', in Taylor and Yapp (eds), *Political Identity*, pp. 78–112.

[32] David Gilmartin, *Empire and Islam: Punjab and the Making of Pakistan* (Berkeley, CA: University of California Press, 1988), pp. 225–33.

[33] Ian Talbot, *Punjab and the Raj, 1849–1947* (New Delhi: Manohar, 1988).

[34] Erland Jansson, *India, Pakistan or Pakhtunistan? The Nationalist Movements in the North-West Frontier Province, 1937–47* (Uppsala: Acta Universitas Upsaliensis, 1981), pp. 159–65.

as unsuccessful as the Punjab Unionists in countering the groundswell of opinion in favour of the Muslim League arising from violence and polarisation of attitudes elsewhere in India. Sarah Ansari has echoed David Gilmartin's findings in Punjab in highlighting the crucial role of sufi *pirs*, in underpinning the Muslim League advance in Sindh.[35] Before these studies, 'high politics' accounts said little more about the role of Islam in mobilising support for Pakistan, beyond the fact that there was popular support for the vague slogan of 'Islam in danger'.

Regional studies of Muslim separatism in Bengal have somewhat lagged behind those on the Muslim-majority provinces in the north-west. The works of Shila Sen, Humaira Momen and Harun-or-Rashid have, however, highlighted the role played by Dacca University in popularising the Pakistan message, paralleling the achievements of University of Aligarh students in the north and west. They have also pointed out the importance of the Muslim *jotedar* peasants' shift in allegiance from the rival Krishak Praja Party of Fazlul Huq to the Muslim League in the run-up to 1947.[36] Suranjan Das has examined the polarisation of attitudes in Bengal from the perspective of communal riots. According to him these transformed community consciousness and thus became increasingly political in their overtones. Sugata Bose, on the other hand, portrays the unravelling of rural society along communal lines due to economic conditions which had been marked by 'symbiosis' as a result of the enmeshing of the agrarian economy in the world market in the 1930s and 1940s.[37]

Overall there are two common characteristics of the regional and local approaches: first, like the all-India studies, they are concerned with *why* partition occurred, rather than with its *consequences*; second, they point to continuities beyond the climacteric of August 1947. The first focus is largely intended as a corrective to the traditional emphasis on high politics, which omits vital details on how precisely support was mobilised, for example, in the Pakistan struggle. The latter stress how the provincial peculiarities – history, economic development, culture, language and, above all, the level of political development – shaped the fortunes of the successor states. As we shall see in subsequent chapters, Pakistan's

---

[35] Sarah Ansari, *Sufi Saints and State Power: The Pirs of Sind, 1843–1947* (Cambridge University Press, 1992).

[36] Shila Sen, *Muslim Politics in Bengal, 1937–47* (New Delhi: Impex India, 1976); Humaira Momen, *Muslim Politics in Bengal: A Study of the Krishak Praja Party and the Elections of 1937* (Dacca: Sunny House, 1972); Harun-or-Rashid, *The Foreshadowing of Bangladesh: Bengal Muslim League and Muslim Politics, 1936–1947* (Dhaka: Asiatic Society of Bangladesh, 1987).

[37] Sugata Bose, *Agrarian Bengal: Economy, Social Structure and Politics, 1919–1947* (Cambridge University Press, 1986).

inheritance of the colonial state's peripheral regions was to leave an indelible imprint on its post-1947 political development.

The historiography of the human dimension of Partition

What has been termed the 'new history' of Partition was pioneered by feminist writers and activists who emerged from an intellectual milieu in the early 1980s provided by the Subaltern Studies school of writing with its desire to restore agency to non-elite groups. As well as feminism and subaltern studies, the other major influences on new history were deconstructionist methodologies of postmodernism, post-structuralism and post-colonialism that sought to place the subject at the centre of their research.[38] In counter-distinction to 'high politics' and official histories, the victims of Partition, and principally women, became the new foci of research, a development reinforced by the contemporaneous revival of mass communal riots symbolised by the 1984 Delhi anti-Sikh riots following the assassination of the Indian premier Mrs Indira Gandhi by her Sikh bodyguards. Indeed, by drawing on the experience of assisting the victims of these riots and the complicity of the state and political groupings in the Delhi violence, Urvashi Butalia undertook a more systematic study of the female victims of the Partition violence. Her work *The Other Side of Silence* formed the seminal text that announced this new departure.[39]

Butalia's approach was extended by Ritu Menon and Kamla Bhasin's equally groundbreaking work entitled *Borders and Boundaries*, which examined in depth for the first time issues surrounding the rehabilitation of women who had been abducted during the 1947 Partition violence.[40] Butalia, Menon and Bhasin all demonstrated that women were the main victims both of 'other' male predators and of their own menfolk who killed them in order to save family and community 'honour'. Further suffering was occasioned by the fact that the Indian and Pakistan states coerced

---

[38] Historians, anthropologists and political scientists have all contributed to the subaltern-studies approach. This rests on the need to move away from a preoccupation with the colonial and nationalist elites and to study the underprivileged communities, not merely as victims or passive bystanders in history, but as agents with their own autonomous consciousness. The concept of a 'subaltern class' is drawn from Antonio Gramsci. The foundations of the Subaltern Studies school of Indian history were laid by Ranajit Guha's *Elementary Aspects of Peasant Insurgency in Colonial India* (Delhi: Oxford University Press, 1983). For an assessment of the achievements of the school of writers see Veena Das, 'Subaltern as Perspective', in Ranajit Guha (ed.), *Subaltern Studies: Writings on South Asian History and Society*, vol. VI (Delhi: Oxford University Press, 1989).

[39] Urvashi Butalia, *The Other Side of Silence: Voices from the Partition of India* (New Delhi: Penguin, 1998).

[40] R. Menon and K. Bhasin, *Borders and Boundaries: Women in India's Partition* (New Brunswick, NJ: Rutgers University Press, 1998).

abducted women to return to their homeland even when they had settled with new husbands and families.

The gendered approach, as its main proponents recognise, is very Indian and Punjab-centred.[41] Only Nighat Said Khan has published on Pakistani women's experience.[42] In fact, relatively little has been written about any aspects of the human dimension of the Pakistan experience, although there are now comparative studies of refugee resettlement in both the Pakistan and Indian Punjab following the work of Talbot and Virdee.[43]

Clearly the 'new history' has not only added a human face to bald statistics of deaths, abductions and refugee migrants, it has also provided victims – and to a much lesser extent aggressors – with a voice. The use of oral testimonies challenge state and community constructions of Partition with alternative sources of knowledge, as well as demonstrating that *all* communities had their own victims and aggressors, thereby undermining the stereotype of the 'other' community as the aggressor and perpetrator of violence. These testimonies have also revealed, as we shall see in chapters three and four, the differential experiences of violence, migration and resettlement that were previously subsumed in uniform official publications.[44]

Another major contribution of the 'new history' is to view Partition as a process rather than as an event confined to August 1947. For many years standard accounts tended to stop in 1947 without seriously considering whether continuities could be seen beyond this date, but recently historians have begun to explore these.[45] Oral testimonies reinforce these

---

[41] For a discussion of the difficulties of undertaking cross-border work, see Papiya Ghosh, *Partition and the South Asian Diaspora: Extending the Subcontinent* (London: Routledge, 2007), pp. xx–xxi.

[42] Nighat Said Khan, 'Identity, Violence and Women: A Reflection on the Partition of India, 1947', in Nighat Said Khan *et al.*, *Locating the Self: Perceptions on Women and Multiple Identities* (Lahore: ASR Publications, 1994), pp. 157–71.

[43] Ian Talbot, *Divided Cities: Partition and its Aftermath in Lahore and Amritsar 1947–1957* (Karachi: Oxford University Press, 2006); P. Virdee, 'Partition and Locality: Case Studies of the Impact of Partition and its Aftermath in the Punjab Region 1947–61', unpublished PhD thesis, Coventry University, 2005.

[44] See Ravinder Kaur, *Since 1947: Partition Narratives among Punjabi Migrants of Delhi* (New Delhi: Oxford University Press, 2007); Ian Talbot, *Divided Cities*.

[45] Ayesha Jalal, *The State of Martial Rule: The Origins of Pakistan's Political Economy of Defence* (Cambridge University Press, 1990); Sarah Ansari, *Life after Partition: Migration, Community and Strife in Sindh, 1947–1962* (Karachi: Oxford University Press, 2005); Ian Talbot, *Pakistan A Modern History* (London: Hurst, 1998); Variza Fazila-Yacoobali Zamindar, *The Long Partition and the Making of Modern South Asia: Refugees, Boundaries, Histories* (New York: Columbia University Press, 2007); J. M. Brown, *Modern India: The Origins of an Asian Democracy*, 2nd edn (Oxford University Press, 1994); Joya Chatterji, *The Spoils of Partition: Bengal and India, 1947–1967* (Cambridge University Press, 2007); Mushirul Hasan, *Legacy of a Divided Nation: India's Muslims since Independence* (Oxford University Press, 1997).

pioneering crossings of the 1947 historical divide by suggesting that, among other things, pre-existing social and economic ties profoundly impacted on resettlement prospects, or that there was often not a single upheaval in 1947, but continuous movement to and fro with refugees in some instances engaged for years of struggle to resume their lives; many wandered from place to place before final resettlement.[46]

However this new history is not without its shortcomings. The collection of ever-increasing numbers of personal testimonies has added immeasurably to the empirical depth of knowledge regarding Partition, though perhaps at the expense of its conceptual and comparative understanding.[47] Too often there are fragmentary and incommensurate points of view that, though they add to subjective experience of suffering, settlement or neglect, pose a difficult task for the historian and the social scientist to construct meaningful narrative, unless it is embroidered with established understandings. Thus the new history runs the risk of reproducing the sense of incomprehension which is frequently all too evident in many of the first-hand accounts of violence and uprooting.

Perhaps, more seriously, there are also methodological concerns surrounding the use of oral testimonies that are prone to a faulty recall and retrospective reconstruction of memory. Individual accounts can – and do – provide a useful source for interrogating official and community histories, but they can often be heavily influenced by them. Take for example the character of the Sikh *sahukar* (moneylender) in the best-selling novel, *What the Body Remembers*. 'Sardar Kushal Singh', recalls one commentator, 'forgets many things now. Only the terrible things the Muslims did to us. He remembers only that … He weeds memories like a *mali* (gardener), ripping out the ones that mar the colours and textures of those he wishes to grow.'[48] Generally silences pervade memories in discussions of violence, female abduction and the relations of authority and subservience which governed everyday life in pre-Partition times. At the same time there is a tendency to exaggerate both attachment to *desh* and the extent of land and property abandoned in the flight across new international borders. Memories can thus be as partial and fractured as historical discourses, and as Pandey has powerfully demonstrated, strongly mediated by community and national consciousness.[49]

---

[46] See Ian Talbot (ed.) with Darshan Singh Tatla, *At the Epicentre of Violence* (New Delhi: Permanent Black, 2005).

[47] Vazira Zamindar's work is an exception in this respect.

[48] Shauna Singh Baldwin, *What the Body Remembers* (London: Black Swan, 2001), p. 527.

[49] Gyanendra Pandey, *Remembering Partition: Violence, Nationalism and History in India* (Cambridge University Press, 2001).

Partition historiography looking beyond Punjab

Traditionally the Punjab has dominated the historiography of Partition beginning with official histories and reflecting the movement from the All-India level to the province. Indeed the iconic images of Partition-related migration are all drawn from this region, whether it is the refugee foot columns, trudging alongside bullock carts to a new homeland, or the trains with their roofs and compartments crammed with refugees. More recently Sarah Ansari, for example, has produced an important study on the impact of partition on urban Sindh and especially on Karachi,[50] and Vazira Zamindar has shown how the return migration of Muslims to India from Sindh in the Spring of 1948 led New Delhi to unilaterally introduce a permit system to restrict this influx across its western frontier on 14 July 1948.[51] Outside of Punjab, however, it is Bengal that has received the lion's share of scholarly attention. Here too there has been a distortion in the literature in that the focus has been overwhelmingly on the experiences of Hindu refugees from East to West Bengal. Regrettably little has been written about the migration of Hindu Bengalis to Tripura and of Muslim migrants from West Bengal, Assam, Tripura, Bihar and Uttar Pradesh to East Pakistan and what is now Bangladesh.

In Bengal, Willem van Schendel, Joya Chatterji and Gyanesh Kudaisya have shown the dramatically different patterns of migration in comparison with Punjab[52] – a theme we examine in chapter four. One of the constant refrains from the literature on West Bengal is how upper-caste Hindus have dominated the post-1947 history of resettlement, to the neglect of the fortunes of lower castes and Muslims. Chatterji to her credit has addressed this serious omission by examining the dislocation, marginalisation and ghettoisation faced by many Muslims after 1947 who either migrated to East Pakistan or faced internal displacement within West Bengal.[53] There

---

[50] Ansari, *Life after Partition*, p. 12.

[51] Zamindar, *The Long Partition*, p. 82. The influx into India of returning Muslim refugees was rooted in the ambivalent attitude of the Pakistan state to the flood of 'surplus' refugees and to the housing crisis in Karachi.

[52] Willem van Schendel, *The Bengal Borderland: Beyond State and Nation in South Asia* (London: Anthem Press, 2005); Joya Chatterji, 'Right or Charity? The Debate over Relief and Rehabilitation in West Bengal, 1947–50', in Suvir Kaul (ed.), *The Partitions of Memory: The Afterlife of the Division of India* (New Delhi: Permanent Black, 2001), pp. 74–110. Gyanesh Kudaisya, 'Divided Landscapes, Fragmented Identities: East Bengal Refugees and Their Rehabilitation in India, 1947–79', in D. A. Low and Howard Brasted (eds), *Freedom, Trauma, Continuities: Northern India and Independence* (New Delhi: Sage, 1998), pp. 105–33.

[53] Joya Chatterji, 'Of Graveyards and Ghettos. Muslims in Partitioned West Bengal, 1947–1967', in Mushirul Hasan and Asim Roy (eds), *Living Together Separately: Cultural India in History and Politics* (New Delhi: Oxford University Press, 2005), pp. 222–50.

was a general movement from urban to rural settings and relocation to emerging Muslim enclaves as in Malda, 24 Parganas and West Dinajpur as Muslim localities in South Calcutta were taken over by Hindu refugees from East Bengal. Chatterji's work has moreover wider resonance in laying bare the often-unspoken concern with the Muslim 'problem' in post-Partition India. She reveals that as in other states, Muslims experienced similar impoverishment, social isolation and ghettoisation. Their abandonment of claims to sacred space and cow slaughter did not soften the 'institutionalised communalism' of West Bengal's police and administration.[54] In one important respect, Chatterji's work reveals a difference in the circumstances of UP and Bengal Muslims who stayed on in India after independence. The UP Muslims continued to congregate in towns, and cities, but the latter, in a reverse of centuries-old trends, moved out to the countryside and clustered in the rural districts bordering East Pakistan.[55]

The widening interest in events in eastern India has also resulted in a number of works on Bihari Muslims, especially by Papiya Ghosh.[56] She chronicled the multiple dislocations which they faced in the aftermath of the October–November 1946 violence which involved migration from Bihar to West Bengal, thence to East Bengal and thence to Pakistan. To date some Biharis are still 'stateless' following the 1971 emergence of Bangladesh. Ironically Pakistan refuses to accept them as refugees notwithstanding the fact that their plight in 1946 was used by the Muslim League to assert the validity of its two-nation theory demand for Pakistan.

The historiography of Partition-related violence

In chapter three we examine in depth the characteristics of Partition-related violence and how this differed from what might be termed 'traditional' communal violence in India. In this section, we provide an appreciation of the main historiographical trends in understanding violence.

The accepted view until the 1980s was that the violence was the result of a 'temporary madness' which had little to do with politics or modernity.[57] Rather violence was a throwback to medieval barbarity. The whole thrust of recent scholarship, in contrast, has been to question these assumptions.

---

[54] Chatterji, *The Spoils of Partition*, p. 199.
[55] Chatterji, *The Spoils of Partition*, pp. 188–90.
[56] On the Bihari Muslims' experience see Ghosh, *Partition and the South Asian Diaspora*; Papiya Ghosh, 'Partition's Biharis', in Mushirul Hasan (ed.), *Islam, Communities and the Nation: Muslim Identities in South Asia and Beyond* (New Delhi: Manohar, 1988), pp. 229–64.
[57] For the view that the violence was spontaneous and unique to the temporary madness of August 1947 in Punjab, see J. Alam and S. Sharma, 'Remembering Partition', *Seminar* 461 (January 1998), pp. 71–4.

Suranjan Das, for one, has pointed out the differences between earlier outbreaks of communal violence and the episodes which began with the Great Calcutta Killing of August 1946.[58] The later episodes, he contends, moved from the public to the private arena, involving attacks on women and children for the first time, and display a clear evidence of planning and political intent. Max Jean Zins has similarly argued that such violence represented a new modern era. Severing the head was an outgrowth of head-counting by the colonial state which had essentialised community identity in an environment of competitive contests for political power. Instead of being evidence of irrationality, 'In its horrible and individual reality, the stabbing and mutilation signified that a point of no return had been reached and that the links with the past had been severed.'[59] Recent work by Talbot has also highlighted the degree of organisation which went into violent episodes such as the 1947 Rawalpindi Massacres, the attacks on refugee trains and the activities of the Sikh *jathas* in East Punjab in August 1947[60] – all of which belie conventional framing of these events as symptoms of anarchy or religious irrationality.

Variza Zamindar has also extended the conceptualisation of the state actors' involvement in Partition-related violence from the chaos of communal conflict to the rational bureaucratic endeavours to manage and control refugees, migration and their property.[61] Definitions of 'abandoned' and 'empty' properties were extended to eventually include those occupied by small minority community family groups. Individuals could be designated as 'intending evacuees' if, for example, they had relatives in Pakistan and their property could not be transferred in any way until the Custodian of Evacuee Property had decided on their case.[62] A visit to a sick relative in Pakistan could result in ancestral property being dispossessed as it was declared evacuee under the powers of the evacuee property laws.[63] This 'punishment' Zamindar claims is worthy of being termed bureaucratic violence.

[58] Suranjan Das, *Communal Riots in Bengal, 1905–1947* (New Delhi: Oxford University Press, 1991).
[59] Max Jean Zins, 'The 1947 Vivisection of India: The Political Use of Carnage in the Era of the Citizen-Massacres', in Mushirul Hasan and Nariaki Nakazato (eds), *The Unfinished Agenda: Nation-building in South Asia* (New Delhi: Manohar, 2001), p. 72.
[60] Ian Talbot, 'The 1947 Violence in the Punjab', in Ian Talbot (ed.), *The Deadly Embrace: Religion, Politics and Violence in India and Pakistan, 1947–2002* (Karachi: Oxford University Press, 2007), pp. 1–15.
[61] Zamindar, *The Long Partition*.
[62] For a discussion of evacuee and intending evacuee categories, see Zamindar, *The Long Partition*, pp. 127–34. The 'intending evacuee' category was not legally removed until 1953.
[63] These were finally abrogated in 1954.

Partition and wider literature

The Partition of India was regarded so long as a unique event that it features little in wider studies of external borders, state downsizing and nation-building, although Gurharpal Singh has drawn attention to the inter-related nature of these features in the case of India and Pakistan.[64] Brendan O'Leary[65] has also pointed out both the characteristics which differentiate the Indian experience from that of the Balkans in the 1990s and the similarities with the Irish and Palestine end-of-empire partitions, while Willem van Schendel has attempted to provide a wider context for understanding the division of India not in terms of partition studies, but borderland studies.[66] The Bengal borderland, which emerged because of the 1947 division and was subsequently affected by the birth of Bangladesh is a lived reality that continues to defy determined efforts at precise demarcation. 'The Bengal borderland,' van Schendel concludes, 'like its counterparts from Tierra del Fuego to Jerusalem, from Dover to the Mekong River, from Lake Victoria to Tijuana, acts as a pivot between territorial states and transnational flows.'[67]

Lastly the Partition experience also surprisingly hardly features in the wider literature on refugee resettlement, despite the fact that it formed the single largest episode of forced migration in the twentieth century. Case studies of the consequences for resettlement of the abandonment of large amounts of property by refugees refer to it only in passing.[68] This neglect may well be due to the fact that the event was overshadowed by the almost contemporaneous Holocaust. However as we move into a post-Cold War world with its massive migration and refugee flows,[69] the Partition, as we shall see in chapter four, offers a rich case-study in addressing the perennial themes of ethnic cleansing, forced migration and refugee settlement.

Conclusion

While the Partition still remains off-limits in Pakistani historiography, elsewhere a veritable cottage industry has emerged during the past thirty years. In the absence of integrating texts or themes, the reader is presented

---

[64] Gurharpal Singh, 'The Partition of India in a Comparative Perspective: A Long-Term View', in Ian Talbot and Gurharpal Singh (eds), *Region and Partition: Bengal, Punjab and the Partition of the Subcontinent* (Karachi: Oxford University Press, 1999), pp. 95–116.

[65] O'Leary, 'Analysing Partition'.   [66] Schendel, *The Bengal Borderland*.

[67] Schendel, *The Bengal Borderland*, p. 385.

[68] See R. W. Zweig, 'Restitution of Property and Refugee Rehabilitation: Two Case Studies', *Journal of Refugee Studies* 6, 1 (1993), p. 56.

[69] See B. S. Chimni, 'The Geo-Politics of Refugee Studies: A View from the South', *Journal of Refugee Studies* 11, 4 (1998), pp. 350–74.

with a bewildering array of conflicting standpoints which variously explain the division as a fulfilment of the Indian Muslim community's natural destiny, a human tragedy on a vast scale, a fatal miscalculation by Congress, or still, as the parting gift of the British strategy of 'divide and rule'. In the last three decades there has been a noticeable shift in academic writing from an All-India perspective to the regions and locality, a development that was strengthened by the Cambridge and Subaltern Studies schools of writing. They have made important interventions as the focus has shifted from 'high politics' to the region and finally to the 'human dimension' of the division of India.

Rarely recognised, but common to both personal testimonies and constructed national and community histories, is the desire to displace blame for the massacres and migrations which accompanied India's Partition. Exactly *how* Partition is understood, therefore, still matters even over sixty years later. It continues to impact on notions of identity and state–society relations, underpinned by the fact that *all* accounts of Partition remain highly contested; and though the 'new history' has been able to transcend some of the old disputes, most valuably by hinting at the differentiated experience of Partition across class, gender and regional divides, it is also prone to the familiar distortions, stereotypes and biases of conventional historical accounts.

Finally, the Punjab experience continues to dominate much of the recent writing. While this undoubtedly reflects both the region's key to the creation of Pakistan and the dramatic intensity of the events which unfolded there from August to November 1947, it has obscured the significant regional variations which are explored in chapter four.

The other predominant characteristic in the literature is the tendency to see the Partition as a unique historical event like the Holocaust. Both have been regarded as *sui generis* and in a sense have been essentialised, rendering them *beyond* historical and comparative analysis. This in part explains why the division of India features so little in comparative studies of ethnic conflict, forced migration and state downsizing.

We attempt in this volume to synthesise the growing literature on Partition and its aftermath with the aim of enabling the reader to move beyond partial understandings, whether these are concerned with violence, identity or loss. Such a synthesis opens up a wider recognition of the issues of refuge rehabilitation and resettlement than is provided by Punjab-centric approaches hitherto. Most importantly, the comparative historical dimensions of this study aim to overcome the fragmentation of writings on Partition and historiography on the subject itself. The return of a subcontinental perspective is not only of academic importance; it is also central to addressing the region's common dilemmas and opportunities at the beginning of the twenty-first century.

2   The road to 1947

When the British divided and quit India in August 1947, they partitioned not only the subcontinent with the emergence of the two nations of India and Pakistan, but also the provinces of Punjab and Bengal. Pakistan received the lion's share of both the old British Indian provinces, while the much smaller areas of West Bengal and East Punjab went to India.[1] The partitioned regions of Bengal and Punjab, far from being identical twins in the new subcontinent, were to experience very different futures. West Bengal and East Punjab were marginalised in India, but West Punjab went on to provide the core of the Pakistan state, while East Bengal in 1971 was to finally break away in the new South Asian state of Bangladesh following a bloody civil war and Indian military intervention.

The existing literature focuses far more on why the subcontinent as a whole was divided than on the partitioning of Punjab and Bengal. Regional accounts of late colonial politics have rightly pointed out that without a Muslim breakthrough in these major centres of population, the credibility of the Pakistan demand would have been in tatters.[2] There is much less reflection, however, on how political and community leaders viewed the prospects for their region within a divided India. Did they merely fall in line at the behests of the Muslim League and Congress High Commands without thought for the future? Or did Punjabi and Bengali political leaders privately regard partition of their home region as an opportunity for 'rightsizing' the state which would ensure untrammelled power, heedless of the economic and human dislocation it might entail?

This chapter addresses these questions by examining the processes which culminated both in the division of the subcontinent and the provinces of Punjab and Bengal. The weaving together of these multi-layered narratives and developments will enable a more comprehensive understanding to emerge than is found in many of the standard accounts. We shall turn

[1] Radcliffe's Award gave West Bengal 28,000 square miles of territory (East Bengal received 49,000 square miles) and East Punjab 35,300 square miles (West Punjab received 63,800).
[2] See, for example, I. Talbot, *Punjab and the Raj, 1849–1947* (New Delhi: Manohar, 1988).

25

Map 1 India, 1947

first to the all-India dimension and understand why a section of the
Muslim political elite had, by 1940, come to demand a separate state.
This will be followed by an assessment of the reasons for both the colonial
authorities and the Congress High Command's reversal of their long-held
commitment to Indian unity. The perspective then switches to the regions
of Punjab and Bengal and the circumstances in which minority populations came to demand division of their homelands. Finally, there is an
assessment of the issue of Partition and the princely states.

Muslim separatism and the demand for Pakistan

The contested history of Muslim separatism and the demand for Pakistan
from 1940 onwards formed the focus of chapter one. Clearly it is impossible

to reconcile conflicting primordialist and instrumentalist perspectives. Our aim here is not to repeat them, but to focus on three key areas which help explain Indian Muslim history during the colonial era: first, the pluralism of the community; second, the different attitudes to constitutional reform espoused by political leaders from the major centres of Muslim population and those in the Hindu majority areas; and third, the consequences of the period of Congress rule in 1937–1939 and the impact of the Second World War for the standing of the All-India Muslim League and the emergence of the demand for Pakistan.

(i)   Muslims of British India

The eventual partition of India was made possible by the fact that though the Muslim community was scattered throughout the subcontinent, for historical reasons there were important clusters of Muslim-majority populations in north-east and north-west India. It was out of these territories that a Pakistan state was to be carved. Paradoxically, the demand for separate political representation and ultimately a separate homeland did not come from Muslims in these areas, but from the minority area of the United Provinces (UP) where they numbered around 8 million or 15 per cent of the total population at the time of the 1941 census. A further 5 million Muslims resided in neighbouring Bihar, where they formed 10 per cent of the population.

It is important to remember that Indian Muslims, like other Indians, were divided by ethnicity, language and sect. The main ethnic division was between the descendants of the Arab, Afghan and Turkish invaders of India (the *ashraf*) and those whose ancestors had been converted from the indigenous Hindu population (the *ajlaf*). A cultivated lifestyle was the hallmark of the *ashraf* who comprised Sayeds, Mughals, Sheikhs and Pathans. It was in UP that the largest proportion claimed foreign descent[3] with Urdu as the lingua franca of the *ashraf* elite. The *ashraf* were drawn from the large landholders and the administrative/professional classes that have been termed as the 'salariat' and have been identified as the prime movers of Muslim separatism because they were the ones who stood to lose most from a future Hindu-dominated India.[4]

The *ajlaf*, on the other hand, comprised the majority of the Indian Muslim community and spoke the regional Bengali, Punjabi, Gujarati

---

[3] The 1931 census provides a figure of 411 per thousand.

[4] Hamza Alavi, 'Pakistan and Islam: Ethnicity and Ideology', in Fred Halliday and Hamza Alavi (eds), *State and Ideology in the Middle East and Pakistan* (New York: Monthly Review Press, 1987), pp. 64–111.

and Tamil languages which cut across religious identity. They tended to be tenant and peasant cultivators, labourers, traders and the skilled artisan classes of, for example, weavers, cloth-printers and locksmiths. Within all the regions of India, agriculturalists formed the bulk of the Muslim population. A sense of relative deprivation vis-à-vis the Hindu upper and middle castes, who had commercially and professionally prospered under British rule, was politically influential.[5]

Of these classes the so-called 'writer castes' of Hindus had taken to the new English language with alacrity. In Bengal, for instance, the high-status *bhadralok* castes, comprising less than one in twenty of the population, monopolised the new educational opportunities. Literacy rates among Khatri, Agarwal and Arora middle-caste trading communities in the Punjab were seven times the average according to the 1891 census. The Muslims' relative educational backwardness was to be a major factor in shaping the emergence of a separatist Muslim political platform and was to gain further strength in communities which experienced relative decline in colonial India and also possessed memories of former rule. Such sentiments were especially pronounced amongst the UP Muslim elite who came to represent the backbone of the demand for Pakistan.

However, Muslim separatism was able to emerge as a political force mainly because the colonial state viewed India in terms of monolithic caste and religious identities. This in part arose from the interaction between British sources of knowledge of native society and perceptions of the significance of religious identity arising from the place of Christianity and the Catholic–Protestant divide in contemporary European ideas. The need to justify their rule also strongly shaped British perceptions about Indian society. The colonial census which was introduced throughout India in 1881 formed the scientific basis for the stereotype of rigid religiously defined communities – a homogeneity which overlooked popular folk beliefs and practices and the influence of *Sufi* and *Sant* traditions which transgressed the boundaries of formal religion[6] – and created the basis of religious majorities and minorities.

---

[5] Asghar Ali Engineer, for example, primarily understands Muslim separatism in terms of the economic imbalances between Hindus and Muslims. Asghar Ali Engineer, *Communalism and Communal Violence in India: An Analytical Approach to Hindu-Muslim Conflict* (Delhi: Ajanta Press,1989).

[6] See Roger Ballard, '*Panth, kismet, dharm te qaum*: Continuity and Change in Four Dimensions of Punjabi Religion', in Pritam Singh and Shinder S. Thandi (eds), *Globalisation and the Region: Explorations in Punjabi Identity* (Coventry: Association for Punjab Studies, 1996), pp. 7–38.

(ii)   Political representation

The collection of census data, 'scientific' mapping of religious communities and the way the British understood Indian society, strongly influenced the colonial state's gradual introduction of representative institutions. This is seen most clearly in the decision to introduce separate electorates for Muslims in 1909 at the provincial level. Although it is facile to argue that this step made the creation of Pakistan inevitable, it strengthened the belief that people following a particular religion naturally shared common interests from which others were excluded. Some Indian nationalist writers, as we saw in chapter one, understand the introduction of separate electorates issue as part of a Machiavellian British divide-and-rule policy in India.

Nonetheless, separate electorates were designed to increase Muslim representation in the system of elective local government which was introduced from the Indian Councils Act (1861) onwards. There were further rounds of reform down to the Government of India Act (1935) which gave Indians control of the provinces, a de facto self-government, while the British reserved power to themselves at the centre. This process of gradual democratisation was unnerving for minority religious communities who were traditionally used to wielding economic and political influence. In the case of UP, the *ashraf* elite feared for the future, and significantly it was here that a sense of a solidified Muslim political interest first emerged.[7]

Muslim anxieties in UP were heightened from the late nineteenth century, with the spread of political representation and the political mobilisation of Hindus in the Hindi–Urdu controversy and the anti-cow-killing riots of 1893.[8] The final catalyst for the movement to a Muslim separatist political identity was provided by the rise of the 'extremist' wing of the Congress and the furore which attended the Viceroy Lord Curzon's controversial decision to partition Bengal in 1905.[9] The delegation of Muslim leaders who visited the new Viceroy Lord Minto at Simla the

---

[7] See Francis Robinson, *Separatism among Indian Muslims: The Politics of the United Provinces' Muslims 1860–1923* (Cambridge University Press, 1974).

[8] Hindi and Urdu shared a common vocabulary, although they were written in the Nagri and Persian script respectively. The issue of which script was used had important repercussions for the administrative class. It became a wider source of conflict as the two communities jockeyed for power and influence.

[9] This decision was taken on administrative grounds, but Indian nationalist writers see it as part of the British divide-and-rule strategy. Resistance to the Partition which was revoked in 1911 boosted the Congress weapons of boycott of British goods and the use of Hindu icons to mobilise support for the *swadeshi* campaign. See I. Talbot, *India and Pakistan* (London: Arnold, 2000).

following year to press for the recognition of a distinct Muslim political interest comprised mainly of upper-class Muslims from the minority provinces, where the fears about future Hindu domination were most apparent. This established a pattern for the future development of the All-India Muslim League which was created at the Dacca 1906 Muslim Educational Conference. The All-India Muslim League membership was limited to just 400, 70 of whom were from the UP quota.[10] Its principal aim was to voice Muslim views during the discussions concerning constitutional-reform proposals which took place from October 1907 onwards. After lobbying in London and organising protest meetings in different parts of India, the League's demands for separate electorates, together with the reservation of seats in the Imperial Legislative Council were duly included in the Indian Councils Act (1909).

The idea that Hindus and Muslims had different political identities had received official sanction in the linking of religion with political representation, power and patronage. The Indian National Congress (INC), which had been established in 1885 as the secular voice of Indian nationalism that would transcend all communities, ultimately acceded to the British grant of separate electorates in its Lucknow Pact (1916) with the Muslim League as a quid pro quo for the latter's support for the nationalist struggle. But if the Lucknow Pact pointed to the possibility of compromise between the Muslim League and Congress in the national cause, it also laid bare the divisions within the Muslim community in which the political interests of Muslims in UP, Bombay, Bihar, Central Provinces and Madras had been secured at the cost of a reduction of Muslim representation in Punjab and Bengal.[11]

From October 1919, the Khilafat struggle (for the restoration of the Caliph in Turkey) was led jointly with the INC's campaign for self-rule.[12] M. K. Gandhi's declaration that he supported the 'just cause' of the Khilafat movement was followed by well-publicised displays of Hindu–Muslim unity, including an all-parties Hindu–Muslim unity conference at Allahabad in June 1920. But this new-found cooperation did not last long. Liberals such as Jinnah were alienated by the growing role of religion in politics and there were also tensions between the Khilafatists and the Gandhians

---

[10] Talbot, *India and Pakistan*, p. 117.

[11] In UP, Muslims were given 30 per cent of the seats despite forming only 14 per cent of the population; in Bengal, Muslims had to accept 40 per cent of the seats, despite forming 52 per cent of the population.

[12] The Khilafat struggle had grown out of increasing Pan-Islamic sentiment. It centred on fears concerning the power of the Ottoman Caliph. See G. Minault, *The Khilafat Movement: Religious Symbolism and Political Mobilization in India* (New York: Columbia University Press, 1982).

over non-violence as a strategy. Muslim co-operation with the Gandhian civil disobedience campaigns ended in disillusionment in 1921–1922. The Khilafat campaign received its *coup de grâce*, when the Turkish National Assembly abolished the office of the Caliph in March 1924.

Pakistani historians have portrayed the period from 1922 onwards as an inevitable 'parting of the ways' between the Muslim League and the Congress. The League's divisions and provincial rivals' growing challenge to its claim to represent All-India Muslim opinion were in reality more important. Mian Fazl-i-Husain's adroit leadership of the Punjab Unionist Party, for instance, enabled it to extend its influence to the national level of politics.[13] In fact, subsequently, Jinnah's famous 'fourteen points' as a condition for India's unity, with the emphasis on strong provinces within a weak Indian federation, largely reflected the interests of the Punjabi-dominated All-India Muslim Conference.[14]

However the development of separate electorates is subsequently interpreted, it is doubtless that they had the effect of consolidating the Muslim political constituency at a time when democratisation was further extended by the constitutional reforms in 1919 and 1935. These increased the opportunities for the Muslim political majorities in Punjab and Bengal to correct the educational and economic imbalance in favour of Hindu and Sikh populations. A similar process also occurred in Congress-dominated provinces. The Muslim backlash against the Congress administration in UP (1937–1939) was to provide the critical catalyst in the demand for a separate homeland.

(iii)   Pre-Partition decade

In the decade before 1947 it was evident that India's unity would be determined largely by political developments. It is true that Chaudhary Rahmat Ali had in 1933 coined the term 'Pakistan', 'the land of the pure' which was to consist of the Punjab, the North West Frontier Province, (Afghania) Kashmir, Sindh and Balochistan, but the pamphlet in which this appeared (*Now or Never*) was largely ignored at the time. In August 1933, a Muslim delegation to the Parliamentary Committee on Indian Constitutional Reforms dismissed Pakistan as 'chimerical and impracticable'. However, two major developments transformed the demand into practical politics. The first was the experience of Congress rule in the Muslim-minority areas following the

[13] David Page, *Prelude to Partition: The Indian Muslims and the Imperial System of Control, 1920–1932* (Delhi: Oxford University Press, 1982).

[14] Ayesha Jalal, *The Sole Spokesman: Jinnah, the Muslim League and the Demand for Pakistan* (Cambridge University Press, 1985), pp. 10–11.

introduction of provincial autonomy in 1937. The second was the impact of the Second World War. Without these contingencies and Jinnah's adroit exploitation of them, it is unlikely that Pakistan would have come into being.

The Government of India Act (1935) introduced a substantial measure of representative government through provincial autonomy. 'Law and order' subjects which had previously been kept under British control in the system known as 'dyarchy' were now handed over to elected Indian representatives. The number of voters throughout India increased to nearly 35 million. The Act, which constituted an important landmark in the democratisation of colonial rule and was to substantially comprise the eventual constitution of India, heightened Muslim-minority anxieties and fears of Hindu domination.

In the elections held for the first time under the new constitutional system in 1937 the Muslim League achieved its best result in the Muslim-minority provinces where it projected itself as the guardian of community interests. In UP it captured twenty-nine of the sixty-four Muslim seats. Yet in the main centres of Muslim population which were later to become Pakistan, notably Punjab and Bengal, regional parties eclipsed its appeal: the Unionist Party formed the government in Punjab; in Bengal, the Muslim League had to be content with a share of power in the coalition government headed by the Krishak Praja Party leader Fazlul Haq.

In contrast Congress won 716 out of 1585 seats in the provincial assemblies, enabling it to form governments in 7 of the 11 Indian provinces. Its manifesto claimed that communalism was not a religious problem and had little interest for the masses as it ignored their social and economic concerns. Nehru continued to act in this spirit after the polls, most notably with the launching in March 1937 of the Muslim mass-contact movement under the leadership of K. M. Ashraf. But the elections had in fact revealed, however, that Congress's appeal to Muslim voters was relatively limited, for it had contested only 58 out of the total 482 Muslim seats and was successful only in 26. Despite these disappointing results, the party continued to claim that it represented all communities. It thus offered a share of government to the Muslim League politicians in UP only if they ceased to function as a separate group, and though there were good parliamentary and ideological reasons for such a stance, it was a grave blunder, which increased the psychological distance between the Congress government and the Muslim masses. This was further accentuated as the new administration enforced cow protection and the use of Hindi. Equally dramatic was the new image of future Congress Raj. As Chandra has commented:

At the headquarters of the Provincial Governments, in the very citadels of the old bureaucracy, many a symbolic scene was witnessed. Now suddenly, hordes of people from the city and the village, entered these sacred precincts, and roamed about almost at will. The policemen and the orderlies with shining daggers were paralysed; the old standards had fallen. European dress, symbol of position and authority, no longer counted. It was difficult to distinguish between members of the legislatures and the peasants and townsmen who came in large numbers.[15]

Whilst the Muslim League investigations into Congress 'oppression' in the provinces in which it formed ministries were exaggerated,[16] nonetheless they gained some credence among the wider Muslim populace. The spectre of Hindu domination had now materialised, and when the Congress provincial ministries resigned en masse in October 1939 in protest at the Viceroy Linlithgow's declaration of war on India's behalf, the Muslim League organised 'Deliverance Day' celebrations throughout India.[17] Separate electorates had appeared hopelessly inadequate as a safeguard for Muslim political interests: the Congress ministries had inadvertently put Chaudhary Rahmat Ali's call for a separate Muslim homeland firmly on the political agenda.

A number of possible constitutional schemes were mooted, before Muslim League representatives from all over India gathered in Lahore in March 1940 for the party's annual session. The event was held in a large tent set up in Minto Park within sight of the imposing Badshahi Mosque. Jinnah, in a two-hour presidential address given in English, spelled out the two-nation theory justification for a separate Muslim homeland. Muslims and Hindus, he insisted, were irreconcilably opposed monolithic religious communities and as such no settlement could be imposed that did not satisfy the aspirations of the former. Although Pakistan was not mentioned by name, the resolution passed by those present on 23 March was subsequently dubbed the 'Pakistan Resolution'. Its third paragraph called for a grouping of contiguous Muslim majority areas in north-west and north-east India into 'Independent states in which the constituent units would be autonomous and sovereign.' Such vagueness may well have been designed to give Jinnah room for manoeuvre, but it also encouraged ideas of a Pakistan confederation which were not fully exhausted even when in 1946 the plural 'states' was excised from the separatist demand.

Although the passage of the Lahore Resolution was an important landmark in the movement for Pakistan, the Muslim League still had an uphill

---

[15] Cited in Bipan Chandra, *India's Struggle for Independence* (Harmondsworth: Penguin, 1989), p. 324.

[16] The Pirpur Report into Muslim grievances in the Congress-ruled provinces was published in November 1938. The Shareef Report which dealt especially with Bihar followed a year later.

[17] Deliverance Day was observed throughout India on 22 December 1939.

task in order to convince the British and the Congress that its demand was credible. The key to achieving this lay in overcoming its traditional weakness in the Muslim-majority areas which would eventually form the basis of a Pakistan state. This, as we have seen in chapter one, has been the focus of much recent historical research, but what is important here is to draw attention to the ways in which the Second World War underpinned the Muslim League advance.

In contrast to the Muslim League, which operated with state patronage, the Congress during the war years devoted its energies to the struggle against the colonial state. Its non-cooperation movement (1939–1942) and the violent Quit India movement (1942) led to the widespread arrests of its national and local leaders at a juncture when the Muslim League was free to popularise the Pakistan demand. British wartime expediency saw the Muslim League – along with the princes, and the Unionists of the Punjab – mobilised as valuable allies who would both work for the war effort and provide essential political ballast against renewed Congress demands for constitutional reforms. The latter were deemed unrealistic at the time, especially the demand for an Indian Defence Minister, as New Delhi and London feared it would imperil the resistance to any future Japanese onslaught. In sum, Congress was the main loser from the policy of disengagement and open hostility, while the Muslim League enjoyed a new credibility and respectability.

A day after the Viceroy Linlithgow declared that India was at war (3 September 1939), Jinnah was invited to see him on an equal footing with Gandhi. When Linlithgow made his statement on war aims on 18 October 1939, he described the Congress as a Hindu organisation, whilst implicitly accepting the Muslim League's claim to speak for all India's Muslims. Linlithgow's August Offer (1940) made it clear that the British would not transfer power to any system of government whose authority was 'denied by large and powerful elements' in India's national life.[18]

Notwithstanding this posture Sir Stafford Cripps, the Leader of the Commons, was sent by Churchill to India in March 1942 to secure Indian support for the war effort with the promise of future constitutional reform. R. J. Moore has described the mission as 'a watershed in the history of partition'.[19] Set against the background of a growing Japanese threat following the fall of Singapore, the need to demonstrate good faith to the Americans (who were now wartime allies and had voiced

[18] H. V. Hodson, *The Great Divide: Britain–India–Pakistan* (London: Hutchinson, 1969), pp. 84–5.
[19] Cited in Nicholas Owen, 'The Cripps Mission of 1942: A Reinterpretation', *The Journal of Imperial and Commonwealth History*, 30, 1 (2002), p. 61.

anti-imperialist sentiment) and the pressure from the Labour Party which was now part of the wartime coalition,[20] Cripps had the onerous task of selling the promise of India's Dominion Status at the end of the war. Cripps's proposals also included a proviso that no part of India would be forced to join the post-war arrangements, and though the mission ended in failure, the Muslim League emerged with its prestige and standing further enhanced. Indeed, Jinnah at the time of his interview with Cripps had been 'rather surprised' to see how far his declaration went 'to meeting the Pakistan case'.[21] An enraged Gandhi, in contrast, informed Cripps that his proposal amounted to 'an invitation to the Moslems to create a Pakistan'.[22] Congress in turn responded by launching the Quit India movement, the most serious threat to British rule in India since the 1857 revolt. This challenge was easily contained. Most of the Congress's front-rank leaders were detained until 1945 while Jinnah was free to concentrate on consolidating the Muslim League's position.

Jinnah's main asset was to sit tight and let his opponents make mistakes. Gandhi's correspondence with Jinnah in the autumn of 1944, in seeking to accommodate Muslim League demands, further legitimised Pakistan's demand while also confirming Jinnah's claim as the sole spokesman of the Muslim community. Jinnah's finest hour came at the June 1945 Simla conference. The Viceroy Lord Wavell had called this in an attempt to break the constitutional impasse between the Congress and the Muslim League. But the conference collapsed when Jinnah refused to yield on his insistence that all Muslim members of the proposed Indian Executive Council should belong to the Muslim League. Jinnah's determined stance won him the day. This outcome was a bitter blow for the Punjab's Unionist Prime Minister, Khizr Hayat Khan Tiwana, who had sought a seat on the Executive Council in order to shore up his position. Jinnah's victory at Simla accelerated the Muslim League advance in the Punjab, which he had called the 'cornerstone of Pakistan'. The Muslim League delivered a crushing blow to the Unionist citadel in the provincial elections of February 1946, recording victories in seventy-five out of eighty-six Muslim seats. This was a decisive verdict in favour of Pakistan, though Khizr Tiwana and a handful of sup-porters clung to office in a coalition with the Akalis and Congress.[23] At the time, the Muslim League overlooked the fact that many of its successful

---

[20] For a revisionist view of the role of the Labour Party pressure, see, Owen, 'The Cripps Mission', pp. 61–98.
[21] Interview with Jinnah 25.3.1942 P&J/10/4 , Transfer of Power Records, Departmental Papers, India Office Records (IOR).
[22] Owen, 'The Cripps Mission', p. 80.
[23] See Ian Talbot, *Khizr Tiwana, the Punjab Unionist Party and the Partition of India: The Subcontinent Divided: A New Beginning* (Karachi: Oxford University Press, 2002), pp. 193–214.

candidates were former Unionist landholders who had opportunistically clambered aboard its bandwagon. This legacy was to produce a faction-ridden Muslim League in the crucial early post-Independence period, which was to undermine democracy in the heartland of Pakistan.

The Muslim League victories in 1946 were equally impressive on paper elsewhere in the future Pakistan areas: it won 439 of the 494 seats reserved for Muslims in the provincial assemblies, capturing 75 per cent of the total Muslim vote in comparison with the derisory 4 per cent it had obtained in 1937. The best result was in Bengal where it secured 113 of the 119 Muslim seats. In the minority provinces the Muslim League vote was consolidated: it won all the Muslim seats it contested in Bombay, Madras, UP and Bihar, and captured 54 of 64 and 34 of 40 seats respectively. The League's claim to speak for Muslim India was vindicated. Only in the North West Frontier Province did the Congress have any legitimate claim to influence as a result of the success of its Pakhtun allies in the Khudai Khidmatgar Party of Abdul Ghaffar Khan. Here Congress captured 30 seats to the Muslim League's 17, including a majority 19 of the 36 seats reserved for Muslims. The Muslim League had barely broken out of its traditional urban strongholds and the non-Pakhtun base of the Hazara district. Yet in the June 1947 referendum the province's Muslims voted overwhelmingly for inclusion in Pakistan.[24]

In the aftermath of the February 1946 provincial elections and the failure of constitutional negotiations, the consolidation of political allegiances around religious community both reflected and contributed to the communal polarisation. British officials and Congress opponents alike regretted the poisoned atmosphere which followed the elections. The Bihari Congress leader Sri Krishna Sinha summed this up when he declared that the Muslim League's success had stemmed from its violent electioneering.[25] The polls paved the way for Pakistan, but also formed a prelude to the violence which accompanied Partition.

Congress and Partition

Until the 1980s, which saw the rise of the Hindu Right and was followed by a growing critique of the secular Nehruvian Congress, the official

[24] For details see Erland Jansson, *India, Pakistan or Pakhtunistan? The Nationalist Movements in the North-West Frontier Province, 1937–47* (Uppsala: Acta Universitas Upsaliensis, 1981); S. A. Rittenberg, *Ethnicity, Nationalism and Pakhtuns: The Independence Movement in India's North-West Frontier Province, 1901–1947* (Durham, NC: Duke University Press, 1988).

[25] Papiya Ghosh, *Partition and the South Asian Diaspora: Extending the Subcontinent* (London: Routledge, 2007), p. 4.

Indian view had been that Partition was a heavy but necessary price to pay for Independence. Gandhi himself had stood out against this at the time – a sentiment summed up in his phrase that Partition was a 'wooden loaf'. The Mahatma was, however, an isolated and somewhat tragic figure by this stage in his life. It was only through the press that he got to hear about the Congress Working Committee's Resolution adopted in March 1947 – that Punjab should be partitioned if Pakistan was created. He publicly stated that he could not 'tolerate' any plan which involved the 'vivisection' of India.[26] Gandhi maintained that Britain did not possess the moral right to impose partition on an 'India temporarily gone mad'.[27] The Attlee administration, mindful of opinion elsewhere in the empire as well as at home, could not however comply with Gandhi's desire to leave 'India to its fate'. In reality many Congress leaders were far less sanguine at the prospect of the dividing-up of the subcontinent. Among these included members of the All-India Congress Working Committee and Punjab's and Bengal's Hindu leaders. How can we explain this outlook given the party's long-term commitment to Indian unity?

Congress leaders, like their Muslim League counterparts, did not antici-pate the vast human tragedy which accompanied Partition. With hindsight this appears remarkable, given the warning signs of politically motivated violence and driving-out of minority populations from the time of the August 1946 Great Calcutta Killing onwards. Yet even the politically astute, who made precautionary moves in anticipation of trouble, did not expect that they would need to permanently quit their homes and busi-nesses. There was thus a widely held belief that Partition could bring a peaceful solution to the violence which had wracked large areas of north India for the best part of a year between 1946 and 1947.

However, Partition was also welcomed by the Congress High Command as it was being implemented in line with its terms. While the end of the Second World War had greatly reduced Jinnah's political role as his usefulness to the British declined, it simultaneously increased the Congress's ability to influence the terms of the transfer of power. The outgoing Raj did not have the stomach for repressing another major nationalist struggle after 'Quit India'. Moreover, it was also increasingly recognised that continued British influence in the region depended on good relations with a successor Indian government. The formation of the Attlee government in 1945 brought politicians into power, such as Cripps,

---

[26] See Sucheta Mahajan, 'Congress and the Partition of the Provinces', in Amrik Singh (ed.) *The Partition in Retrospect* (New Delhi: Anamika Publishers, 2000), p. 232.

[27] Cited in B. R. Nanda, 'The Tragedy and Triumph of Mahatma Gandhi', in Singh (ed.), *The Partition in Retrospect*, p. 54.

who had long sympathised with the Indian nationalist struggle. There was thus a gradual convergence of interests around the need for a swift and smooth transfer of power. Jinnah's stonewalling approach, which had previously served him well, was now perceived as an irritant. The British shared with the Congress the commitment to Indian unity, if this was possible, or failing that, a partition that did not threaten balkanisation. Despite the hopes of Sikhs, Pakhtuns, Tamils and assorted princely rulers, there was to be just one partition. Moreover, if Jinnah was to secure Pakistan, it would be a significantly truncated state. Despite the alarm that Nehru felt when he saw the first draft partition plan, by the time of the final 3 June agreement, the Congress could rest content that Pakistan had been drastically cut back to size. If, for example, there had been any prospect that Calcutta would have fallen into Jinnah's lap, it is unlikely that Congress would have accepted the division of territory.

The Congress High Command was assisted in the task of confining Pakistan by the British belief that the subcontinent's future strategic and economic stability depended on the existence of a powerful Indian territorial unit. The national leadership was also boosted by local Congressmen and other opponents of the Muslim League in Bengal and Punjab who demanded the partition of their provinces. This made it impossible for the Muslim League to secure a homeland without paying its own price: the division of the major Muslim-majority provinces of Punjab and Bengal. The mixed motives and unexpected outcomes surrounding these territorial divisions will be considered later in the chapter; suffice it to say here that local pressures for provincial partition were useful for Congress in its all-India strategy.

It was of course easier for an individual such as Sardar Vallabhbhai Patel, the future deputy prime minister of India, to contemplate partition than it was for Nehru. The redoubtable Congress hardman was in much closer sympathy with Hindu right-wing attitudes. It has been claimed that he cynically accepted Pakistan's creation in the belief that the country would collapse and its leaders would be forced to come back cap in hand to India. Certainly, Patel's membership of the Partition Council, established after the acceptance of the 3 June Plan, would have alerted him to the unfavourable economic prospects of the new state. Nehru, as ever, was concerned with the bigger picture and did not immerse himself in the minutiae of division. So why did he concur?

Nehru's commitment to a secular vision for the subcontinent's future has remained unquestioned. His perspective on Hindu–Muslim relations had been initially framed by his upbringing in the cosmopolitan elite UP culture, and the socialist ideals imbibed during education in England. He came increasingly to the view that the Hindu–Muslim conflict had nothing to do with religion, but was located in its exploitation by the self-styled communal leaders of the Muslim League and the Hindu Mahasabha who encouraged a 'communal consciousness' in order to protect their privileged status. As early as 1933, he was advocating the election of a Constituent Assembly by universal suffrage that would confront the real bread-and-butter economic issues and bypass the elites who used communalism 'to take as big a share of power and privilege for themselves as possible'.[28] Yet by accepting the Pakistan claim less than a decade and a half later, he appeared to validate the two-nation theory he had always denigrated.

One reason for this change of tack was the violence that limited other constitutional options and made it inconceivable that the Muslim community could be corralled in India against its will. Indeed, Nehru justified to Gandhi the Congress Working Committee's acceptance early in March 1947 of the possibility of Punjab's partition precisely in these terms.[29] Four months previously he had seen at first hand the devastation in Bihar, where Muslims had been the victims of mass killings. Almost as sobering had been Nehru's experience of the workings of the Interim Government, in which he functioned as a prime minister in waiting. The Viceroy Lord Wavell's hope that the Interim Government, sworn in on 2 September 1946, would act as a bridge between the Congress and Muslim League was confounded. When the latter belatedly decided to enter the new arrangement on 13 October, the earlier smooth proceedings were disrupted. Rather than functioning as a coalition the two parties acted as warring blocs. This was hardly surprising given the Muslim League's continued boycott of the Constituent Assembly and the mistrust which festered after the failure of the Cabinet Mission proposal. There is evidence however that Nehru drew the lesson from the Interim Government experiment that a continued Muslim League presence would stymie his hopes for post-Independence Indian economic and social development.[30] Partition would thus remove a major irritant and enable the Congress to press ahead with the nation-building tasks in the areas it controlled.

The British and Partition

The closing period of British rule laid bare the contradictions between the short-term tactic of boosting the Muslim League and the long-term imperial commitment to a united India. The latter was not just a matter

[28] Cited in Judith M. Brown, *Nehru: A Political Life* (New Haven, CT: Yale University Press, 2003), p. 118.
[29] Brown, *Nehru*, p. 171.   [30] Brown, *Nehru*, pp. 167–8.

of pride in bringing administrative unity to the subcontinent. Most British officials possessed serious reservations about Pakistan's economic viability and so the epithet of reluctant partitionists may be deserved.

The Cabinet Mission in March 1946 represented the final hope for keeping India united. The issue was not whether power would be transferred but what form the post-imperial order was to take. The 'three magi', of Pethick-Lawrence, Stafford Cripps and A. V. Alexander, as Wavell referred to the members of the Cabinet Mission, preferred an option for a united India on strategic grounds. After fruitless negotiations with Indian leaders, they put forward their own proposal. This included the establishment of an All-India Union government whose powers would be limited to defence and foreign affairs. All remaining powers were to reside in the provinces which would be free to form three groups: section A that included Madras, Bombay, the Central Provinces, UP and Bihar; and sections B and C that comprised the Muslim-majority regions of north-west and north-east India. Congress was to later raise objections to the compulsory grouping of Assam in section C and the North West Frontier Province (then under a Congress government) in section B, which were Muslim League-dominated blocs. It was when Nehru publicly raised doubts about the feasibility of such grouping that the Muslim League reversed its earlier acceptance of the scheme. Notwithstanding the claims of revisionist historians that the acceptance by the Muslim League indicated that Pakistan was no more than a bargaining chip, the scheme offered the prospects of achieving Pakistan by other means, though with a proviso that it would have to wait until the agreement was reviewed in ten years when the provinces could opt for self-determination.

The collapse of the Cabinet Mission proposals not only brought increasing political deadlock, but formed the backdrop, as we shall see in chapter three, to a cycle of violence which swept north India from August 1946 onwards. Wavell responded to the deteriorating situation by pressing a breakdown plan for a phased British withdrawal. His ideas of a deadline for the British departure and a phased withdrawal were regarded by the Cabinet as defeatist. When Wavell persisted with his proposals, the decision was taken to replace him with Lord Mountbatten. Ironically, Mountbatten would only agree to take on the role of Viceroy if a deadline was announced for the British departure. On 20 February 1947, Prime Minister Attlee coupled the announcement of Mountbatten's appointment as Viceroy with the statement to the House of Commons that the British would withdraw from India by a date no later than June 1948. The Opposition condemned the new policy as 'an unjustifiable gamble', but the Attlee declaration set the scene for the endgame of empire in India.

A measure of British commitment to the idea of a united India, albeit one with a weak centre, can be seen in the fact that despite the violence and the Muslim League boycott of the Constituent Assembly, when Mountbatten arrived in India on 22 March 1947 as the last Viceroy, he still hoped to resurrect the Cabinet Mission proposal. It was only after he embarked on a series of interviews with Indian leaders that it became clear that partition was now a more realistic option. Although great controversy still surrounds Mountbatten's timing of partition and the boundary and security arrangements which accompanied it, there is little evidence for the claim that he imposed partition on reluctant and unsuspecting Indian leaders. Partition was not a 'parting gift' of outgoing imperial masters: it was self-consciously willed by the All-India Congress and Muslim League leaders and, above all, reflected their fears and mistrusts, as well as hopes, that a 'right-sized' state would deliver to them the power to construct a new political, economic and social order in a free subcontinent.

Plans from mid-April onwards were drawn up for a partition proposal. A working committee comprising General Ismay (the Viceregal chief of staff), Sir Eric Mieville (the Viceroy's principal secretary) and George Abell (the Viceroy's private secretary) worked under Mountbatten's direction. After prolonged discussions, the Indian leaders were presented with the Partition Plan on 2 June.[31] The Viceroy received favourable responses and was relieved of any last-minute anxieties that Gandhi might torpedo it when he chose not to break his day of silence. The following day the Plan was announced in a series of radio broadcasts. Mountbatten also tabled a paper on the 'Administrative Consequences of Partition'. The leaders' acceptance that they would have power transferred as dominions enabled the Indian Independence Bill to be drafted in time for a transfer of power on 14/15 August. Jinnah had very reluctantly acquiesced to the 3 June Plan as it involved the partition of Punjab and Bengal.

Punjab and Partition

Punjab's future was settled in Delhi. Nevertheless, provincial politicians both influenced this process and had their own reasons for division. At one level, this could be understood as a knee-jerk reaction by the Hindu and Sikh leaders to the gathering support for the Pakistan scheme. But like

---

[31] Mountbatten had to overcome Nehru's objections to the draft plan. He returned to London on 19 May to discuss its revision with Attlee and the India and Burma Committee of the Cabinet.

the UP Muslim elite's espousal of separatism, Hindus and Sikhs in the Punjab drew on a store of historical memories, as well as contemporary fears. Sikhs looked back to the brief golden era of Ranjit Singh's nineteenth-century Kingdom of the Punjab, as well as earlier memories of Mughal oppression in laying claim to sovereign rule. The Hindu golden era in the Punjab was as far back as the Vedic era, but nineteenth- and twentieth-century reformers had popularised the concept of Punjab as 'holy land'. In 1909 the Arya Samajist missionary Bhai Parmanand called for a partition of the region to ensure that this holy land was under Hindu control. Such imagined pasts provided inspiration for communities whose privileges were increasingly threatened. The spread of representative politics was also threatening to undermine the financial power of Punjab's Hindu leaders as increasing restrictions were imposed on the lucrative rural moneylending activities of the Bania and Khatri castes and the introduction of communal quotas in educational institutions, designed to improve the prospects of the educationally backward Muslim-majority community, offered the prospect of more educated and mobilised Muslim social groups.

Such Punjabi Muslim leaders as Mian Fazl-i-Husain and Sikander Hayat had skilfully used the powers devolved to them in the 1920s and 1930s to bolster the position of the Muslim landowners. At the same time they had recognised the need for support from Hindu and Sikh Jats in order to construct the cross-communal support base of the Unionist Party. By deliberately targeting urban professional interests – overwhelmingly dominated by mercantile Hindu castes – the Unionists were able to deflect most of the religious design. Right until March 1947 the Unionist Party functioned as a cross-community organisation.

Punjabi urban Hindu elites, in contrast, who had historically remained locked out of the Unionist Party grand coalition turned successively to the Hindu Mahasabha and Congress to safeguard their privileges, espoused religious reform to strengthen community solidarity, and toyed with the idea of partition long before it became an actual reality. Swami Shraddhananda had echoed upper-caste Hindus' anxieties in his influential book, *Hindu Sangathan-Saviour of the Dying Race* (1926). The Punjabi Hindu leader Lala Lajpat Rai, as early as September 1920, had suggested that:

The Punjab should be partitioned into two provinces, the Western Punjab with a large Muslim majority to be a Muslim-governed province, and the Eastern Punjab with a large Hindu-Sikh majority to be a non-Muslim governed province.[32]

[32] Cited in S. M. Burke and Salim Al-Din Qureshi, *Quaid-i-Azam Mohammad Ali Jinnah: His Personality and His Politics* (Karachi: Oxford University Press, 1997), p. 253.

Yet over a quarter of a century was to pass before the Congress could contemplate this territorial arrangement; and then it was not to pull the irons out of the fire for the privileged Punjabi Hindu elite, but in response to all-India developments in which the spectre of an enlarged Pakistan that included the whole of Punjab threatened to extend the borders of the new states to the outskirts of Delhi.

The division of Punjab along Hindu–Muslim lines was further complicated by the presence of the Sikh community which laid claims to the historic governance of Punjab before the onset of colonialism. Unlike the Hindu elite, Sikh demands for the Punjab's partition arose much later and were more clearly responses to the Pakistan demand. The main Sikh political party, the Shiromani Akali Dal (SAD), floated the idea of Azad Punjab in March 1942 that excluded the Muslim-majority areas of the whole of the Rawalpindi division and most of the Multan division but produced a new Punjab state in which Sikhs with 20 per cent of the population would hold the balance between the Muslims and Hindus with 40 per cent each. Congress dubbed the proposal 'anti-national and reactionary'. Sir Bertrand Glancy, the Punjab governor, regarded the scheme's practical objections to be 'even greater' than those that lay in the path of Pakistan.

Yet Sikh unease increased further in 1944 following the Gandhi–Jinnah talks. Even after their failure in September, many Akalis believed that the Congress might come to an agreement concerning Pakistan over their heads. The SAD thus raised the demand for a Sikhistan state which was to be a federation comprising the most populous Sikh districts of the eastern and central Punjab, and the neighbouring Sikh princely states of Patiala, Nabha, Jind, Faridkot, Kalsia and Kapurthala. The scheme singularly unimpressed the Cabinet Mission team because it further complicated the task of securing an all-India agreement between the Congress and the Muslim League. Its chances of success were also handicapped as there was no one of Jinnah's calibre to advocate Sikh demands. Fatal to SAD's hopes however was the fact that the community lacked a majority in any district of the Punjab which could form the territorial basis for a separate state and was evenly divided between East and West Punjab. Given the British reluctance to concede to the demands of the Muslim League, it is small wonder that the Sikh case received such short shrift.

After the failure of the Cabinet Mission proposals, Sikh leaders became more wary of the imminence of Pakistan. It should be remembered here that the SAD was the standard-bearer of a reformed Sikh identity that had been partly constructed by Singh Sabha reformers around the history of martyrdom at Mughal hands. In the immediate aftermath of the passage of the Lahore Resolution, the SAD leader, Master Tara Singh, had made the uncompromising response that he would 'fight Pakistan tooth and nail'. It was his unsheathing of a sword outside the Punjab Assembly when the Khizr government resigned on 2 March 1947 that sparked off the violence that led to so many deaths in the Rawalpindi Massacres (see chapter three). These killings, which claimed numerous Sikh victims, convinced the SAD that there was no alternative to the partition of the Punjab. There is evidence that, at the same time, clandestine preparations were made for attacks on the Muslim community in the East Punjab which would not only exact revenge, but clear out the Muslims for the resettlement of Sikhs from the prosperous Canal Colonies that would be allotted to Pakistan, and lay the basis for an independent Sikh state.

The role of Muslim League members, sympathisers, officials and police in the Rawalpindi Massacres is examined in chapter three. The motives for this action remain a matter for conjecture: did the desire for loot encourage the brutalities? Or rather, was it an unmistakeable claim for future dominance? Did the perpetrators act in ignorance of possible minority-community response and, thereby, score the massive 'own goal' of creating the circumstances for the demands for the partition of Punjab? Is it possible to discern a cynical and careful decision behind the violence? Did Punjab's Muslim leadership decide that they could best rule the roost in a truncated province and therefore take steps which would encourage this eventuality, even if it flew against the wishes of the All-India leadership? Clearly a united Punjab would have made Pakistan economically stronger, but its large Hindu and Sikh populations would have frustrated the Muslim landed elite's will to power and would have posed a permanent ideological threat to the two-nation theory.

Against this backdrop SAD's public acceptance of the 3 June Plan was accompanied by hopes that the Punjab Boundary Commission, which was established to demarcate the boundaries between the new Punjabs, would take into consideration 'other factors' than the unfavourable Sikh demographic equation when drawing up its lines. Sir Cyril Radcliffe, the vice-chairman of the General Council of the English Bar chaired the Punjab and Bengal Boundary Commissions. He had been recommended by Mountbatten for this appointment after the Congress had opposed Jinnah's suggestion that the UN should appoint an impartial non-Indian commission.[33] Radcliffe only arrived in India on 8 July 1947 and power was to be transferred on 15 August. In the absence of agreement between

---

[33] Mountbatten also opposed the UN involvement as it would delay the process of boundary delimitation. There were also of course wider imperial objections to a UN presence in the transfer of power in India as this could undermine British prestige in the eyes of other colonial populations.

the Congress and Muslim League nominated members of the Commissions, Radcliffe became the final arbiter.

Naturally the most intense lobbying involved the Punjab Commission which sat in Lahore from 21 to 31 July. The Congress and Muslim League delegations were led by the eminent lawyers, Motilal C. Setalvad and Sir Zafrullah Khan. Oskar Spate, the Australian geographer, was the only technical expert present amongst the crowd of lawyers. This surprisingly received no adverse comment. Spate represented the case of the heterodox Muslim Ahmadi community whose headquarters were based in the contested Gurdaspur border district. Spate's Lahore diary provides a vivid account of the chaotic and politically charged public hearings of the Boundary Commission.[34] In many respects, they were a microcosm of the wider Partition process. This was marked by the drive to capture state power by Indian politicians with little thought for how Partition would affect minority groups, physical infrastructure and economic activities, and secondly, by a desperate British attempt to retain a semblance of control. The Boundary Commission, like the Partition Council, was fatally flawed because it had been established on the precept of political cooperation when there was none to be found in an atmosphere vitiated by hostility and mistrust. When Radcliffe recommended that disruption to Punjab's intricate canal system be minimised by India and Pakistan jointly operating the headworks, Jinnah replied that 'he would rather have Pakistan deserts than fertile fields watered by the courtesy of the Hindus', while Nehru, 'curtly informed [Radcliffe] that what India did with India's rivers was India's affair'.[35] Disputes over water and territory along the Punjab border arising from river-bed changes following the monsoon floods persisted until 1960.

The delegations not only openly exchanged information with the Commission judges who had been nominated by their parties, but pressed for the greatest possible territorial award. Sardar Harnam Singh who put forward a seventy-five-page memorandum in support of the Sikh case used the historical significance of Guru Nanak's birthplace, which lay in the Muslim-majority Sheikhupura district, to push boundary claims as far as the Chenab River. In fact, 8 July 1947 had been observed as Nankana Sahib Day. Mr M. C. Setalvad argued on behalf of Congress that Lahore should be awarded to India because of the non-Muslims' cultural attachments to the city and because of their property ownership. Sir Muhammad Zafrullah Khan, on behalf of the Muslim League, countered

[34] See O. H. K. Spate Papers, Centre for South Asian Studies, Cambridge.
[35] Leonard Mosley, *The Last Days of the British Raj* (New York: Harcourt, Brace & World, 1962), p. 199.

the Hindu and Sikh demands with the argument that on demographic and natural frontier grounds the Sutlej should form the boundary.

The Punjab Boundary Commission's deliberations were accompanied by increasingly vociferous statements to the press. Master Tara Singh talked of the 'extinction' or perpetual 'enslavement' of the Sikh community if it did not receive justice from Sir Cyril Radcliffe.[36] *Dawn* carried a series of letters and statements from East Punjab Muslim *anjumans* which called for facing all eventualities if the boundary award went against them and of fighting to maintain territory with the 'last drop of blood'. Such pronouncements were not sheer bravado, as communities had been arming themselves for several months.

Controversy still surrounds the Punjab Boundary Award. Pakistan writers claim that far from being an independent judicial decision, Mountbatten influenced Radcliffe to award the Muslim-majority *tehsils* of Ferozepore and Zira, which had respective Muslim majorities of 55.2 and 65.2 per cent, to India.[37] They also maintain that the Gurdaspur district which had a bare (0.8 per cent) Muslim majority was awarded to India because of the access it provided to Jammu and Kashmir, with the Hindu-majority Chittagong Hill Tracts in the east going to Pakistan to 'balance' the award. It is also claimed that the delay in its publication until 17 August was a contributory factor in the Partition-related massacres because of the confusion this generated.

Lucy Chester's study[38] demonstrates that the Pakistan claims over Gurdaspur are unfounded. She supports the view, however, despite the absence of direct evidence, that Mountbatten may have influenced the Ferozepore award to India. This followed the threat of the Maharajah of Bikaner to accede to Pakistan, if the boundary placed the Ferozepore canal headworks in Pakistan control. Rather than regarding this as 'improper', she regards Mountbatten's 'intervention' as symptomatic of a process shot through with politics, despite the facade of judicial objectivity. Strikingly she maintains that the Punjab Award, 'rushed and inexpert' as it was, may have minimalised the violence. Although Chester does not fall into the trap of presenting the award as Radcliffe's *fiat*, she underplays the role of Indian leaders in accepting the state downsizing implicit in the new

[36] *Tribune* (Lahore) 20 June 1947.
[37] These claims were fuelled by the sketch map sent by George Abell, Mountbatten's private secretary, on 8 August to the Punjab Governor, Sir Evan Jenkins, which showed what was termed the Ferozepore salient comprising the three *tehsils* of Ferozepore, Zira and Fazilka in Pakistan. Two days later, Jenkins received a cryptic telegram which read 'Eliminate salient'.
[38] Lucy Chester, *On the Edge: Borders, Territory and Conflict in South Asia* (Manchester University Press 2008).

Map 2 Post-Independence India and Pakistan

boundaries. She also passes lightly over the fact that the sittings of the Commission and the media's fevered reporting of rumours where the boundary might fall had themselves turned up the political temperature.

The Partition Council decided upon the formation of a Punjab Boundary Force to maintain order. This came into being on 22 July 1947 under the command of Major-General Rees with Brigadier Dhigambir Singh as the senior Indian officer and Ayub Khan (President of Pakistan, 1958–1969) as his counterpart. The force had British officers and Gurkha troops among its 55,000-strong contingent. Nevertheless the majority of the ordinary soldiers were drawn from the increasingly polarised Punjabi Muslim and Sikh communities. Its capability was further undermined by the vast 37,500 square mile area it had to police that included 17 towns, nearly

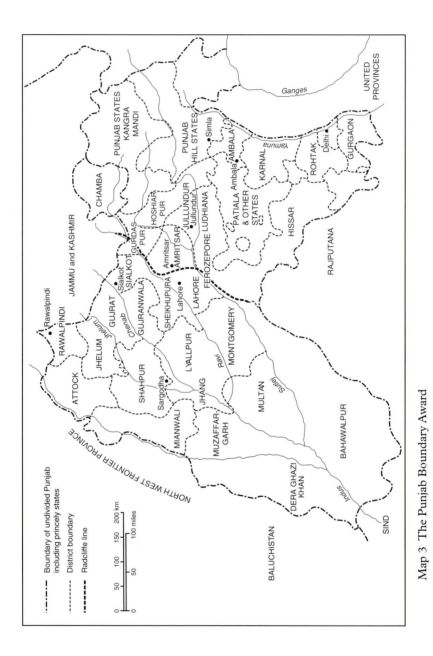

Map 3 The Punjab Boundary Award

17,000 villages and a population of 14.5 million in the 12 districts of the central Punjab. Of all the Partition arrangements, the Boundary Force was the most flawed: it was wound up on 29 August following a Joint Defence Council meeting in Lahore.

The Punjab Boundary Force was no match for the Sikh and Muslim war bands. The Sikh *jathas*, as we shall see in chapter three, were ruthlessly efficient killing machines as they sought to regain on the ground what the Radcliffe Commission had denied them on the map. Once the dislocation arising from the collapse of administrative structures in East Punjab had ended, the authorities called a halt to their mayhem. The Sikhs were not to realise a separate state of their own, but their post-1947 accommodation within the Indian Union, as we shall in chapter five, was to remain difficult with periodic assertions of autonomy and claims of separatism.

Bengal and Partition

Joya Chatterji's study has shed much light on the previously uncharted territory of the Partition of Bengal.[39] According to her, the Congress High Command and the Bengal Hindu elite had 'quite different reasons' for accepting the division of the province. The former saw this as opening the way for independent India to have a strong centre, 'without weightages, reservations and other such devices'.[40] A strong central government was deemed necessary to hold India together amidst the possibility of economic and political chaos. Such a government would only be possible if the Muslim-majority tracts, 'with their awkward demands for special representation', were got rid of.[41] Local protagonists for Bengal's division, on the other hand, saw Partition as a means to restore their influence which had declined with the introduction of 'dyarchy' and provincial autonomy. It would 'deliver them from the tyranny of a Muslim majority'.[42]

Chatterji reveals how the demands placed before the Boundary Committee were determined more by the contending political groupings' interests in running a future partitioned West Bengal state than in maximising its resource base. This, she maintains, displays both a lack of understanding of the economic dislocation attendant on Partition and any awareness that the division could spark off large-scale migration. In the event, migration both exacerbated the loss of access to such vital raw materials as jute and upset the carefully laid plans for a 'rightsized' state. The *bhadralok* instead found themselves competing for both jobs and power with a huge influx of refugees within a greatly diminished

[39] Chatterji, *The Spoils of Partition.*   [40] Chatterji, *The Spoils of Partition*, p. 315.
[41] Chatterji, *The Spoils of Partition*, p. 314.   [42] Chatterji, *The Spoils of Partition*, p. 314.

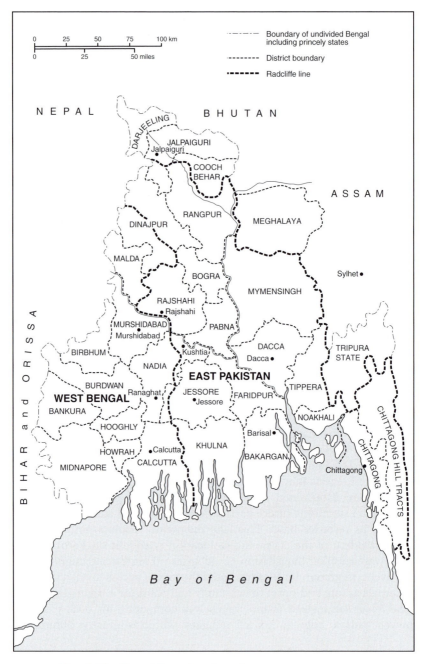

Map 4 The Bengal Boundary Award

territorial base. To further compound matters, the loss of over 21 million people diminished the region's voice in all-India politics. It was thus unable to secure adequate resources from the Centre to fund its development. The *bhadralok* expectations of Partition delivering a 'small, manageable Hindu-dominated state', a 'lost golden age of ... power and influence' were to be cruelly unrealised.[43]

Yet the Bengal Congress did not wholly support the province's Partition, which, it should be noted, was also urged by the Hindu Mahasabha. Surat Bose and Kiran Shankar Roy both supported the United Bengal scheme which was raised in April 1947 by the Muslim League Prime Minister Huseyn Shaheed Suhrawardy. Although the latter was out of favour with the All-India Muslim League leadership, nevertheless Jinnah supported his moves, despite their implications for the two-nation theory. Chatterji has noted both the Congress High Command's and Bengal Provincial Congress Committee's opposition to the scheme, leading her to describe the proposal as 'never more than a pipedream'.

Unlike Punjab, where local demands for Partition followed the Rawalpindi riots, Hindu leaders did not demand a separate West Bengal province in the wake of the Calcutta and Noakhali riots (1946), but only after Attlee's February 1947 declaration which signalled an imminent British departure and raised the prospect of some kind of Pakistan state. Instead of riots, far more important was the Muslim League's success in mobilising peasant support against landlord and moneylender along communal lines, a process that had began with claims that the Hindu merchants and *zamindars* had caused the devastating Bengal Famine (1943); it continued with the sloganising at the time of the 1946 elections that the creation of Pakistan would bring 'land to the tiller'. At its Gaffargaon Conference in January 1946, under the Presidency of the UP landlord and right-hand man of Jinnah, Liaquat Ali Khan, the Muslim League revealed that its objective was to abolish the *zamindari* system in Bengal.[44] This struck at the heart of the interests of the *bhadralok* rentier class. The following April, the Suhrawardy government tabled the State Acquisition and Tenancy Bill to redeem this promise.[45] Such measures emboldened Muslim peasant attitudes towards the Hindu landlords and moneylenders which were motivated by the belief that they had become 'independent'.

---

[43] Chatterji, *The Spoils of Partition*, p. 314.

[44] Interestingly Liaquat Ali Khan who had lost his UP powerbase following Partition, was eventually nominated a place in the Pakistan Constituency Assembly from an East Bengal constituency.

[45] For details, see Taj-ul-Islam Hashmi, 'Peasant Nationalism and the Politics of Partition: The Class-Communal Symbiosis in East Bengal 1940–1947', in Ian Talbot and Gurharpal Singh (eds), *Region and Partition*, p. 32.

This acting-out of a 'peasant utopia' in acts of killing, forced conversion and looting was summed up by an elderly peasant following the mass exodus of Hindus from riot-torn Noakhali and Tippera. He declared that they had 'achieved Pakistan' as the region between Feni and Chandpur had been 'liberated'.[46]

The highly charged class conflict in the East Bengal countryside explains the vehement opposition to the United Bengal Scheme by the *bhadralok*. Their expectations that Partition would bring security and restore their former fortunes were unfounded. Nevertheless they secured the veto of the Suhrawardy-Bose-Roy formula for an independent Bengal by Nehru and Patel. It is important to understand Bengali Muslim support for the proposal as being far more than a belated response to the threat of the province's partition. While the Urdu-speaking business classes of Calcutta and the conservative landed families of Dacca supported the idea of an East Pakistan zone within a single Pakistan state, a section of Bengali-speaking Muslim Leaguers were committed to the ideal of a sovereign East Pakistan state that would be the realisation of the distinctive Bengali cultural identity and would be the authentic reading of the Lahore Resolution (1940) which had spoken of 'Pakistan states'. This idea, which contradicted the All-India Muslim League two-nation theory was propounded by the Muslim League members active in the East Pakistan Renaissance Society (founded in 1942) which argued for a *Purba* (eastern) Pakistan. The conflict between the Bengali and Urdu-speaking Muslim elites remained incipient in the pre-Partition period: it was to subsequently dominate east–west Pakistan relations and contribute to the 'second partition' of 1971. The seeds of this conflict had been sown as early as July 1933 when the All-Bengal Urdu Association declared that 'Bengali is a Hinduised and Sankritised language' and that 'in the interests of the Muslims themselves it is necessary that they should try to have one language which cannot but be Urdu'.[47]

The attempt to keep Bengal united, despite its ultimate failure, throws interesting light on the wider Partition process. First, it provides evidence that Jinnah could adopt a flexible position even if it contradicted the two-nation theory in the bid to improve the Muslim League position and avoid provincial partition. Second, it points to the intermeshing of all-India and provincial pressures which culminated in the Partition of Bengal and Punjab. Finally, it reveals again the importance of Indian political leaders' complicity in Partition outcomes. Rather then imposing the

[46] Hashmi, 'Peasant Nationalism', p. 31.
[47] Harun-or-Rashid, *The Foreshadowing of Bangladesh: Bengal Muslim League and Muslim Politics, 1936–1947* (Dhaka: The Asiatic Society of Bangladesh, 1987), p. 45.

Partition of Bengal, Mountbatten entered into full consultations on the issue, and both he and the provincial governor Sir Frederick Burrows were in fact sympathetic to the United Bengal scheme. Indeed, Mountbatten advised Suhrawardy that he should offer joint Hindu–Muslim electorates in order to increase the chances of its success.[48]

The issue of Indian political leaders' complicity in Bengal's Partition has been explored most fully by Chatterji in terms of the popular mobilisation of the Bengal Congress and the Mahasabha, and the memoranda put forward to the Boundary Commission. She argues that the attempts to influence the framing of a future West Bengal state by the 'minimalist' dissident Congress groups so as to increase their post-Independence political prospects, clearly dispels the orthodox view that Radcliffe imposed his 'fiat from above'.[49] Unlike the figure in Auden's famous poem, 'Partition', Radcliffe did not singly settle the fate of millions by the stroke of his pen. In short, he provided a useful 'screen' for the Indian politicians to hide behind when the new boundary lines evoked their inevitable hostility.

In fact in Bengal the Radcliffe award more or less followed the Congress submissions. The Muslim League argued that Calcutta should go to East Pakistan, on the grounds that its jute mills, railway workshops and ordnance factories were vital to East Bengal's economy, communications and defence. Radcliffe however conceded the Congress argument which meant that East Bengal without Calcutta was consigned to its fate as a 'rural slum'. The region which produced the bulk of the world's raw jute supply was left without a single mill. Radcliffe also awarded the Hindu-majority population, tea-producing areas of Darjeeling and Jalpaiguri to West Bengal, despite the Muslim League claims. In all West Bengal received just over a third of the total area (some 28,000 square miles) and population, including a sizeable Muslim minority of 29 per cent of the population. Hindus made up a similar percentage of the total population of 39.11 million in East Bengal.

The princes and Partition

The end of colonial rule also had profound implications for the patchwork of princely states which spread across the subcontinent and covered almost one third of the total territory. As rulers of nominally independent territories, the princes had direct treaty relations with the British Crown, but their apprehensions concerning their future relations with a self-governing India had increased in the 1930s because the Congress had

---

[48] Hodson, *The Great Divide*, pp. 246–7.   [49] Chatterji, *The Spoils of Partition*, p. 19.

encouraged the States' Peoples Conference movements for political reform within their borders and also because their hopes of a role as a conservative bulwark in an All-India federation had collapsed. The princes' predicament worsened the nearer the British departure appeared. The princely state traditionally had lower incidences of communal conflict than in British India, but tensions arose in those states such as Jammu and Kashmir and Hyderabad which had rulers drawn from a different religious community than the majority of their population.

The modern history of Jammu and Kashmir is normally dated from the Treaty of Lahore (1846) which ended Sikh rule in the province and marked the beginning of a Hindu monarchy that lasted almost a century. During this period the Hindu elite established an ethnically and economically stratified society in which the status of the vast majority of Muslims was reduced to that of a heavily exploited and servile peasantry. In the 1930s, as the nationalist movement sent ripples of political awakening across the province, Sheikh Abdullah, later to be known as the 'Lion of Kashmir', launched the popular National Conference, an ethnosocialist movement that campaigned against feudal oppression but also became the champion of Kashmiri identity. At the height of the Congress–Muslim League impasse between 1945 and 1946, Kashmir's struggle for self-determination led by Abdullah was portrayed by the Communist Party of India as a viable 'third way' – as an alternative to a Congress-dominated India or a Muslim Pakistan.

Hyderabad, the largest princely state, was ruled by a Muslim nizam, though 85 per cent of its 16 million inhabitants were Hindus. The nizam toyed with the idea of Dominion Status. The main drawback was its landlocked status making it both vulnerable to a hostile independent India and commercially dependent on it. The nizam's sympathies lay with Jinnah who attempted to dissuade him from acceding to India. The militant Ittehad-ul-Muslimeen, which drew support from the privileged Muslim elite, threatened violence. During the closing period of British rule, the nizam stood aloof from the pressures for accession, studiously avoiding a meeting with the viceroy to discuss the state's future. There had been no progress about accession by 15 August 1947. Indian troops were eventually to invade Hyderabad on 13 September 1948 in a 'police action' while Pakistan was distracted by the death of its founding father Mohammad Ali Jinnah.

The intervening period between the acceptance of the 3 June Plan and the British transfer of power were filled with efforts to ensure that the princes fall into line and accede either to the dominion of Pakistan or India. These efforts were overseen by the newly constituted States Department which took over from the Political Department responsibility for the states. There was at first misgiving in Whitehall as the policy was also opposed by Sir Conrad Corfield of the Political Department who was against the princes being pressured to accede before the transfer of power. This stance led Nehru to claim that Corfield was acting against India's interests and that a judicial enquiry should be launched into his behaviour. The Congress had always been suspicious of the Political Department as it had traditionally sided with the interests of the rulers rather than the States' Peoples Conference. Mountbatten shared the view held by Nehru that independence for the larger princely states, or for groupings of them, would result in a fragmented and inherently unstable subcontinent. By mid-June, a combination of Nehru, Patel and Menon had kicked into touch Corfield's stand against accession. Mountbatten charmed, while Sardar Vallabhbhai Patel and V. P. Menon bullied rulers to accede.[50] Corfield left India at the end of July 1947, 'with a feeling of nausea, as though my own honour had been smirched and I had deserted friends'.[51]

Mountbatten, in his role as Crown Representative, followed up a persuasive speech in favour of accession to the Chamber of Princes on 25 July with lobbying of those who still wavered. General chaos was avoided. The princely states acceded to either India or Pakistan. The rulers of the Sikh states of the Punjab (see chapter three) did link up with SAD and attempt to carve out a Sikhistan area amidst the administrative collapse in the region. The other problems surrounded the three princely states of Jammu and Kashmir, Hyderabad and Junagadh. The latter, geographically isolated on the tip of the Kathiawar peninsula, a Hindu-majority state of some 700,000 people ruled by a Muslim family for the last 200 years, announced its accession to Pakistan without warning on 15 August. These states' eventual incorporation in India was to result in bitter recriminations and, in the case of Jammu and Kashmir, armed conflict between India and Pakistan.

Patel and his Secretary V. P. Menon at the States Department, within the space of a couple of years, oversaw the whittling away of the princes' powers and the amalgamation of their territories or their merger into neighbouring provinces. The princely states' absorption added over a half a million square miles and 90 million people to the Indian Union. The bitter pill of the ending of the old order had been sugared by the tax-free pensions linked to the former state's revenue levels and by making

---

[50] Patel had insisted that Menon be appointed as Secretary to the States Department on 5 July. For an insight into Menon's great influence on the transfer of power arising from the trust he had from Mountbatten in his role as Constitutional Advisor and his links with Patel and Nehru, see Hodson, *The Great Divide*, p. 366.

[51] P. Ziegler, *Mountbatten: The Official Biography* (London: Phoenix Press, 2001), p. 408.

some of the rulers of the larger states *rajpramukhs* (governors) of the new administrative entities. This peaceful political revolution was a major achievement in the early stage of nation-building in India.

Pakistan also needed to address the problem of the amalgamation of princely states, some of which, such as Bahawalpur and Kalat, had pretensions of independence. The issue was further compounded by the fact that small tribal states, such as Swat and Dir, occupied strategically sensitive locations in the borderland regions with Afghanistan. Chitral, the northernmost state in the subcontinent was a suzerain of the Maharajah of Jammu and Kashmir with the result that India did not legally recognise its accession to Pakistan on 18 February 1948. Bahawalpur itself, the largest of the Pakistan region princely states, lay on the sensitive Punjab border with India.[52] Its ruler claimed the new title of king on 14 August 1947. He was vacationing in Britain during the communal violence which spilled over into the state from the neighbouring Punjab province. It was only with some reluctance that an instrument of accession to Pakistan was signed on 5 October. The presence of some 400,000 refugees in the state, along with its border location undermined the attempts by its ruler to limit Pakistan's paramountcy and maintain his political power. It was not, however, until January 1951 that the last vestiges of his power were removed. Bahawalpur's democratic experiment was, however, to shrivel in the desert. The 49-member assembly was dismissed by the Governor-General Ghulam Mohammad in October 1954. The following year Bahawalpur along with the other former princely states was steamrollered into the One Unit arrangement of West Pakistan.[53]

Pakistan's greatest problem of state integration occurred with respect to the Balochistan states. The ruler of Kalat (Khan-i-Azam) had proclaimed independence basing this on the 'legally indistinct' character of the state's sovereignty.[54] The non-accession in a strategic and mineral-rich area was of immense concern to the Pakistan government.[55] It also complicated the position of the other Balochistan princely states, such as Kharan, over which Kalat claimed sovereignty. The state's sensitive nature was further highlighted by the support which the Khan received

---

[52] It covered an area of over 17,000 square miles. Its population was enumerated in 1951 at 1.8 million.

[53] For a narrative of developments in Bahawalpur, see W. A. Wilcox, *Pakistan: The Consolidation of a Nation* (New York: Columbia University Press, 1966).

[54] The Khan claimed he was allowed privileges not dissimilar to those of the king of Nepal. He boycotted the Chamber of Princes for this reason. Wilcox, *Pakistan*, pp. 76–7.

[55] The Khan was aware of the Burmah Oil Company's interests in the Sibi and Bolan areas which he had leased to British Balochistan and sought to claim back with the lapse of paramountcy.

in his non-accession stance from Baloch nationalists. The first but by no means the last of the troubles in the area occurred following the state's unconditional accession to Pakistan in March 1948. The Khan's youngest brother Prince Karim was involved in a series of military clashes with Pakistan forces until his eventual arrest on 16 June. In 1951, Kalat became part of the Balochistan States Union. This pill along with the later incorporation into the One Unit Plan, as the Kalat Division, was sugared by central government subsidies and privy purses. Nevertheless, the Khan could not be bought easily even with his allowance being increased in 1955 from 425,000 to 650,000 rupees per annum.[56] He saw One Unit as a step too far in integration. In October 1958, he announced his secession from Pakistan claiming that the government of unbelievers led by Jinnah and Liaquat Ali Khan had forced him to accede to Pakistan. His tribal party was no match for the Pakistan army. He was arrested on 6 October and divested of his privileges. The tribal revolt had repercussions far beyond the 70,000 square miles of remote Kalat countryside, for President Iskander Mirza used the Khan's attempted secession as justification for the coup which brought to a close Pakistan's first experiment with democracy.[57]

Conclusion

It is important to remember that Partition was not the inevitable outcome of entrenched Hindu–Muslim differences. Notions of what constituted a religious community in the subcontinent had always been more plural, flexible and malleable than either census enumerators or religious reformers would countenance. Political separatism based on religion therefore was an ideology which resonated only in particular contexts. Its importance strengthened against the background of several intersecting developments – the fears stoked by democratisation in the 1930s, the Second World War, Congress's anti-war stance, the open declaration of the British in the early 1940s that they would leave India and the near-civil-war conditions between 1946 and 1947. Even at the height of communal polarisation in 1946–1947, there were well-documented cases where people, political parties and national political leaders refused to accept the official registers which defined the political categories of Hindus and Muslims.[58]

---

[56] Wilcox, *Pakistan*, p. 187.
[57] Talbot, *Pakistan*, p. 152.
[58] See Anindita Dasgupta, 'Denial and Resistance: Sylheti Partition "Refugees" in Assam', *Contemporary South Asia* 10, 3 (2001), p. 345.

Nor was Partition the inevitable fulfilment of the British ruling presence in India. There is no linear progression from the introduction of separate electorates to Pakistan. If anything the division of the subcontinent was contingent on a range of political choices made by both the British and India's political elites within the context of the impact of the Second World War on the subcontinent. It is true the British risked their long-term goal of Indian unity for the short-term policy of hiding behind the Muslim League's 'skirts' in order to frustrate constitutional reform. But then the Congress also made a series of tactical errors in dealing with the Muslim League's threat, as for example, during the 1944 Gandhi–Jinnah talks. Jinnah brilliantly turned the wartime opportunities to his advantage and bolstered the claim that the Muslims were a separate political nation. His rising status put pressure not only on the remaining Muslim nationalists, but also on his regional opponents. And though an almost millenarian religious sentiment marked grass-roots attitudes, political elites were concerned mainly with capturing state power, cynically using violence to further their aims. The 1946 elections completed political consolidation on communal lines, but it was only after the cycle of violence in north India which began with the Great Calcutta Killing of August 1946 that Partition became inevitable.

Nehru's vision for a state-directed modernisation was diametrically opposed to a weak centre and powerful provinces desired by the Muslim League, and though Partition was a blow to his belief in a united India, it ended the interminable wrangling with the Muslim League. Conversely, the latter saw a sovereign state as the solution to perpetual minority status in a representative political system. Jinnah hoped for a large Pakistan containing a considerable non-Muslim population because that would guarantee that the Muslims left behind in India would not fall victim to Hindu majoritarianism. He eventually had to settle for a 'moth-eaten' Pakistan shorn of the partitioned East Punjab and West Bengal. Paradoxically, the political leadership of Hindu and Sikh religious minorities of these states began to view Partition as a means to escape future Muslim 'tyranny', an opportunity to use state power to claw back their privileges and power which was threatened by Muslim majoritarianism in these provinces. Sadly, neither Jinnah, Nehru nor the provincial political elite anticipated the scale of the social dislocation which Partition would bring, or factor in the economic consequences arising from the division.

Bengal Muslim Leaguers' attempts to head off Partition were frustrated by the local *bhadralok* resolve for division and the Congress High Command's veto of the United Bengal scheme. Similarly, the Punjab Muslim Leaguers' lust for state power prevented any meaningful efforts at reconciliation with the Sikh community after the Rawalpindi Massacres.

SAD leaders, thereafter, harboured only thoughts of revenge. The use of force to carve out a Sikh state comprising areas of former British territory and the Sikh princely states was effectively thwarted by the Congress regime which took power in 1947.

The division of territory in 1947 was accompanied by massive social dislocation. The unforeseen consequences of mass migration presented huge problems for provincial authorities throughout north India and were to shape their dealings with the Centre and impact on community formation as well souring the relations of the fledgling Indian and Pakistan states.[59] While some of the migration had been voluntary, for most it was a response to the violence. It is to this that we will turn in our next chapter.

---

[59] As late as May 1960, the joint Indo-Pakistan Punjab Partition Implementation Committee was still sifting through various financial disputes, relating to government revenues, pensions of the victims of the 1947 disturbances, third-party claims and public investments. American Consul Lahore to Department of State, 25 May 1960. 790D.00(W)6–162–790D1/2–1060 US National Archives at College Park.

3　Violence and the Partition

The Golden Temple is an oasis of calm amidst Amritsar's cacophony of traffic and street noise. The press of people and surrounding buildings are such that one almost stumbles upon the main eastern entrance of the Sikh faith's holiest shrine. Stairs lead down from the entrance to the *Parkarma* (walkway) around the *Amrit Sarowar* (Tank of Nectar). Underneath them, there is a marble plaque which commemorates the victims of the Partition violence in the village of Bhuller in the Montgomery district of West Punjab. The 300 Sikhs who were 'martyred' there on 29 August 1947 have come to symbolise their community's heroism. They are also commemorated in folk song and story.[1] Their fate was shared by hundreds of thousands of others drawn from all communities: their deaths are not memorialised,[2] nor until recently[3] have they formed a significant element in histories of the Partition.

This chapter argues that the Partition-related violence was qualitatively different from earlier communal riots. It was not only more extensive and brutal, but was clearly linked with political developments. Heated debates about the creation of Pakistan and its consequences shifted from the drawing rooms to the streets of north India at the time of the 1946 provincial elections. Violence emerged both as a political resource and as a reaction to the increasingly vitiated political atmosphere. Each outbreak created more fear and distrust: the pool of trained killers was larger than ever. But the Partition massacres were also an outgrowth of the dislocations of the war years, the weakening of the *esprit de corps* it brought to the Indian Army[4] and

---

[1] Mohindar Singh Randhawa, *Out of the Ashes: An Account of the Rehabilitation of Refugees from West Pakistan in Rural Areas of East Punjab* (Chandigarh: Public Relations Department, Punjab, 1954), p. 15.

[2] A number of peace activists have attempted to set up a permanent memorial to the victims at the Wagah border crossing. See www.groups.yahoo.com/group/asiapeace.

[3] See the work of Gyanendra Pandey, *Remembering Partition: Violence, Nationalism and History in India* (Cambridge University Press, 2001).

[4] Similarly to the First World War, recruitment extended beyond the traditional recruits drawn from the 'martial castes' of the Punjab.

the legacy of a flood of weapons and demobilised soldiers in north India. The latter helped to train up volunteer movements which bombastically paraded and drilled in the streets of northern cities throughout the closing months of colonial rule. There were 58,000 members of the Hindu volunteer movement the Rashtriya Swayam Sevak Sangh in the Punjab alone. Their fascistic trappings alert us to the fact that the 1947 killings have as much in common with the brutalities of modern Europe as a throwback to the horrors of a medieval past.[5]

The chapter widens the scope from August 1947 to discern a cycle of violence that began in August 1946 and continued until March 1950. In contrast to the more conventional accounts of Partition-related violence from August to November 1947, it examines the violence's variegated nature – by region, locality and social patterns. Finally, we argue that throughout the period 1946–1950, communal violence was organised with the singular objective of clearing out minority populations. The state's response crucially determined whether violent episodes were contained or spiralled out of control, creating large numbers of casualties and refugees. The transition from a collapsing colonial state to its national Indian and Pakistani successors both reduced the capacity to maintain law and order and created a psychological environment which hindered the ability to protect minority populations. The potential for serious conflict in August 1947 was further increased by the existence of princely states, some of which harboured political ambitions or ideas of independence, thereby resulting, especially in the Punjab region, in the assaults on their minority populations as well as refugees who traversed their territory. Drawing on recent works on ethnic conflict in South Asia and new empirical findings from local research, we question the view, popularised by both nationalist and imperialist historiography, that the outbreaks of violence were 'irrational' and 'spontaneous' occurrences. But before we proceed, it is necessary to consider the issues of casualty numbers, the attempts at 'blame displacement', and the glorification of valour and martyrdom which characterise community and nationalist accounts of the violence.

Casualty figures

The exact number of those killed in Partition violence will never be known. Monsoon floods, mass disposal of bodies and administrative collapse meant that many corpses were never fully recovered, or enumerated.

---

[5] See, for example, Tapan Raychaudhuri, 'Shadows of the Swastika: Historical Perspectives on the Politics of Hindu Communalism', *Modern Asian Studies* 34, 2 (May 2000), pp. 259–79.

Most authors base their numbers on contemporary press reports, fragmentary official records and calculations made at the time. Figures vary from the low estimate of 200,000 by the British civil servant Penderel Moon[6] to those of 2 million. The Indian judge G. D. Khosla put the total at 500,000 with an equal number of Muslim and non-Muslim casualties.[7] The Mohajir Qaumi Mahaz (MQM) in its 1990s publications maintained that as many as 2 million *mohajirs* died. Such writers as Patrick French[8] have adopted a median figure of a million casualties. Propagandists inflated the numbers whether this aimed to promote community sacrifice and victimhood, indict the Mountbatten administration, or to 'demonise' the aggressor 'other' community. In the absence of verifiable figures, Gyanendra Pandey has correctly pointed out that the historical discourse on the killings, 'continues to bear the stamp of rumour'.[9]

Whatever the numbers, immense human suffering[10] occurred in a peacetime situation in which governments demonstrated a lamentable inability to provide basic security for minority communities. This failing was to have important repercussions on how nationalist accounts portrayed the violence; it was also, as we shall see in the next chapter, to encourage celebratory accounts of the state's role in rehabilitating the millions of refugees who fled the violence.

Community and nationalist accounts

The earliest accounts were designed to 'displace blame' for the onset of violence on to the 'other' community by documenting, albeit one-sidedly, the events surrounding Partition. G. D. Khosla's study *Stern Reckoning* exemplifies these aims. It is based on the researches of the Fact Finding Commission of the Government of India's Ministry of Relief and Rehabilitation. The Commission collected statements of refugees' maltreatment to counterbalance Pakistani charges of genocide in East Punjab. *Stern Reckoning* details, village by village, Muslim atrocities committed on

---

[6] Penderel Moon, *Divide and Quit*, new edn (New Delhi: Oxford University Press, 1998), p. 293.

[7] Gopal Das Khosla, *Stern Reckoning: A Survey of Events Leading up to and Following the Partition of India*, 2nd edn (New Delhi: Oxford University Press, 1999), p. 299.

[8] Patrick French, *Liberty or Death: India's Journey to Independence and Division* (London: Flamingo, 1998), p. 349.

[9] Pandey, *Remembering Partition*, p. 91.

[10] Personal testimonies reveal the brutality and sudden nature of the violence. They also attest to the agony arising from separation from loved ones and not knowing their fate. There are also graphic accounts of bloated corpses floating in the canals and water courses, of bodies piled high on the main migration routes and of vultures so sated by the feast of corpses that they ultimately only picked at the victims' livers.

the Hindu- and Sikh-minority populations of the West Punjab. It is only in a brief final chapter that it acknowledges that Muslims were also attacked in the Indian Punjab. These assaults are portrayed, however, as retaliation for the earlier Muslim violence. Khosla remains more reliable, however, than such community-biased accounts as that produced by, for example, *jathedar* Giani Partap Singh in *Pakistani Ghallughara*.[11]

The need to 'blame' rivals has resulted in diametrically opposed accounts in such riot-torn cities as Amritsar.[12] Personal testimonies as well as documentary records are concerned to portray violence as self-defence or retaliatory. The post-Independence governments sought to set the record straight. The West Punjab Government produced a series of reports in 1948–1949 designed to show evidence of a Sikh 'Plan' to ethnically cleanse Muslims from the East Punjab. They included studies of para-military communal formations such as the Rashtriya Swayam Sevak Sangh.[13] This was a counterpoint to Indian accounts which heaped the blame for the communal violence on the 'war unleashed by the Muslims of the Punjab' on the Hindus and Sikhs.[14] The emphasis of publications on the Punjab region reflects the reality that this was at the epicentre of the violence.

Community histories also emphasised heroism and sacrifice. Sohan Singh Seetal in *Punjab da Ujaarha*,[15] for instance, details the sufferings of Hindus and Sikhs in West Punjab. The author resided in the Qasur *tehsil* of the Lahore district. The new border eventually placed his village just two miles into Pakistan. There are also a number of Urdu-language accounts of the 'heroism' of the East Punjab Muslims. Mashkur Hassan's moving account of what befall his family in Hissar forms the focus for his

---

[11] The author published the text (*The Pakistan Massacre*) on 16 August 1948. The book is organised around three divisions: Rawalpindi (pp. 143–72), Lahore (pp. 273–353) and Multan (pp. 354–416); with details of events and casualties under district-wise categories that are based on personal testimonies. Their accuracy has been called into question. See Giani Partap Singh, *Pakistani Ghallughara* (Ludhiana: Lahore Bookshop, 1948).

[12] See for example the conflicting accounts in S. Gurbachan Singh Talib, *Muslim League Attack on Sikhs and Hindus in the Punjab 1947* (Allahabad: Shiromani Gurdwara Parbandhak Committee, 1950), and Khawaja Iftikhar, *Jab Amritsar jal raha tha*, 9th edn (Lahore: no pub., 1995).

[13] See Government of West Punjab, *The Sikhs in Action* (Lahore: Government Printing Press, West Punjab, 1948); Government of West Punjab, *Notes on the Sikh Plan* (Lahore: Government Printing Press, West Punjab, 1948); Government of West Punjab, *RSSS in Punjab* (Lahore: Government Printing Press, West Punjab, 1948).

[14] Talib, *Muslim League Attack*, p. vi.

[15] Sohan Singh Seetal has produced in *Tragedy of Punjab* a largely autobiographical account which is interspersed with other personal testimonies. Sohan Singh Seetal, *Punjab da Ujaarha* (n.p.: Mater Sher Singh Khazan Singh, 1948).

autobiography.[16] Even more popular in Pakistan is Khawaja Iftikhar's autobiographical work *Jab Amritsar jal raha tha*[17] (When Amritsar Was Burning).[18] Iftikhar was vice-president of the Amritsar branch of the Muslim League. He portrays the Muslims as non-aggressors who valiantly defended their honour in the face of overwhelming odds. S. Gurbachan Singh Talib paints a similar picture from a Sikh perspective. He details the 'memorable and heroic battles given by Sikhs' at Bhuller in the face of an attack by 25,000 Muslims. It was only after the armed police and Baloch military assisted the 'Muslim Mob' that the Sikhs were defeated.[19]

The concept of upholding honour runs through the recently recovered historical discourse surrounding one of the most troubling aspects of the 1947 violence: the killing of female family members in order to protect them from defilement at the hands of the rapacious males of 'other' communities. Talib records of the Bhuller episode, 'Finding that the fight was unequal, Sikhs decided to die fighting, and killed their own womenfolk to save them from dishonour.'[20] Muslim women similarly leaped into wells in Bihar during the October/November violence in 1946. Rather then being a matter of shame, suicide, which in some instances may have been coerced, is portrayed as a reflection of community pride and moral superiority.[21] The most dramatic manifestation involved the collective suicide of 105 Sikh women at the village of Thoa Khalsa by jumping into the village well.[22] The episode provided the inspiration for a fictional episode in Bhisham Sahni's powerful Partition novel *Tamas*.[23] The Thoa Khalsa episode has been interrogated by Pandey and Butalia for what it reveals about the Punjab's notions of community honour and gender relations, and how such 'celebrations of martyrdom'

[16] Mashkur Hassan, *Aazaadi ke charaagh*, 3rd edn (Lahore: no pub., 1986).

[17] Iftikhar, *Jab Amritsar jal raha tha*. The work ran to nine editions in the space of a decade. Its author has been awarded the gold medal of the Pakistan movement and the epithet, *Musavvir-e-Haqiqat* (The Painter of Realities).

[18] V. N. Datta, the leading Indian historian and expert on Amritsar has criticised the work for being 'one-sided, partial and perverse'. He points out that there is no reference to the protection afforded to Muslims at personal risk by such prominent citizens as Sir Buta Singh, Sohan Singh Josh, Dr Baldev Singh, Pandit Amar Nath Vidyalanker, Sant Ram Seth, Brahm Nath Data, Qasir, G. R. Sethi and Bhai Jodh Singh among many others. V. N. Datta, 'Amritsar: When Riots Shattered a Heritage', *The Sunday Tribune* (Chandigarh) 26 April 1998.

[19] Talib, *Muslim League Attack*, p. 173.   [20] Talib, *Muslim League Attack*, p. 173.

[21] Sikhs in community discourses contrast their refusal at all costs to convert to Islam with the behaviour of beleaguered Hindus.

[22] The village had been surrounded by 10 to 12,000 armed Muslims on 12 March 1947.

[23] He sets the event in the village of Sayyedpur. For a discussion of this novel, which evoked considerable controversy when it was dramatised for Indian television in 1988, see I. Talbot, *Freedom's Cry: The Popular Dimension in the Pakistan Movement and Partition Experience in North-West India* (Karachi: Oxford University Press, 1996), pp. 122–3.

neglect the question of female choice. 'The Sikh ladies in their extremity either committed suicide or entreated their husbands and fathers to kill them', declares one such account. 'This was done. Thus the ladies saved their honour.'[24]

Transition from 'traditional' to 'communal' violence

The transition from 'traditional' to 'communal' violence can be dated earlier to the time of the Great Calcutta Killing of August 1946. The cycle then continued, to include the massacres in Noakhali, Bihar and at Garhmukhteshwar in the autumn of that year. The following spring, violence spread to the Punjab which remained disturbed throughout the final months of British rule. The August 1947 violence also had its epicentre in the Punjab. In the weeks after Independence, the shockwaves spread to Delhi and later to Sindh. The cycle ended where it had begun: with riots in Calcutta and East Bengal in February and March 1950. These episodes, spread over a forty-two-month period, can be seen as forming a cycle in part because of their political dimensions. They either precipitated the partition of the subcontinent or flowed from its consequences, and also possessed common elements which mark them off from earlier colonial communal riots.

Plate 1 Calcutta police use tear-gas bombs during an attempt to set fire to a Hindu temple during riots in the city in August 1948.

[24] Talib, *Muslim League Attack*, p. 352.

Before the 1940s 'traditional' communal riots often occurred at times of heightened religious tension when Hindu–Muslim festivals coincided. They were frequently occasioned by clashes over procession routes, or when loud music was played outside of mosques during prayer times. Trivial episodes could spark a spontaneous riot. These could be anything from name-calling, an alleged slight on the honour of a woman by men from the 'other' community, or the throwing of a single stone. Communities continued to live alongside each other, once the violence had subsided.[25]

Five features differentiated the end of empire violence from 'traditional' communal riots. First, it contained a desire to squeeze out, or in modern parlance, to ethnically cleanse minority populations. This was evidenced both in the high casualty figures and the destruction of dwellings and businesses. Community life was so shattered that it could not be reconstituted in the affected locality. Second, violence was not about religious differences as in the 'traditional' riot, but occurred within the end of empire political context of the contest for power and territory. Local struggles responded to the wider issue of Pakistan. At various stages they either attempted to pre-empt the boundary award, or responded to it.[26] Muslim victims of the violence in Bihar, for instance, tried to persuade Jinnah to argue for the 'establishment [of] an independent homeland for us in some part of the province of Bihar, where we may be able to concentrate our entire population'.[27] Third, the Partition violence was more intense and sadistic than anything that had preceded it. Victims were not only brutally done to death, but were maimed and tortured. The body, especially the female body, became a physical symbol of community identity and honour. It was thus vulnerable to disfigurement by the hostile 'other'. Fourth, linked with the previous characteristic, the violence spread from its traditional public arena of conflict to invade the private sphere. Women and children were caught up in the outbreaks and shown no mercy. Fifth, the violence evinced a high degree of planning and organisation by para-military groups. As in post-Independence pogroms, their task was assisted by the quiescence, if not active involvement, of state agents. These included policemen, soldiers, civil servants and railway

---

[25] See Suranjan Das, *Communal Riots in Bengal, 1905–1947* (Delhi: Oxford University Press, 1991).

[26] This was clearly evidenced in the endemic violence in Lahore and Amritsar from March 1947 onwards. For details, see I. Talbot, *Divided Cities: Partition and its Aftermath in Lahore and Amritsar 1947–1957* (Karachi: Oxford University Press, 2006).

[27] The Bihar Muslim League held a Division of Bihar conference at Gaya in April 1947 when this demand was raised by its President Jafar Imam. See Papiya Ghosh, 'Partition's Biharis', *Comparative Studies of South Asia, Africa and the Middle East* 17, 2 (1997), p. 24.

officials who divulged the running times of the refugee specials so that they could be waylaid along their routes.

The violence from August 1946 onwards differed from earlier episodes in that it contained dimensions of 'ethnic cleansing'. Communal riots previously had been about the 'renegotiation of local hierarchies of power'.[28] This is in essence what disputes over the routes of religious processions were about. The resulting clashes have been termed by some scholars as 'consensual' in character.[29] The signs of 'ethnic cleansing' are first evident in the Great Calcutta Killing of 16–19 August 1946. Over 100,000 people were made homeless. They were also present in the wave of violence which rippled out from Calcutta to Bihar, where there were high Muslim casualty figures,[30] and to Noakhali deep in the Ganges-Brahmaputra delta of East Bengal. With respect to the Noakhali riots, one British observer spoke of a 'determined and organised' Muslim effort to drive out all the Hindus, who accounted for around a fifth of the total population.[31] Similarly, the Punjab counterpart to this transition in violence was the Rawalpindi Massacres of March 1947. The level of death and destruction in such West Punjab villages as Thoa Khalsa was such that it was impossible for communities to live together in its wake. The massacres paved the way for the later August violence both in that they created a Sikh desire for revenge and revealed the ease with which minority communities could be expelled in the absence of effective law enforcement. About 40,000 Sikhs had been left homeless. The August 1947 Punjab violence repeated this uprooting on a huge scale. It formed the context for the largest exchange of population in modern history. Further refugee migrations followed the spread of violence to Delhi and Karachi and the 1950 killings in Bengal prompted a further flood of refugees in a region which had been relatively peaceful at the time of Partition.

There are numerous eyewitness accounts of the maiming and mutilation of victims. The catalogue of horrors includes the disembowelling of pregnant women, the slamming of babies' heads against brick walls, the cutting off of victims' limbs and genitalia and the display of heads and corpses. While previous communal riots had been deadly, the scale and

---

[28] See Veena Das and Ashis Nandy, 'Violence, Victimhood and the Language of Silence', in Veena Das (ed.), *The Word and the World: Fantasy, Symbol and Record* (New Delhi: Sage, 1986), pp. 177–90.

[29] Shail Mayaram, 'Speech, Silence and the Making of Partition Violence in Mewat', in Shahid Amin and Dipesh Chakrabarty (eds), *Subaltern Studies IX: Writings on South Asian History and Society* (New Delhi: Oxford University Press, 1996), pp. 126–65.

[30] See *Report on Disturbances in Bihar and UP* (Muslim Information Centre, 1946). P/T 3363, IOL.

[31] Das, *Communal Riots*, p. 199.

level of brutality was unprecedented. Although some scholars question the use of the term 'genocide' with respect to the Partition massacres, much of the violence manifested itself as having genocidal tendencies. It was designed to cleanse an existing generation as well as prevent its future reproduction.[32]

The repertoire of the 'traditional' communal riot had not included attacks on women. It had taken place in public arenas, frequently around procession routes and disputed sacred space where men from rival communities contested these disputes and were the main victims. Domestic space which was reserved to women was rarely invaded. The violence from August 1946 onwards, however, marked a shift from the public arena to the private sphere. Women were in many respects the 'chief sufferers'.[33] They endured such terrible cruelties as the lopping of their breasts and noses and impregnation by sticks and metal rods. Their targeting for murderous assaults and sexual humiliation represented a new feature of violence.[34] In one such episode, Muslim women were paraded naked through the streets outside Amritsar's Golden Temple. Women were targeted primarily at this time because they were seen as upholding the *izzat* (honour) of their community.[35]

Partition cycle of violence

(i)   *The Great Calcutta Killing: 16–19 August 1946*

Suranjan Das has carefully constructed the background to this episode. It is significant because it marks the transition from 'traditional' communal riots in north India and triggered the spiral of killings that resulted in partition. Das highlights the brutalising effects of wartime inflation, unemployment and population influx into the city in the wake of the 1943 famine. He also points out the 'corrupting' influence of the quartering of US troops[36] who encouraged a rise in prostitution, black marketing and the selling of weapons to para-military organisations. Most importantly

---

[32] See Paul R. Brass, 'Victims, Heroes or Martyrs: Partition and the Problem of Memorialisation in Contemporary Sikh History', *Sikh Formations* 2, 1 (June 2006), pp. 17–31.

[33] See Andrew J. Major, '"The Chief Sufferers": Abduction of Women during the Partition of the Punjab', in D. A. Low and Howard Brasted (eds), *Freedom, Trauma, Continuities: Northern India and Independence* (New Delhi: Sage, 1998), pp. 57–73.

[34] An integral part of the violence was what might be termed 'power rape'.

[35] See Ritu Menon and Kamla Bhasin, *Borders and Boundaries: Women in India's Partition* (New Brunswick, NJ: Rutgers University Press: Kali for Women, 1998).

[36] Das, *Communal Riots*, pp. 162; 180. Weapons had been purchased by rich Marwari businessmen.

Plate 2 Rioters on the streets of Calcutta at the time of the August 1946
Great Calcutta Killing.

the violence was occasioned not by spontaneous religious passions, as in the
past, but by political parties who carefully planned the assaults.

Like other major communal episodes, controversy surrounds the death
toll and the instigation of the trouble, with the figure of 4,000 deaths
officially quoted. An English official maintained that this was 'a new order
in communal rioting', describing the riot as a 'cross between the worst of
London air raids and the Great Plague'.[37] Despite the Muslim League's
denials, the outbreak was clearly linked with the celebration of Direct
Action Day. Muslim processionists who had gone to the staging ground of
the 150-feet-high Ochterlony Monument on the maidan to hear the
Muslim League Prime Minister Suhrawardy, attacked Hindus on their
way back. They were heard shouting such slogans as 'Larke Lenge Pakistan'
(We shall win Pakistan by force). Violence spread to North Calcutta
when Muslim crowds tried to force Hindu shopkeepers to observe the
day's strike (*hartal*) call. The circulation of pamphlets in advance of
Direct Action Day made a clear connection with the use of violence and
the demand for Pakistan. One which depicted Jinnah with a sword in hand
declared:

Oh! *Kafir* your doom is not far and the general massacre will come. We shall show
our glory and will have a special victory.

---

[37] Das, *Communal Riots*, p. 171.

Another proclaimed:

We are starting a Jehad in Your (God's) name. We promise before You that we entirely depend on you. Make us victorious over the *Kafirs*, enable us to establish the kingdom of Islam in India.[38]

Posters were also prominently displayed which declared that the 16 August Direct Action Day would bring independence and break the 'shackles of slavery'.[39] The scene was set for violence when the Hindu Mahasabha issued its own pamphlets calling on Hindus to give a 'clear answer to this act of effrontery'. 'It is the duty of every Hindu', the pamphlet *Beware* declared, 'to carry on his normal occupation. Remember that to join the *hartal* is to support the demand for Pakistan.'[40]

Although three times as much Hindu property was destroyed in arson attacks as that belonging to Muslims, the casualty figures were about equal for the two communities. The Muslim League used this to counter the claim that the Suhrawardy Ministry had instigated the violence. It also questioned why Calcutta, where Muslims formed only a quarter of the population, should be planned as a site for violence.

Women were brutally attacked – unlike in the 1918 and 1926 Calcutta riots. The other new feature was the post-riot movement of population. Around 10,000 people shifted out of the city. Within Calcutta, people moved from mixed localities to Hindu or Muslim enclaves. This consolidation of population occurred in riot-torn towns and cities across north India during the following months. In Calcutta, as in such Punjabi cities as Lahore and Amritsar, 'no-go' areas emerged with their barricades and iron gates. Their existence hampered everyday life for all but Europeans and Indian Christians who could still freely move around. Well before August 1947, in parts of north India, the urban landscape had undergone a visible transformation and trust had completely broken down between the various communities.

(ii)   Noakhali: 10 October 1946

Seven weeks after the Great Calcutta Killing, violence spread to this south-eastern district of Bengal which is now in Bangladesh. From Noakhali it fanned out to the Tippera district. In all 350 villages were affected in the two districts. The disorders were only finally brought under control by the deployment of around 2,500 troops and police. The minority Hindu populations living in inaccessible villages were the victims.

[38] Das, *Communal Riots*, p. 168.   [39] Das, *Communal Riots*, p. 169.
[40] Das, *Communal Riots*, p. 169.

There were a large number of cases of abduction of women, forced conversion and the destruction of the property of shopkeepers who had profiteered at the expense of the Muslim peasantry at the time of the 1943 Famine.[41] At least 2,000 shops and houses were destroyed in the two districts with many large bazaars gutted. Violence was not only provoked by economic grievances against the wealthier Hindu population, but by rumours of Muslim casualties in Calcutta. Despite Gandhi's well-publicised efforts at peacemaking, the restoration of normal life was difficult. Like other episodes of end of empire violence, population dislocation was the outcome. Around 50,000 people took refuge in relief camps. They were settled as far away as Assam where a 'Noakhali Colony' was set up in the Silpukhari area of Gauhati. Noakhali's other shared features with the cycle of violence was the dishonouring of women, the ineffectiveness of the police and the organised attacks on minorities. Demobilised soldiers helped to orchestrate the pogrom and were careful to cut communications between the district and the outside world.

(iii)   Bihar: 25 October 1946

The violence in south Bihar began on 25 October 1946. It spread from the Saran to the Patna, Gaya and Monghyr districts. During the two weeks of violence, entire Muslim villages were wiped out. Khawaja Nazimuddin, the Bengal Muslim League leader, put the death toll at between 10 and 20,000. The Congress-led government of Bihar made a more conservative estimate of 5,000 casualties.[42] Even this figure was in excess of the death toll in Calcutta and Noakhali. The Viceroy Lord Wavell declared that the Bihar killings were 'far beyond anything that I think has yet happened in India since British rule began'.[43] When Jinnah addressed a Bihari refugee camp in Karachi on 23 February 1947, he declared that he was 'really proud' of the Biharis who had 'sacrificed so much' and had 'certainly brought the goal of Pakistan nearer and shown our readiness to make any sacrifice for its attainment'.[44]

The October–November 1946 massacres were followed by large-scale displacement. Some refugees were still in camps in Bihar as late as September 1947. The Sindh government allocated 10,000 acres for the

---

[41] Das, *Communal Riots*, p. 197.
[42] Sucheta Mahajan, *Independence and Partition: The Erosion of Colonial Power in India* (New Delhi: Sage Publications, 2000), p. 258.
[43] Mahajan, *Independence and Partition*, p. 262.
[44] Papiya Ghosh, *Partition and the South Asian Diaspora: Extending the Subcontinent* (London: Routledge, 2007), p. 3.

construction of a Bihari colony in Golimar, Karachi.[45] By March 1947 there were about 1,000 Bihar refugees in the province. The majority of refugees (some 60,000 in April 1947) were located in West Bengal, the first of a series of dislocations involving migration from West Bengal to East Bengal after independence and then back to Pakistan after the emergence of Bangladesh. The 1946 Bihar massacres were again accompanied, like others in the cycle, by what Gyanendra Pandey has termed a 'war on women'.[46] Four thousand girls were abducted in the Patna district alone.[47]

Nehru who rushed to Bihar was taken aback. 'Hindu peasant mobs have behaved in a manner that is the extreme of brutality and inhumanity', he wrote privately. 'To think that the simple, unsophisticated, rather likeable Bihar peasant can go completely mad en masse', he continued, 'upsets all my sense of values.'[48] In reality, however, it was not a spontaneous moment of madness. Bihar had been in economic and political turmoil for months. The province had been wracked by strikes and agrarian unrest caused in part by food scarcities. In the weeks before the outbreaks, there were seventy-two incidents of the looting of food from goods trains on the Bengal–Nagpur line.[49] Communal violence increased opportunities for looting by an angry and impoverished peasantry; it may also have provided a useful distraction for the *zamindars* who were locked in disputes with tenant cultivators.[50]

The Congress government in Bihar, rather than damping down feelings in the wake of the Noakhali massacres, sought to turn them to its political advantage. In an event – which had striking parallels with the 2002 Gujarat pogrom – the Congress ministry on the eve of the outbreak of violence called a Noakhali Protest day to 'remember' the Hindu victims. Once violence had started the officials refused calls for the use of troops: the Prime Minister S. K. Sinha declared that 'the problem of mob violence would be solved not by firing, but by prayer'.[51] It was only after Nehru arrived on the scene on 3 November that Sinha imposed a curfew and

---

[45] Ghosh, *Partition and the South Asian Diaspora*, p. 8.
[46] Pandey, *Remembering Partition*, p. 69.
[47] Ghosh, *Partition and the South Asian Diaspora*, pp. 44–5.
[48] Pandey, *Remembering Partition*, p. 260.
[49] Vinita Damodaran, *Broken Promises: Popular Protest, Indian Nationalism and the Congress Party in Bihar 1935–1946* (New Delhi: Oxford University Press, 1992), p. 322.
[50] This was the Communist Party explanation of the violence. Damodaran finds some support for this in the *zamindars'* orchestration of violence including the provision of weapons. There was extensive violence in such districts as Monghyr where Hindu and Muslim peasants had been previously collaborating in anti-landlord movements. Damodaran, *Broken Promises*, p. 338.
[51] Damodaran, *Broken Promises*, p. 355.

banned assemblies. Few of the perpetrators were punished. The governor, Hugh Dow, noted that out of 100 persons arrested in Bhagalpur, where many Muslims died, the magistrate acquitted 80; a further 15 were acquitted by the Sessions Court. The High Court freed 4 more and the Ministry was likely to pardon the only one who got through the net.[52]

The Muslim minority in Bihar was more vulnerable than in other Indian provinces because the police lacked impartiality: Muslim officers formed only around a fifth of the force. Eventually the trouble was only quelled following the deployment of troops. Ineffective policing sustained the violence and encouraged impoverished lower-caste cultivators to loot Muslim homes. The Congress claimed that the Muslim League capitalised on the violence as all refugee aid in Bihar was channelled through it. Congress also maintained that the League discouraged riot victims from returning to their villages, preferring to oversee their evacuation to Bengal. Yet the levels of violence and destruction in some villages displayed signs of the desire to permanently remove the minority population with incidences of women drowning themselves in wells to escape the community dishonour of rape. 'When I visited the village [of Kanchanpur]', the Sub Divisional Officer of Bihar Sharif, noted, 'I found a smell coming from the house of Pahar Mian. The well in the house was full of dead bodies, and we filled it up with earth ... It is said some of the rioters raped the women and killed them. Seeing this some of the other women threw themselves in the well of the house and committed suicide.'[53] Within less than a month, 60,000 refugees had left the province,[54] many taking shelter in the camps run by the Muslim League in West Bengal.

(iv)   Garhmukhteshwar: 6 November 1946

Muslims were also the victims at Garhmukhteshwar, a small town in the Meerut district of western UP. The violence had begun at a fair three miles outside of the town. The annual *Kartik Purnima Mela*, encamped over an area of 12 square miles, drew upwards of three quarters of a million pilgrims from the surrounding areas and as far away as Punjab. Indeed, it was alleged that Jats from its Rohtak district were the main aggressors. The trouble began after an alleged insult to a Hindu woman who was watching a wall-of-death motorcycling display. Muslim shopkeepers were attacked at their stalls on the evening of 6 November. Official reports put the number of casualties at forty-six. Thus far the episode had many features of the traditional north Indian communal outbreak with the

---

[52] Cited in Damodaran, *Broken Promises*, footnote p. 355.
[53] Damodaran, *Broken Promises*, p. 344.   [54] Pandey, *Remembering Partition*, p. 264.

eruption of violence over a 'trivial' event. The massacre[55] of Muslims in Garhmukhteshwar the following afternoon bore all the features of the transition from 'traditional' communal violence. As in Calcutta, Bihar, Noakhali – and later in Punjab – the violence spread from public arenas to private spheres, accompanied by atrocities against women, including parading them naked through the streets, forced conversions and the destruction of Muslim homes and businesses that had been singled out with chalk marks.[56]

The official report into the riot declared that the attacking crowd was 'well organised'. Other accounts[57] point to the role of RSS volunteers and ex-servicemen in which mounted horsemen directed operations. The 'mob' which destroyed the Muslim quarter of Garhmukhteshwar came equipped with petrol and other chemicals, and the assailants went about their deadly and brutal task without any check from the police or the military. According to the report on the disturbances by the former Indian National Army hero, Major General Shah Nawaz Khan, 'Had the police acted more vigorously and promptly, much of the destruction to life and property could have been prevented.'[58]

The events at Garhmukhteshwar were a powerful indictment of the Congress UP government. For Muslim League propagandists they revealed a deep-laid plot against the minority which made it impossible for Hindus and Muslims to live together. *Dawn* proclaimed that the tragedy of Garhmukhteshwar was as serious as that of Bihar, albeit in a 'more concentrated form'.[59] The violence of August–November 1946 had established its own grisly repertoire. It was in Punjab the following March that this was to receive a further performance, after which the partition of the province along with that of the subcontinent became inevitable.

(v)   Punjab: March 1947

The precipitating event which triggered the violence in Punjab was the resignation on 2 March 1947 of the cross-community coalition government led by the Unionist Prime Minister Khizr Hayat Khan Tiwana. The

---

[55] As in all communal violence, casualty figures are notoriously unreliable. The provincial government put the figure at around 200, the Muslim League reckoned on 2,000. This number was also cited by Lieutenant General Francis Tuker in his memoir, *While Memory Serves: The Last Two Years of British Rule in India* (London: Cassell, 1950), p. 200.

[56] See chapter 5 of Pandey, *Remembering Partition*.

[57] See Pandey, *Remembering Partition* for an incisive analysis of the different uses made of the violence in nationalist, Muslim League, colonial and communist accounts.

[58] Pandey, *Remembering Partition*, p. 98.   [59] Pandey, *Remembering Partition*, p. 107.

Muslim League's six-week agitation from 24 January 1947,[60] ostensibly in the name of civil liberties, but in reality to unseat the Unionist administration,[61] heightened communal tension in the Punjab's twin cities of Lahore and Amritsar. This had already been raised by the election campaign which the Muslim League had presented as a referendum on Pakistan. But the outbreak of violence is linked in the popular imagination with Master Tara Singh's melodramatic unsheathing of a sword on the steps of the Punjab Assembly building on hearing the news of the resignation.[62]

Violence in Lahore on the morning of 4 March claimed five lives. It was the prelude to an afternoon of rioting which saw the first arson attacks on Hindu businesses in the walled city, and despite the introduction of a curfew and direct governor's rule, disturbances continued on 5 and 6 March. Hindu properties in the walled city bore the brunt of the damage, while most of the casualties were Sikhs. Simultaneously rioting had begun in neighbouring Amritsar on 5 March and rapidly became more serious than in Lahore. 'The devastation (in Amritsar) was so complete', the All-India Congress Committee Report into the disturbances declared, that 'enemy action from the air in any war zone could not have done greater damage.'[63] The trouble that had started in Chowk Mani spread to the Hindu commercial areas of Katra Karam Singh, Lohgarh, and Hall Bazaar. Shops were systematically looted and burned by Muslims from the neighbouring localities. According to the AICC Report about 8,000 houses were reported to be destroyed with an estimated cost of Rs 8 *crores*.[64]

The outbreak of violence in Lahore rippled out to the Attock, Rawalpindi, Jhelum and Multan – all Muslim-majority districts of the West Punjab. In the three districts of Attock, Rawalpindi and Jhelum the loss of life was estimated to be between 7 and 8,000, and of property between 40 and 50 *crores* of rupees.[65] About 40,000 people, mainly Sikhs, took refuge in

[60] For the background to both the agitation and to Punjab politics after the formation of the Unionist Coalition, see Talbot, *Khizr Tiwana, The Punjab Unionist Party and the Partition of India*, pp. 145–56.

[61] Attlee's announcement on 20 February 1947 that the transfer of power would take place no later than 30 June 1948 made it even more imperative for the Muslim League to unseat its Unionist rivals in what Jinnah had termed the 'cornerstone' of Pakistan.

[62] See Syed Nur Ahmad, *From Martial Law to Martial Law: Politics in the Punjab 1919–1958* (Boulder, CO: Westview Press, 1985), p. 226.

[63] Report on the Recent Disturbances in the Punjab (March–April 1947), All India Congress Committee File (AICC) No G-10/1947, Nehru Memorial Museum and Library (NMML).

[64] Report on the Recent Disturbances.

[65] For a detailed first-hand account, see C. Dass Dutt, *The Punjab Riots and Their Lessons*, 30 April 1947. S. P. Mukherjee Papers IV File 17, NMML.

hurriedly established camps. In Rawalpindi, the destruction and looting was greatest in the Ratta, Kartarpur and Shivala area near the *jamma masjid*.[66] Outlying villages such as Thamial, Kahuta, Jikka Gali, Daulatala, Kuri and Thoa Khalsa witnessed shocking violence: in the Gujjar Khan and Campbellpur districts, in March 1947 villages were completely wiped out, corpses of young children were found hanging from trees and girls as young as 11 years old were victims of gang rape. Such bestial violence abated only after the arrival of troops, armoured cars and tanks.

Despite the naming and shaming by citizens' fact-finding committees, few of those involved in the March disturbances were brought to justice. The leading Sikh organisation, the Chief Khalsa Diwan,[67] had issued a direct appeal to the government to suspend all officers and employees who had been engaged in violence and called for the army rather than the police to protect the minorities. It also demanded that the administration in minority areas should be staffed by non-Muslims and the recruitment of Hindu and Sikh police personnel should be raised to 50 per cent. Most importantly, the Chief Khalsa Diwan urged that 'impartial officers' should investigate the cases against those who had planned the assaults.[68]

However, political circumstances frustrated such accountability. The British instituted an enquiry into the worst cases of official negligence and threatened to relieve the guilty of all their titles and grants of government land.[69] Yet this was an empty threat because Muslim League promises and warnings carried more weight than those of the outgoing British. During a tour of the riot-torn Attock district, for example, a prominent League politician promised future protection for those who had been arrested and threatened recriminations against those officials who had attempted to maintain law and order.[70] These events, with their direct capture of law-and-order machinery and the official regime, were to set a deadly precedent. In more ways than one, they were to presage the development of what Brass terms the institutionalised riot system in post-Independence India.[71]

---

[66] Report on the Recent Disturbances in the Punjab (March–April 1947) AICC File No. G-10/1947, NMML.

[67] The Chief Khalsa Diwan was founded in 1902 as a central body to represent Sikh opinion to the Colonial State. It also ran schools, orphanages, hospitals and possessed its own printing press.

[68] Chief Khalsa Diwan, *Amritsar, Happenings of 1947 Atrocities and Brief Notes* (Translation from Punjabi) (Amritsar: Chief Khalsa Diwan n.d.), pp. 32–4.

[69] *Civil and Military Gazette* (Lahore) 16 March 1947.

[70] Jenkins to Mountbatten, 30 April 1947, N. Mansergh (ed.), *The Transfer of Power 1942–1947*, vol. 10 (London: HMSO, 1981), p. 506.

[71] P. R. Brass, *The Production of Hindu–Muslim Violence in Contemporary India* (Seattle, WA: University of Washington Press, 2005).

(vi)   The August–November 1947 Violence

The violence that accompanied India's independence repeated on a larger scale the patterns which had been evident since the Great Calcutta Killing. Even New Delhi, the capital of newly independent India, was affected. The radical Urdu writer Shahid Ahmad has left a vivid account of the September 1947 disturbances in his work *Dilhi ki Bipta*.[72] He describes how Muslim houses in such localities as Karol Bagh were marked so they could be identified by assailants. He also details the defence systems of gates on streets, guard groups, and coloured lights: red if riots threatened, green as an all-clear signal. Another eyewitness account is provided by John Turner. He was the only British Newsreel cameraman in Delhi at the time of the Independence Day celebrations. He recalls that much of the violence took place around Chandni Chowk in the commercial centre of the city and near to the Imperial Hotel where he was staying. 'In New Delhi in the early morning', he remembers, 'there were bodies lying in the streets in Connaught Place and Connaught Circus ... some brutally butchered and mutilated.'[73] Vazira Zamindar has provided oral testimonies of the violence which resulted in the 'destruction' of such Muslim areas as Karol Bagh, Sabzi Mandi and Paharganj. Official accounts blamed the 'orgy of murder, loot and arson' on Punjabi Hindu and Sikh refugees.[74]

However it would be misleading to portray the whole of the subcontinent as awash with refugees and blood. Even in the most disturbed Punjab region not everywhere was similarly affected. The small Muslim-ruled princely state of Malerkotla, for instance, was an oasis of peace. In the riot-ravaged cities of Lahore and Amritsar, the destruction was confined to the inner-city areas,[75] with the suburbs largely unscathed.[76] The famous Sikh novelist Khushwant Singh, who was living in Lahore on the eve of Partition, recalls that while the walled city was engulfed in flames, 'We went about in our cars to our offices, spent evenings playing tennis at

---

[72] This is contained in the collection edited by M. Shirin, *Zulmat-e-Neem Roze* (Karachi: no pub., 1990). See pp. 145–7.

[73] John Turner, *Filming History: The Memoirs of John Turner Newsreel Cameraman* (London: British Universities Film and Video Council, 2001), p. 123.

[74] Zamindar, *The Long Partition*, pp. 22–7.

[75] According to the District Taxation and Excise Officer in Amritsar nearly 10,000 buildings had been burnt down. *Tribune* (Simla) 10 November 1947. In Lahore, 6,000 houses had been destroyed. M. Baqir, *Lahore Past and Present* (Lahore: Panjab University Press, 1952), p. 309.

[76] A good account of the unruffled calm in the upper-class Model Town suburb of Lahore is provided by a former Hindu resident Som Anand in *Lahore: Portrait of a Lost City* (Lahore: Vanguard Books, 1998).

the Cosmopolitan or Gymkhana Club, had dinner parties where Scotch which cost Rs 11 per bottle flowed like the River Ravi.'[77]

In Sindh, where non-Muslims comprised a quarter of the population, there was calm in the weeks after Partition. The first serious outbreak of communal violence occurred in Karachi on 6 January 1948, and claimed around 200 lives and was accompanied by widespread looting in the city centre.[78] According to Gurbachan Singh Talib, even the police and employees of the High Court of Sindh joined in. Following the disturbances, 10,000 Hindus crowded into refugee camps in the city, before their evacuation to India.[79] The outbreak was linked with the flood of refugees, mainly from Delhi, into the city who had survived violence in India, only to find that the Pakistan state was 'appeasing Hindus' in Karachi. While the flashpoint of the riots was the desire for revenge, they are best understood as an escalation of 'everyday' violence of house-breaking and property seizures arising from the city's acute housing shortage. The Hindus had to be pushed out to accommodate the growing number of *mohajirs*.

Bihar, Bengal and western UP which had suffered considerable earlier bloodshed were relatively undisturbed in this same period, although Hindus in East Bengal suffered the 'quiet violence' of requisitioning of property in Dacca and robberies, threats and insults to their women.[80] How can we account for the differential levels of physical violence at this time? They were undoubtedly to have important repercussions for migration patterns.

Part of the answer lies in the fact that not all communities were equally vulnerable. The prosperous Sikh farmers, who migrated from the West Punjab Canal Colonies, were well organised and armed. They were thus a more difficult target to attack. Wealthier localities could be more easily defended than poor slum areas, especially those in mixed localities. These had borne the brunt of urban violence since the time of the Great Calcutta Killing. The city's relative calm, less than a year after the violence which had claimed upwards of 4,000 persons, was attributed to Gandhi's moral influence. He stayed in a poor Muslim neighbourhood, living with Suhrawardy, the alleged instigator of the Great Calcutta Killing, where he prayed and fasted for peace. Mountbatten dubbed him a 'one man

[77] Khushwant Singh, 'Last Days in Lahore: From the Brittle Security of an Elite Rooftop, a View of a City Burning', *Outlook* (Delhi) 28 May 1997.
[78] See Sarah Ansari, *Life after Partition: Migration, Community and Strife in Sindh 1947–1962* (Karachi: Oxford University Press, 2005), p. 56.
[79] Talib, *Muslim League Attack*, p. 213.
[80] On this 'quiet violence', see, for example, Tathagata Roy, *My People Uprooted: A Saga of Hindus of East Bengal* (Kolkata: Ratna Prakashan, 2002), pp. 159–60.

boundary force'. 'Having drunk the poison of mutual hatred', Gandhi declared, 'this nectar of fraternity tastes all the sweeter.'[81]

When Gandhi returned to Delhi in October, he sought to end the violence that had left some 20,000 Muslims dead in India's capital and had rendered thousands more homeless, as they either fled the killing or had their homes forcibly seized. Sumit Sarkar has termed Gandhi's intervention his 'finest hour'.[82] Gandhi also exerted his moral authority in favour of improved relations between India and Pakistan. He viewed with increasing alarm and impotence the unfolding power politics and escalating hostilities over Kashmir. He declared to his close followers: 'The freedom that came was not true freedom ... my eyes have now been opened ... Today everybody in the Congress is running after power. That presages grave danger.'[83] Nehru refused to agree to Gandhi's offer to go to Pakistan at the head of a non-violent Indian *shanti-sena* (army of peace). The Kashmir fighting profoundly troubled Gandhi. 'For so long we fought through the *charkha* [spinning wheel]', he declared, 'and the moment we have power in our hands we forget it. Today we look up to the army.'[84] Gandhi abhorred not only India's mounting war costs, but the cynical view that the Kashmir war would bankrupt Pakistan. He thus fasted to secure the release of the 550 million rupees which India was withholding from Pakistan although it was a promised part of Pakistan's share of British India's cash assets. The Indian Cabinet agreed to transfer the funds, but Gandhi's action was a provocation for Hindu extremists, who were dubbing him 'Mohammad' Gandhi because of his concern for Muslim interests. Less than a fortnight later, on 30 January 1948, he was shot dead by Nathuram Godse in the grounds of Birla House, New Delhi where he was staying and conducting prayer meetings. 'The light has gone out of our lives and there is darkness everywhere', a solemn Nehru declared over All-India Radio. Gandhi, in death, achieved as much for communal harmony as in life, for Nehru was able to clamp down on the activities of the extremist Rashtriya Swayam Sevak Sangh with which Godse had been associated.

Gandhi's influence was not the only moral imperative in favour of harmony in a hate-filled northern India. The peace in August 1947 in the small Muslim-ruled Punjab princely state of Malerkotla[85] also raises

---

[81] Cited in S. Wolpert, *Shameful Flight: The Last Years of the British Empire in India* (New York: Oxford University Press, 2006), p. 174.

[82] S. Sarkar, *Modern India, 1885–1947* (New Delhi: Macmillan, 1983), p. 437.

[83] Wolpert, *Shameful Flight*, p. 189.   [84] Wolpert, *Shameful Flight*, p. 190.

[85] See P. Virdee, 'Partition and Locality: Case Studies of the Impact of Partition and Its Aftermath in the Punjab Region 1947–61', unpublished PhD thesis, Coventry University (2005), pp. 91–124.

the question as to whether there were moral constraints to violence in some localities. The surrounding Ludhiana district of the former British Punjab was wracked by violence and the neighbouring Sikh State of Patiala witnessed horrific communal massacres in which its ruling authorities were implicated.[86] In these circumstances, Malerkotla became a safe haven for Muslims. In contemporary Indian Punjab, Malerkotla city remains the only Muslim-majority area. The popular myth is that the *haa da naara*, or protest, to Emperor Aurangzeb by the state's ruler Sher Mohammad Khan in 1705 at the bricking-alive in Sirhind of Guru Gobind Singh's two sons, resulted in his 'blessing' on the state. This ensured its protection from attack by the Sikhs in the troubled eighteenth century and at Partition. The myth raises the important issue that a sense of traditional obligation and of *izzat* could inhibit violence, as well, as we have seen earlier, instigate it.

Although the belief in the Guru's blessing can be dismissed as 'sentimentality', comparative research on ethnic violence has acknowledged that social disapproval is an important factor in limiting killings.[87] The Guru's blessing alone might, however, have been insufficient to protect Malerkotla's Muslim community and rapidly swelling refugee population. The ruler, Nawab Ali Khan, used the state police and military to patrol the borders to deter attacks. He also kept a tight rein on internal security, acutely aware that any communal clashes would imperil the state's stability in the post-Independence Indian Union. Malerkotla thus points to the fact that a crucial determinant of the level of violence was both the existence of a functioning authority and a political will to deploy force to stamp out disorder.

Nonetheless violence was most intense in East Punjab because the region exhibited a fatal combination of administrative collapse in the former British areas and of princely rulers who, far from maintaining law and order, aided and abetted attacks on the Muslim minority.[88]

[86] State troops in Patiala regularly preyed on refugee trains passing through from Delhi to Lahore. They murdered 450 Muslim railway employees and their families at Bathinda. In Barnala, 3,000 Muslims were killed by the state military and the police. Mudie Papers Mss. Eur. F. 164 IOR. For a measured analysis of the role of the Sikh princes in the East Punjab massacres, see Ian Copland, 'The Master and the Maharajas: The Sikh Princes and the East Punjab Massacres of 1947', *Modern Asian Studies* 36, 3 (2002), pp. 657–704.
[87] See chapter 12 of Donald Horowitz, *The Deadly Ethnic Riot* (Berkeley, CA: University of California Press, 2001).
[88] British observers commented that refugees fleeing from Jullundur and Ludhiana experienced, 'far worse treatment than anything ... in Montgomery and Lahore'. Report of Mr. Hadow's tour of Jullundur, Hoshiarpur, Ludhiana and Ferozepore Districts. 7 January 1948. East Punjab Affairs 1947–50. G2275/80 Do. 35 3181, Dominions Office and Commonwealth Relations Office PRO.

This organised violence aimed at ethnically cleansing the Muslim population was intended to create the space for the resettlement of Sikh refugees from West Punjab and was, in some measure, motivated by a desire to forge a Sikh state. During the closing weeks of British rule, 'ungraded' intelligence reports were filtering through to the Punjab Governor linking the neighbouring Sikh princely states with plans for a terror campaign in East Punjab.[89] While leading Sikh politicians[90] maintained that the 'Sikh Plan' was a fabrication of Muslim CID officers designed to discredit the community, it is clear that the attacks on East Punjab Muslims were abetted by the Sikh princes: such rulers as Yadavindra Singh of Patiala.[91] The rulers of the states of Faridkot and Jind had dramatically increased the size of their armed forces as the British departure grew closer.[92] They also provided weapons to the irregular Sikh armed bands (jathas) that were being organised in the British-administered territory.[93] The princes themselves denied that they had contacts with the jathas, but high-ranking court state and military officers such as Bir Davinder Singh and Colonel Bhagwan Singh of Patiala, along with the chief minister of Jind, were widely believed to have connived at their activities.[94] The fact cannot be denied that troops from the princely states attacked their Muslim inhabitants and passing refugee trains; they also joined in assaults on neighbouring districts of the former British-administered Punjab. Trains coming from Ludhiana and Hissar were detained at Dhuri in the Patiala State, where their passengers were systematically butchered and their possessions looted. The military and the police were so involved in the violence that it was almost impossible for a Muslim to pass safely through the state.[95] Patiala authorities also assisted jathas in the systematic murder of Muslim residents. The attack on the Muslims of Barnala in Patiala which claimed 3,000 lives was preceded by the enforcement of a curfew only on their community.[96] Violence

---

[89] S. Abbott to R. Brockman n.d. Ungraded Intelligence Report, R/3/1/145 IOR.
[90] See, for example, Statement of Baldev Singh on Present Situation, n.d., R/3/1/174 IOR.
[91] Copland, 'The Master and the Maharajas', p. 678. Yadavindra Singh claimed he had no part in the killings which ethnically cleansed Muslims from his state. He was, it is true, residing at his summer palace at Chail at the time, but was in telegraphic communication with ministers. It is also true that from the middle of September 1947 he ordered the district nazims to oversee the safety of Muslim refugees, but it could be argued that, by this time, the killings and lootings had already spent their course and Muslims had almost disappeared not only from his state, but throughout the East Punjab.
[92] Copland, 'The Master and the Maharajas', p. 681.
[93] Copland, 'The Master and the Maharajas', p. 680.
[94] Copland, 'The Master and the Maharajas', p. 693. Copland in fact cites evidence that the rulers of Kapurthala and Faridkot had direct contact with the jathas.
[95] Copland, 'The Master and the Maharajas', p. 401.
[96] Copland, 'The Master and the Maharajas', p. 409.

followed personal assurances from the Maharaja that the Muslim minority was safe. Its removal enabled the state to receive large numbers of incoming refugees from Pakistan.

Critical to all these cases was the role of the administration in curbing violence. The example of UP provides an instructive counterfactual case study. This province had suffered considerable violence in 1946. On the eve of the British departure, it shared many of the Punjab's characteristics as weapons were stockpiled and political parties and communal organisations developed their own extensive para-military volunteer forces. In UP there were around 25,000 members of the Muslim League National Guards, and RSS and Hindu Mahasabha volunteers between them numbered 40,000.[97] By August, a further combustible element had been added with the presence of around half a million refugees with their tales of atrocities in Pakistan sparking off retributive violence against local Muslims. Nevertheless, much to Nehru's relief,[98] despite isolated attacks on trains and stabbings, the deaths in the province were far lower than in neighbouring Punjab. This outcome was largely the result of the resolute law and order enforcement measures taken by the UP Congress government that had been genuinely shocked by the earlier carnage at Garhmukhteshwar. As a consequence an emergency ordinance was introduced in May 1947 that sanctioned a police shoot-to-kill policy for curfew breakers. Severe punishments were also introduced for acts of forced conversion and marriage. The UP Congress Prime Minister, Govind Ballabh Pant, overrode his own party members' opposition as well as that of the RSS to justify the deployment of tanks to quell disturbances in Meerut.[99] There was also much greater control over the press with the establishment of a Press Consultative Committee which helped to limit the spread of rumour and the publication of inflammatory articles.[100] Finally, officials were disciplined if they failed to deter communal violence: the district magistrate in Dehra Dun was, for example, dismissed in this manner.

(vii)   East and West Bengal: February–March 1950

I visited Muladi ... where I found skeletons of dead bodies at some places. I found dogs and vultures eating corpses on the riverside. I got the information there that

---

[97] Note on Volunteer Organisations in UP, June 9 1947. IOR, L/PJ/5/276.

[98] 'If the disturbances had not been halted in western UP, he wrote in a letter of 15 October to Provincial Prime Ministers they would eventually have spread eastwards right up to Bihar and West Bengal and the whole of northern India would have been in chaos.' Cited in Yasmin Khan, 'Out of Control? Partition Violence in Uttar Pradesh', in Talbot (ed.), *The Deadly Embrace*, pp. 36–60.

[99] Khan, 'Out of Control?', p. 50.

[100] Moreover, some Urdu papers even published 'communal harmony' issues.

after the wholesale killing of all adult males, all the young girls were distributed among the ringleaders of the miscreants.[101]

This was not Punjab in August 1947, but East Bengal in February 1950. Violence had started in Dacca, but spread within a few days to the Tippera, Noakhali, Sylhet and Barisal districts. The coastal district of Barisal witnessed severe disturbances as four villages were completely burned down. Muladi was one of its important riveraine ports. Most of its Hindu victims died in the compound of the police station where they had taken shelter. The officer in charge was later found in possession of large amounts of looted property.[102] In the Sylhet district, over 200 villages were devastated and 800 Hindu temples desecrated.[103] In large areas, the repertoire familiar since 1946 was repeated of forced conversions, dishonouring of women and attacks on trains.[104] The latter lasted from 11 to 14 February and claimed many victims on the Chittagong Mail. The bodies of at least a hundred Hindus were buried by the side of the railway line.[105]

Similar scenes of violence occurred in West Bengal. There were widespread disturbances in the Muslim localities of Calcutta, such as Bagmari, Beliaghatu and Goolpara. Houses were looted and burned along with mosques. According to the *Civil and Military Gazette* newspaper, nearly 10,000 Muslims from Chinsurah, Paikpara, Goolpara and Telnipara had to leave their homes and take shelter in open fields opposite the Victoria Jute Mills. Muslims were also attacked in Jalpaiguri town. Two hundred shops were looted in the Muslim-controlled bazaar of Karimgunj in Assam.[106] Muslim refugees from Karimgunj and Hailakandi claimed that the police led the looters.[107] Certainly more resolute law enforcement would have cut short the disturbances. Their continuation sparked the largest wave of migration in the eastern Indian region since 1947.

---

[101] This report was made by the Scheduled Caste former Minister for Law and Labour in the Pakistan Government, Jogendra Nath Mandal. He resigned in the wake of the East Bengal killings. A. J. Kamra, *The Prolonged Partition and Its Pogroms: Testimonies on Violence against Hindus in East Bengal 1946–64* (New Delhi: Voice of India, 2000), pp. 173–4.

[102] Kamra, *Prolonged Partition*, p. 63.   [103] Kamra, *Prolonged Partition*, p. 76

[104] The trains packed with up to 4,000 refugees had been easy targets in August 1947, despite the presence of armed escorts. Blood-splattered trains arrived in both India and Pakistan with whole compartments of butchered corpses.

[105] Kamra, *Prolonged Partition*, p. 89.

[106] *Civil and Military Gazette* (Lahore) 22 March 1950.

[107] *Civil and Military Gazette* (Lahore) 22 March 1950.

Partition violence: spontaneous madness or organised mayhem?

Javeed Alam has suggested that the Partition massacres were indulged in 'By people at a moment of loss of judgement, of a sense of proportion, at a moment of frenzy.' According to him, there was 'No involvement of large organisations or the state as the instrument of mass killings.'[108] This reading of the 1947 violence suggests that it cannot be rationally explained, is unique and beyond comparative analysis. In contrast Paul Brass's work on violence in such UP localities as Aligarh and Meerut and the writings of Romila Thapur, Imtiaz Ahmed and Dipankar Gupta on the 2002 Gujarat carnage,[109] have all drawn attention to such key features in situations of endemic and intensive communal conflict as: the 'functional utility' of riots for politicians, state complicity in the perpetration of organised acts of violence and delays in securing justice for the victims. The latter sends out a clear message to would-be rioters that no harm will come to them, allowing in Brass's words, the 'repeat performances' of riot production.

Clearly all of these features are evident in the cycle of violence from 1946 to 1950. Far from a spontaneous and temporary aberration, the violence of this period was frequently marked by its cold-blooded planning and execution. Attacks on foot convoys and refugee trains were frequently made with military precision.[110] Their attackers had been assisted by complicit railway officials who had revealed the timing of the refugee specials.[111] The killings were not the work of a few frenzied hotheads, but were carried out, in many instances, by large organisations such as Sikh *jathas* and Muslim tribal war parties. These gatherings were far from spontaneous: they acquired their fearsome weaponry with planning and organisation. In the case of the Rawalpindi massacres, for example, the sources are unanimous that violence was carefully planned. It is a mistake to call what happened in Rawalpindi area 'Communal riots', the AICC Report records:

---

[108] Cited in Pandey, *Remembering Partition*, p. 58.

[109] Brass, *The Production of Hindu–Muslim Violence in Contemporary India*. Dipankar Gupta and Romila Thapur, 'Who Are the Guilty? Punishment and Confidence Building in Gujarat', *The Hindu* (Chennai), 2 April 2002; Imtiaz Ahmed, 'Has Communalism Changed?', both in Asghar Ali Engineer (ed.), *The Gujarat Carnage* (New Delhi: Longman, 2003), pp. 108–11; 137–41.

[110] In one such attack on a train outside Khalsa College, Amritsar, 1,200 Muslim refugees were massacred. *Civil and Military Gazette*, 14 September 1947.

[111] See Swarna Aiyar, '"August Anarchy": The Partition Massacres in Punjab, 1947', in D. H. Low and Howard Brasted (eds), *Freedom, Trauma, Continuities: Northern India and Independence* (New Delhi: Sage, 1998), pp. 15–39; also published in special issue of *South Asia* 18 (1995), pp. 13–36.

These were not riots but deliberately organised military campaigns. Long before the disturbances broke out secret meetings were held in mosques under the leadership of Syed Akbar Khan ex-MLA, Captain Lal Khan of Kahuta, Tehsildar and Police Sub Inspector Kahuta, Maulvi Abdul Rehman and Kala Khan MLA in which *jihad* was proclaimed against the minorities and emissaries were sent out to collect volunteers from the rural areas ... The armed crowd which attacked Kahuta, Thoa Khalsa, and Nara etc. were led by ex-military men on horseback armed with Tommy Guns, pistols, rifles, hand grenades, hatchets, petrol tins and even some carried field glasses.[112]

The following strategy, the report continues, was used wherever the mobs attacked:

First of all minorities were disarmed with the help of local police and by giving assurances by oaths on holy Quran of peaceful intentions. After this had been done, the helpless and unarmed minorities were attacked. On their resistance having collapsed, lock breakers and looters came into action with their transport corps of mules, donkeys and camels. Then came the '*Mujahadins*' with tins of petrol and kerosene oil and set fire to the looted shops and houses. Then there were *maulvies* with barbers to convert people who somehow or other escaped slaughter and rape. The barbers shaved the hair and beards and circumcised the victims. *Maulvis* recited *kalamas* and performed forcible marriage ceremonies. After this came the looters, including women and children.[113]

The parallels with accounts of the 2002 Gujarat attacks on the Muslim minority in which RSS activists came equipped with gas, oxygen cylinders and petrol and in which 'respectable' people joined in the looting are chillingly apparent.[114] Equally, Suhrawardy's behaviour during the earlier Great Calcutta Killing also provides echoes of the Gujarat pogrom. Like many a latter-day Indian politician, he interfered with police operations and with his parliamentary associates 'spent a great deal of time in the police control room directing the operations'.[115]

Hindu 'mobs' and the Sikh *jathas* were no less organised than Muslim war parties. The *jathas* led the attacks on Muslims that ethnically cleansed them from the East Punjab. From May 1947 onwards, there had been a widespread collection of funds, manufacture and import of weapons and the establishment of an organisation of 'dictators', 'company commanders' and village 'cells'. Little is known about their total numbers, the second rank of leaders, or their composition, save that many ex-servicemen from both

---

[112] Report on the Disturbances in the Punjab (March–April 1947) AICC File No. G-10/1947 NMML.

[113] Report on the Disturbances.

[114] K. N. Panikkar, 'The Agony of Gujarat', in Engineer (ed.), *The Gujarat Carnage*, p. 93; Uday Mehta, 'The Gujarat Genocide: A Sociological Appraisal', in Engineer (ed.), *The Gujarat Carnage*, p. 191.

[115] Das, *Communal Riots in Bengal*, p. 178.

the British Indian Army and the INA were in their ranks.[116] During the final days before the publication of the Radcliffe Boundary award,[117] *jathas* commenced heavy raids on Muslim villages in 'border' areas.[118] The *jathas* were ruthlessly efficient killing machines which carefully targeted their victims.[119] They were well armed with sten guns, rifles, pistols, spears, swords and *kirpans* (steel sword/dagger) and the largest had contingents around 3,000 strong.

Similarly the Hindu rioters in Calcutta in August 1946 were directed by searchlights and microphones fixed to the housetops. The rioters placed Red Cross symbols on their vehicles to escape police detection and Hindu shops were marked so that they would be spared arson and looting.[120] The Congress general secretary reported the gathering of attackers in Garhmukhteshwar on horses, cycles and even camels in a makeshift army unit.[121] The Viceroy Wavell informed the secretary of state that he was also certain that the violence was organised 'and organised very thoroughly' by 'the lower strata of the Congress' without the knowledge of their leadership, just as the Muslim League had been responsible for violence in Noakhali.[122] In Sonepat, in the East Punjab Rohtak district, wealthy Hindus contributed 100,000 rupees to finance mob attacks on the Muslims. Traders and merchants were also prominent in organising violence in Chapra Town in Bihar. *Zamindars* too played a role in the incitement and collection of rioters. In Masaurhi where there were large Muslim casualties, the owner of the rice and flour mills summoned the crowd to attack by means of the factory hooter.[123]

The involvement of the police in violence is a constant feature throughout the period surrounding 1946. It provides another parallel between the Partition killings and post-Independence communal violence. Such behaviour is by no means unique to the subcontinent, but has been reported across the globe.[124] It flows from the depth of communal animosity in situations of endemic conflict, lack of professionalism and the skewed ethnic composition of forces. In pre-Partition Punjab, for example, just under three-quarters of the police force were Muslims and they sided with their co-religionists. In independent India, Hindu

---

[116] See Copland, 'The Master and the Maharajas', for a discussion of the scanty data that does exist.
[117] This demarcated the new international border in the Punjab region. Its judgements were controversially delayed until after the British transfer of power.
[118] Punjab FR 30 July 1947; 13 August 1947. L/P&J/5/250 IOR.
[119] Copland, 'The Master and the Maharajas', p. 687.
[120] Das, *Communal Riots in Bengal*, p. 180.   [121] Cited in Khan, 'Out of Control?'.
[122] Khan, 'Out of Control?'.   [123] Damodaran, *Broken Promises*, p. 345.
[124] Horowitz, *The Deadly Ethnic Riot*, pp. 354–5.

predominance in such forces as the Provincial Armed Constabulary has resulted in the disproportionate number of Muslim casualties in commu-nal riot situations.[125]

Indeed there are many reports, for example, of Muslim Punjabi police-men aiding and abetting the March 1947 violence, or of being inordinately slow in responding to appeals for assistance. The Hindu residents of Traggar in the Multan district were attacked for eleven hours on 10 March but received no assistance from the police until after troops arrived. A police contingent in the city of Multan stood by while a prominent Sikh leader and President of the Minorities Board, Sardar Nanak Singh, was done to death. The police then abandoned the areas outside the walls where many Hindu businesses were located, leaving them at the mercy of looters. Hindu residents complained bitterly to the Congress investigators in a refrain frequently repeated by the Muslim minority in independent India: that the police were the main cause of their 'misfortune'. They said that they could better defend themselves if the police were removed from the scene.[126]

Hindu policemen were equally culpable in East Punjab. The ring-leaders of the attacks in Sonepat included a couple of honorary magis-trates and the sub-inspector of police.[127] Similar help was provided by the sub-inspector of police in organising attacks on Muslims at Jagraon in the Ludhiana district. On 24 August 1947, the Muslim policemen at Ludhiana were disarmed and replaced by ex-INA men. Shortly thereafter, the Muslim localities of Fieldganj and Abdullahpur were attacked and looted.[128] Hindu and Sikh policemen led by a sub-inspector joined in an assault on the Muslims of Hansi in the Hissar district that claimed 300 lives.[129] Hindu policemen displayed a similar partiality in the Bihar vio-lence of October–November 1946. The sub-divisional officer and the deputy superintendent of police failed to halt the Beniabad massacre which sparked off widespread rioting. The Muslim League alleged that the sub-inspector of police at Chapra instigated the violence in the town. When the deputy inspector-general visited the scene he did not leave any police behind. The trouble was only quelled when the commissioner requested the 43rd Gurkha Regiment to take over the town.[130]

[125] Brass, *The Production of Hindu–Muslim Violence*, pp. 60–1; 169–71; 177–8.
[126] Report on the Disturbances in the Punjab (March–April 1947) AICC File No. G-10/ 1947, NMML.
[127] Rukhsana Zafar (compiler), *Disturbances in the Punjab 1947* (Islamabad: National Documentation Centre, 1995), p. 410.
[128] Zafar, *Disturbances in the Punjab*, p. 407.   [129] Zafar, *Disturbances in the Punjab*, p. 400.
[130] See Damodaran, *Broken Promises*, p. 354.

Nor did the military always adequately protect minorities. There are accounts of Baloch forces harassing and attacking Hindu refugees.[131] Yet the most tragic failure involved the Punjab Boundary Force.[132] When it was not standing by helplessly, it actually added to the carnage.[133] By the beginning of September 1947, the Punjab Boundary Force was dissolved. The task of protecting the huge numbers of refugees who were engaged in a chaotic two-way migration across the India and Pakistan Punjab borders was given to the Military Evacuation Organisation of India and Pakistan (see chapter four).[134]

Studies of ethnic violence from across the world (see the Kanpur riots in 1994, Central and East Java 1980) reveal that where the police or the army move quickly to suppress violence, escalation is limited, with few casualties.[135] Although it is unpalatable for Indian and Pakistani nationalist historians, it is clear that casualties would have been much lower in the Partition violence, if the forces of law and order had acted more impartially.

Of course some of the 1946–1947 violence was retributive, motivated by atrocity tales and the arrival at railway stations of train loads of corpses. Individual rioters may also have been motivated by lust for loot or women, but they were operating in an environment in which such violence was *socially* sanctioned. Indeed, there are reports that *goondas* from Lahore were taken to such places as Lohianwala in the Gujranwala district to loot and murder.[136] Whatever the truth behind such allegations, *goondas* were unlikely to be apprehended for their crimes in circumstances in which officials and police largely condoned and contributed to Partition-related violence because they could act with impunity. In a real sense, therefore, the failure to prosecute those involved in the March Rawalpindi Massacres paved the way for the communal holocaust in the Punjab in August 1947. The contrast with the post-Garhmukhteshwar situation in UP is striking.

Conclusion

Standard accounts of the 1947 communal violence concentrate on the 'summer madness' of mid-August. They also focus on the disorder in the

---

[131] See Talib, *Muslim League Attack*, pp. 173–5.

[132] The 23,000-strong force was formed by Muslim and non-Muslim troops drawn largely from the 4th Infantry Division at Jullundur and was commanded by Major General Thomas Rees.

[133] For details, see M. K. Sinha, Report of the Deputy Director Intelligence Bureau n.d., R/3/1/173, IOR.

[134] See Brigadier Rajendra Singh, *The Military Evacuation Organisation 1947–48* (New Delhi: Government of India Press, 1962).

[135] Horowitz, *The Deadly Ethnic Riot*, pp. 490–1.

[136] Talib, *Muslim League Attack*, p. 184.

British-administered areas rather than in the surrounding princely states. These accounts situate the massacres in a moment of transition between empire and nation-state when the machinery of government was in the process of being dismantled and even the boundary demarcation was uncertain. Violence is thus linked with state collapse. The chronological concentration on August 1947 also locates the violence in a 'special' time of flux and transition[137] when conventional mores failed and anarchy prevailed.

However, in reality, Partition-related violence should be seen as beginning in the second half of 1946 when there was a transition from the 'consensual' traditional communal riot to the 'genocidal' violence which marked the later communal holocaust. Violence not only became more intense, but it became organised. It reached its climax in August 1947 when it displayed elements both of opportunism and purposefulness. In some situations, it thrived because of the existing power vacuum. But in others, because of the complicity and involvement of the forces of law and order and in a context of ethnic cleansing, it was able to take hold and intensify. Functioning administrations could inhibit violence: they only acted to do so when there was political advantage in this. In different circumstances they were likely to be implicated in killings. The lid was kept on violence in situations significantly where there was both a strong administration and political motive for quiescence. This was the case with both the Pant Congress Government in UP and the Nawab of Malerkotla's government.

Violence differed across north India not only in its intensity, but in its timing. It peaked in Bihar, Bengal and UP late in 1946. It only began in Punjab in March 1947 and then continued almost uninterrupted until Independence. In Sindh and Delhi it only began after the arrival of Partition refugees. While some wealthy Hindus and Sikhs had migrated from the future Pakistan areas well before the British departure, most of the eventual migrants in north India left only under the extreme circumstances of a threat to their life. In Punjab, mass migration came to an end within a couple of months of Partition. In Bengal, on the other hand, it was to continue for years on a much smaller scale. It is to this differential experience of migration and the problems that it brought for refugee resettlement that we will turn in our next chapter.

---

[137] For theories that link times of transition with increased potential for violence, see for example Tamotsu Shibutani and Kian M. Kwan, *Ethnic Stratification: A Comparative Approach* (New York: Macmillan, 1965), p. 377.

4   Migration and resettlement

Partition was accompanied by the largest uprooting of people in the twentieth century. Despite warning signs of population movement accompanying violence from the time of the Great Calcutta Killing onwards, the migration was wholly unanticipated by the Indian political leaderships as well as by the colonial authorities. Nationalist historiography in both India and Pakistan made much of the role of the state in rehabilitating the flood of refugees. Recent research, however, suggests that the experience of forced migration[1] and settlement was far from uniform as was suggested in official literature; rather, migrants suffered numerous vicissitudes and their experiences were heavily mediated by social class, ethnicity, language, caste and the unspoken assumptions about gender. In this chapter we examine how the historical understanding of migration and settlement has changed by discussing, first, the overemphasis on the Punjab experience and then exploring the diversity of migration and settlement in both the east and the west. The chapter concludes with an overview of the ways in which migration transformed the urban landscape of leading cities in the subcontinent.

Punjab and dominant images of the refugee experience

The Punjab has provided the iconic images of the 1947 migration (see photographs): men, women and children with their heavily laden bullock carts travelling across tracks of ground inundated by the monsoon rains; trains with not only their carriages, but running boards and roofs, packed with refugees; and, more disturbingly, trains arriving at their destination stacked with mutilated corpses. The drama and intensity of violence and uprooting in Punjab in part explains why it has come to represent

---

[1] In the literature on Partition the terms 'migrants' and 'refugees' are used interchangeably without some of the contemporary distinctions that attach to these concepts. Our coverage reflects this usage though we recognise that the movement across borders was rarely voluntary.

Plate 3 A part of the last big Muslim refugee foot column marching from Ambala to Pakistan. This shot was taken from the Dakota aircraft of the Indian Governor-General, Lord Mountbatten.

Plate 4 Lady Mountbatten with West Punjab and Pakistan government officials discussing the refugee situation.

the Partition experience. After all, the region was at the epicentre of the holocaust and mass exodus in 1947, when around 10 million Punjabis were caught up in a chaotic two-way flight during the 'August anarchy'.[2] Moreover, it proved far easier to bolster India's nation-building by

---

[2] See Aiyar, '"August Anarchy"', in Low and Brasted (eds), *Freedom, Trauma, Continuities*, pp. 15–39.

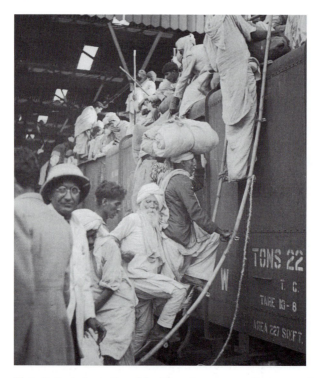

Plate 5 Ambala station: Muslim refugees crowding on to the roof of a train going to Pakistan. The owner of the flimsy bamboo ladder is charging the luckless passengers 2 annas a trip to the roof of the truck.

drawing on the Punjabi success story of refugee rehabilitation than the more problematic Bengal experience. Indeed, very early on, Nehru was acutely aware of the need to counteract the 'stress [that] had been laid in newspapers throughout the world on the destructive aspect of the recent happenings'. He was especially keen on producing the right publicity about the 'work done on rehabilitation, relief and evacuation'.[3]

Publications such as *Stern Reckoning* and *Out of the Ashes*[4] did much to privilege the Punjab experience, and later generations of historians' dependence on documentary, oral and fictional sources about Punjab have

---

[3] Emergency Committee 26th Meeting 7 November 1947 MB1/D275, University of Southampton.

[4] G. D. Khosla, *Stern Reckoning: A Survey of the Events Leading up to and Following the Partition of India* (New Delhi: Oxford India paperbacks, 1989); M. S. Randhawa, *Out of the Ashes: An Account of the Rehabilitation of Refugees from West Pakistan in Rural Areas of East Punjab* (Chandigarh: Public Relations Department, Punjab, 1954).

Plate 6 Part of the last great Hindu and Sikh refugee road column going from Pakistan to India. These were the lucky ones going by lorry and tonga; many thousands were on foot.

Plate 7 Dejected refugees in the back of a lorry; this picture is from the last great Hindu and Sikh road column on its way to India. On the top of the truck are charpoys turned upside down so passengers can be carried on the roof.

further reinforced this bias. There are, of course, short stories and novels of the Partition drama in all languages and from all the affected regions of the subcontinent,[5] but the most well known works are those by Punjabi

---

[5] See Alok Bhalla's collection, *Stories about the Partition of India* (New Delhi: Indus, 1994).

Plate 8 Soldier, police and volunteer camp officials outside the Khalsa College refugee camp, Lyallpur, where Sikh evacuees await trains to take them to India.

Plate 9 Part of the crowd of 30,000 evacuees awaiting trains to take them from Lyallpur to India.

Table 1: *Monthly Statement of the Evacuation of Non-Muslims from West to East Punjab Carried out by the Military Evacuation Organisation India from 23 August 1947 to 27 May 1948*

Date	By foot	By military transport	By rail
23–31 August 1947	258,160	107,590	101,500
September	824,000	18,116	189,000
October	477,160	21,622	276,500
November	885,000	16,594	245,500
December	31,714	24,060	70,000
January 1948	–	7,945	21,000
February	–	8,620	10,500
March	8,000	5,270	18,500
April	–	1,300	35,000
1–27 May	–	3,200	7,000
Total	2,484,034	214,317	974,500

Source: Lt Col. Mohammad Sadiq Comd. MEO Pak Lahore 29 May 1948

authors written in English or translated from Punjabi, Urdu or Hindi.[6] In this genre there is little mention of such Bengali publications as Sabitri Roy's *Swaralipi* (Musical Notations) or Tulsidas Lahiri's controversial play *Banglar Mati* (The Earth of Bengal).[7] Similarly, films such as Nemai Ghosh's *Chhinnamul* (Uprooted, 1951) and Ritwik Ghatak's classic *Meghe Dhaka Tara* (The Star Veiled by Clouds, 1960) are not widely known beyond Bengal; but Khushwant Singh's *Train to Pakistan* has been internationally acclaimed, while Saadat Hasan Manto's short story, *Toba Tek Singh* has become the premier symbol of Punjabi identity torn asunder by Partition.

Clearly the suddenness of 'ethnic cleansing' in Punjab made it the centre of Partition discourses. Tables 1 and 2 provide a summary of the flows of migrants across the province after the announcement of the Radcliffe Award. By the end of November 1947, the two-way flow had peaked, with only nominal movement after December.

---

[6] The writings of Manto, Amrita Pritam, Kartar Singh Duggal and Bhisham Sahni have all become well known to western audiences following their translation.

[7] For a discussion of the works see Tapati Chakravarty, 'The Paradox of a Fleeting Presence: Partition and Bengali Literature', in S. Settar and Indira B. Gupta (eds), *Pangs of Partition: The Human Dimension*, Vol. 2 (New Delhi: Manohar, 2002), pp. 261–83; and Jayanti Chattopadhyay, 'Representing the Holocaust: The Partition in Two Bengali Plays', in Settar and Gupta, *Pangs of Partition*, pp. 301–13.

Table 2: *Monthly Statement of the Evacuation of Muslims from East to West Punjab Carried out by the Military Evacuation Organisation Pakistan from 23 August 1947 to 27 May 1948*

Date	By foot	By military transport	By rail
23–31 August 1947	36,000	15,742	101,500
September	566,300	46,882	189,000
October	625,500	41,568	276,500
November	838,740	34,964	352,500
December	274,500	16,443	108,500
January 1948	–	32,276	21,000
February	–	18,875	16,400
March	–	3,695	31,274
April	–	6,153	40,800
1–27 May	–	1,807	19,000
Total	2,341,040	218,405	1,156,474

Source: Lt Col. Mohammad Sadiq Comd. MEO Pak Lahore May 1948

Once the violence started the Military Evacuation Organisations (MEOs) in India and Pakistan undertook to organise the movements of populations which resulted in virtual de-population of East Punjab by Muslims and of West Punjab by Hindus and Sikhs. This mutually organised transfer of population reinforced popular notions of a 'hard' border-line which ripped across the historic province conforming to the nationalists' ideal of the new nation-states.

In contrast, India's eastern border with Pakistan in Bengal was to undergo a less cataclysmic change, but in the long run was to see a huge concentration of refugee population. By 1973, refugees formed 15 per cent of West Bengal's entire population.[8] For many migrants of the 'Partition-in-the-East' the key date was not 1947 but 1950. As we saw in chapter three, it was in that year that disturbances on both sides of the Bengal border sparked off migration flows that were far greater than at the time of the transfer of power, with particular intensity of outflows from East Bengal to Assam. Migration of Hindus continued in Bengal (see Table 3) throughout the decade which followed the Great Calcutta Killing, and these periodic bursts were undoubtedly a key factor in the Indian state's less effective response in the east than in Punjab where there was a more concentrated outflow.

---

[8] Chatterji, *Spoils of Partition*, p. 151.

Table 3: *Month-wise Figures of Refugee Influx to West Bengal: 1953–1956*

Month	1953	1954	1955	1956
January	5,248	4,077	15,674	17,011
February	5,961	5,710	22,848	42,360
March	7,507	5,821	26,503	15,167
April	6,900	6,002	15,070	18,039
May	6,032	6,656	18,190	34,657
June	4,798	6,354	21,146	24,734
July	5,026	6,208	22,957	27,442
August	4,147	8,127	13,813	–
September	3,223	10,644	9,371	–
October	4,379	10,352	13,757	–
November	3,212	11,073	11,535	–
December	4,214	22,776	18,709	–
Total	**60,647**	**103,800**	**209,573**	**179,410**

Source: *Relief and Rehabilitation of Displaced Persons in West Bengal* (Calcutta: Home (Pub.) Department, Government of West Bengal, 1956), p. 17

Bengali refugees from East Pakistan argued that they were the principal victims of the creation of Pakistan because of the Indian government's half-hearted approach to their rehabilitation.[9] One writer summed up the official attitude by depicting the refugees as *Natun Yehudi* (The New Jews). Other writings on migrants elsewhere in the eastern zone, on the other hand, dispel this image of refugee as victim. Some portray upper-caste Bengali migrants from Sylhet as comfortably settled in the towns of Assam, who by the early 1960s dominated trade, commerce and the professions because of their educational qualifications and social networks. In a provocative counter-image, some have described the refugee as 'tourist', who came with 'camera in hand, clicking random pictures of the city (of Gauhati); they thought Assam was a jungle and were so excited.'[10] For them the term refugee was a 'slur' on their social status and 'implied they had no source of income outside Sylhet'.[11]

Borders and migration flows

One Punjab-centred generalisation has been to accord permanence to the 1947 borders which they have only acquired gradually. Talbot and

---

[9] For a discussion of these claims, see Joya Chatterji, 'Right or Charity? The Debate over Relief and Rehabilitation in West Bengal, 1947–50', in Suvir Kaul (ed.), *The Partitions of Memory: The Afterlife of the Division of India* (New Delhi: Permanent Black, 2001), pp. 74–110.

[10] Dasgupta, 'Denial and Resistance', p. 345.

[11] Dasgupta, 'Denial and Resistance', p. 344.

Zamindar have shown how formal immigration controls were only slowly extended on the western border,[12] and when the violence subsided, there was considerable movement back and forth.[13] Anand recalls the presence of Hindu professionals in post-Partition Lahore, where like his father, they continued to fill important niches in the fledgling Pakistan banking system.[14] The border was even more porous in the east: the existence not only of cross-border marketing, but cross-border cultivation 'continued for years without much trouble' as families adopted creative strategies to circumvent the new borderline. 'When Partition took place', notes van Schendel,

Haru Mondol, then a young boy, found that the border ran right through the family's ancestral land. Haru's father stayed put in what was now India, but Haru's uncle built a new house on the land just across the border. In this way, the two brothers and their offspring became citizens of two countries but continued to cultivate the family land jointly.[15]

Such strategies were possible because in Bengal, the border resembled a patchwork quilt rather than a natural boundary. While the Bengal Boundary Commission divided East and West Bengals, the border to the east with the princely state of Tripura, which joined India in 1949, had no contiguous link with any Indian territory, and the boundary in the north-west, with two districts that joined India in 1947 and the princely state of Cooch Behar that joined in 1950 also, had no contiguous territory with India.[16] Continuously shifting topography in the delta plain, moreover, made demarcation of many segments impossible, creating a permanent source of conflict that would last until the present day.

Even in Punjab, where a tide of humanity swept across the new international boundary between August and November,[17] migration was not just a single journey. Many refugees, especially those from an urban background, travelled from place to place in their new homeland before finally settling

---

[12] See I. Talbot, *Divided Cities: Partition and its Aftermath in Lahore and Amritsar 1947–1957* (Karachi: Oxford University Press, 2006); Vazira Zamindar, *The Long Partition and the Making of Modern South Asia: Refugees, Boundaries, Histories* (New York: Columbia University Press, 2007). The Indo-Pak passport and visa scheme was introduced on 15 October 1952.

[13] G. D. Khosla, *Memory's Gay Chariot: An Autobiography* (New Delhi: Allied Publishers, 1985).

[14] Som Anand, *Lahore: Portrait of a Lost City* (Lahore: Vanguard Books, 1998).

[15] Cited in Willem van Schendel, *The Bengal Borderland: Beyond State and Nation in South Asia* (London: Anthem Press, 2005), p. 123.

[16] van Schendel, *The Bengal Borderland*, pp. 42–4; 53–65.

[17] Brigadier F. H. Stevens, Commander of the Pakistan Military Evacuation Organization, computed the Muslim exodus at 4,680,000. Quoted in *Eastern Times* (Lahore), 25 December 1947. More than a million and a quarter Hindus and Sikhs travelled by train alone in the same period. *Statesman* (Calcutta), 16 November 1947.

Mr. Ram Narain, Stenographer, Punjab Registered (I. & S.) Stock-holders' Association Ltd., Saddar Bazar, Ambala Cantt. wants to know from any refugee from Lyallpur the whereabouts of Ch. Kanshi Ram Sub-Inspector of Police, lately incharge Traffic and Special Branch, Lyallpur and family.

Mr. D. R. Varma, S.D.O., Central P.W.D., 486, Madan Mahal Road, Wright Road, Jubbalpur (C. P.) wants information about L. Wazir Chand, Harnamdas, and L- Jagdish Ram Marwaha previously working in the office of the Chief Engineer, Northern Command, Rawalpindi. He will also like to hear from or about L. Panna Lal Gaind, B.A., LL.B., originally of Pasrur, employed in the Municipal Committee, Gujrat.

NOTE. L. Tara Chand of the Tribune' is working in the office at Simla.

V. N. Dogra Esq. P. W. D. B, & R. Sectt. Simla East would like to get the whereabouts of his brother Sardarilal Dogra Karachi Police, and brother-in-law Mr. Shiv Kumar Parcel Clerk, Quetta.

Mr. Dina Nath of the "Tribune," wants to know the whereabouts of his wife, Sh. Maya Vanti with two children and his uncle Munshi Diwan Chand, Village. Wasu in Gujrat.

Mr. Daya Nand Kohati Block C House No. 20 Sriganganagar (Bikaner State) wants to know the whereabouts of:—

1, L. Sàda Nand Batra R. M. S. Multan. 2. Mr. S. N. Dudeja of Radhu & Co. Rawalpindi 3. Seth Shanu Ram & Seth Narain Dutt Prop. Imperial Talkies Multan 4. Dr. Chaman Lal, Kohat City.

Mr. Dewan Chand of Nurpur Thal, District Sargodha, now at Simla, wants to know the whereabouts of his brothers Messrs. Bhagwan Dass and Meghraj and their families residing in Douglaspura, Jhang Bazar, Lyallpur, his brother B. Jaswant Rai and family residing at Nurpur Thal, Wanti and her husband, S. Jagdish Singh Nawanshehr Multan Cantt.

Mr. Hans Raj Sahnan of Tribune, Lahore informs all his relatives and friends that he has reached Simla safely and is staying at Bantony, The Mall, Simla He wants information about L Daulat Ram, Proprietor American Watch Co., Lahore and Mr Daulat Ram Sabharwal, Assistant Manager, American Watch Co. Lahore.

Principal H. C. Batra informs that he is safe and so are his wife and son.

Mr. G. L. Duggal, of the Telegraphs Department, Simla, wants to know the whereabouts of his father-in-law, L. Ramji Dass Khuller, Commission Agents, Kanak Mandi, Gujranwala.

L. Kahan Chand- Chopra, Wine Shop, Chhota Simla E., wants to know the whereabouts of Mr. Sukh Dev Khanna, Imperial Bank of India Akalgarh, Gujranwala District.

Dr. B. L. Saxena, 91, Lower Bazar, Simla, enquires about the whereabouts of Dr. Pooran Singh Mahendru of Amritdhara Road, Lahore and G. E. C. Lahore staff.

Mr. Nathu Ram Malhotra Jamandar, Trikhian Street, Multan City, wants to know the whereabouts of L. Anant Ram Khanna, proprietor Machinery and Foundry Works, Sidhusam, Railway Road Multan City. He left by a police special train on Sept. 12. His mother-in, law is very anxious about him.

Mr. Shanti Sarup Premi, clerk, office of the Accountant General, G. H. Q. Buildings, East Pb. Simla wants to know the whereabouts of the following :

(1) Dr. Pran Nath Phiranda, Jagan Nath and Raj Kumar Phiranda of Tulamba, Distt- Multan and their families.

(2) Mr. Raghunandan Lal Sharma Ziladar- of village Kabirwala, Tehsil Khanewal Distt. Multan.

Figure 1 Refugees Forum *Tribune* 8 October 1947.

permanently. For some families there were to be years of wandering,[18] loss and the psychological trauma of separation that was poignantly reflected in the 'missing persons' columns which were published under the heading 'Refugees Forum' in most of Punjab's newspapers. (See p. 99 above.)

Similarly, Ansari's work on Sindh reveals a much longer timescale of migration and settlement than is contained in conventional accounts.[19] Sindh was home to a large Hindu and Sikh minority (a quarter of the population) before 1947 and remained calm in the immediate aftermath of Partition. As we saw in chapter three, the first serious outbreak of communal violence occurred in Karachi in January 1948, when 10,000 Hindus crowded into refugee camps in the city before their evacuation to India.[20] Violence was provoked by the flood of Muslim refugees from India into the city. Ayub Khuhro, the Sindh premier, had been reluctant to accept refugees who could not be absorbed in West Punjab but was pressured into accepting an additional 200,000 – a figure which was eventually to rise higher than this following the closure of the Punjab camps in October 1948. Migration from India continued well into the 1950s. Eventually, around 60 per cent of the *mohajirs* from UP resettled in Karachi, Hyderabad and some of the smaller towns in the interior. By 1951, *mohajirs* numbered 616,906 and accounted for 58 per cent of Karachi's population.[21] As we shall see in chapters five and six, the creation of a UP Urdu-speaking enclave in the sands of Sindh was to have profound consequences for Pakistan's politics.

In short, the experience of Sindh, Bengal and the neglected histories of Punjabi migrants, suggests that migration and settlement were difficult and long-term processes that have perhaps been coloured by over-generalisation of the narrative in Punjab. Indeed, it is to correct this imbalance that we now turn to a more detailed consideration of the Bengal experience.

Bengal, migration and Partition

The Bengal Boundary Commission's decision left approximately 4 million Muslims in West Bengal and nearly 11 and a half million Hindus in East Pakistan. At the time of Independence only 344,000 Hindu refugees entered West Bengal.[22] This initial trickle formed the prelude to a flood

---

[18] See Ian Talbot (ed.) with Darshan Singh Tatla, *Epicentre of Violence: Partition Voices and Memories from Amritsar* (Delhi: Permanent Black, 2006).
[19] See Sarah Ansari, *Life after Partition: Migration, Community and Strife in Sindh 1947–1962* (Karachi: Oxford University Press, 2005).
[20] Talib, *Muslim League Attack*, p. 213.   [21] Ansari, *Life after Partition*, p. 110.
[22] Kudaisya, 'Divided Landscapes', p. 108.

which continued for several decades. By mid-1948 refugees from East
Bengal had risen to 786,000, reaching a peak of 1,575,000 a year later. In
the following years the flow stabilised at around 200,000 per annum (see
Table 3 above). Displacement continued periodically, though the West
Bengal government wound up the work of rehabilitation in March 1958.
Between this date and 1 January 1964, fresh arrivals were not recognised
as displaced persons in need of assistance. The troubled final years of East
Pakistan's existence encouraged a further massive movement of population: those who entered India between 1 January 1964 and 25 March 1971
were termed as 'new migrants' to differentiate them from the Partition-
related displaced persons. West Bengal because of its existing population
density and weak regional economy struggled to cope with this burden.
Partition left it as the smallest and most densely populated state in India
and the effects of the refugee influx were felt particularly in the 24
Parganas, Nadia and Calcutta districts in which two thirds of the refugees
from East Pakistan were concentrated.

As well as the 'waves' there were also the regular flows. Muslim inhabitants of Tripura, for instance, were still crossing over to East Pakistan at
the beginning of the 1960s, sometimes after having exchanged property
with Hindus who made the reverse journey.[23] The latter's migration from
East Pakistan to Tripura is one of the untold stories:[24] mostly Bengali,
their economic and cultural influence was eventually to create violent
tensions with an indigenous tribal population which saw the state's identity threatened.[25] The movement of Muslim East Bengalis into Assam
also sparked tension. However the most tragic long-term consequences of
Partition-related migration were to be felt by the Muslim refugees from
Bihar after the emergence of Bangladesh. These included 'twice migrants'
who had settled in West Bengal after the violence of October–November
1946, as well as those who had left India for East Bengal in August 1947
and in February 1950.[26] Pakistan accepted less than a fifth of the Biharis
who applied for 'repatriation' after the 1971 war. In the mid-1990s, there
were still around a quarter of a million 'stateless' Biharis eking out a
miserable existence in Dacca's refugee camps.[27]

---

[23] Sen, 'Tripura: The Aftermath', p. 125.
[24] Harihar Bhattacharyya has briefly reflected on the Tripura situation. See
    H. Bhattacharyya, 'Post-Partition Refugees and the Communists: A Comparative Study
    of West Bengal and Tripura', in Talbot and Singh (eds), *Region and Partition*, pp. 325–46.
[25] Bhattacharyya, 'Post-Partition Refugees', p. 343.
[26] Police harrassment and near-famine conditions in north Bihar encouraged the post-
    August 1947 migration, while the communal riots in February 1950 sparked a second
    much larger exodus.
[27] Ghosh, *Partition and the South Asia Diaspora*, p. 43.

In total, West Bengal received the lion's share of non-Muslim migrants with an estimated figure by 1957 of 3.2 million with 400,000 going to Assam and 350,000 to Tripura.[28] East Bengal/Pakistan received much smaller numbers. There were around 350,000 Muslim refugees from Orissa and Madras, 1 million Urdu-speaking refugees mainly from Bihar and West Bengal and about 200,000 Bengali-speaking migrants.[29]

Differences in migration patterns in Bengal and Punjab

In both provinces, despite anticipatory flight of Hindu capital, there was no expectation of a permanent uprooting at the time of partition. Migration was very much a response to the threat of actual violence or fear of future persecution. The levels of violence in August 1947 (see chapter three) were much higher in the Punjab than the Bengal region; and as violence spiralled out of control, the two dominions agreed on what was a virtual exchange of population in the Punjab under the control of Military Evacuation Organisations (MEOs).[30] MEOs set up headquarters on both sides of the new international boundary, organised road transportation in army trucks and requisitioned civilian vehicles. Joint civilian machinery was also established consisting of chief liaison officers who held the status of deputy high commissioners. District officials provided funds, escorts and scarce supplies of petrol to facilitate their work. The Joint Evacuation Plan agreed on 20 October between the two MEOs set a December target for the evacuation of 10 million refugees from both sides of the Punjab.[31] This elaborate machinery brought some order to the migration process, though not to the extent that official histories maintain.[32] Minority populations had no choice but to leave their ancestral homes, even when they were not always in imminent threat of attack, resulting in the denuding of Hindus and Sikhs from Pakistani Punjab and Muslims from the Indian Punjab. Further state control over the migration process was exerted by settling rural refugee populations together in designated localities.[33] Both populations and land were in effect

[28] Pranati Chaudhuri, *Refugees in West Bengal: A Study of the Growth and Distribution of Refugee Settlements within the CMD*. Occasional Paper No. 55 (Calcutta: Centre for Studies in Social Sciences, March 1983), p. 23.
[29] Chaudhuri, *Refugees in West Bengal*, p. 169.
[30] For the work of the Indian Military Organisation see Brigadier Rajendra Singh, *The Military Evacuation Organisation 1947–48* (New Delhi: Government of India, 1962).
[31] Ravinder Kaur, 'Narratives of Resettlement. Past, Present and Politics among 1947 Punjabi Migrants in Delhi', unpublished 2004 Ph.D. thesis, Roskilde University Centre, Denmark, p. 97.
[32] Kaur, 'Narratives of Resettlement', pp. 101–3.
[33] For details of this process with respect to Indian Punjab, see Kirpal Singh, *The Partition of the Punjab* (Patiala: Punjabi University, 1989), pp. 181–3.

being exchanged. It was less easy, however, to direct urban migrants. Where possible such direction was encouraged, for example in the case of skilled labour,[34] but by and large this migration was less well coordinated.

In the Bengal region, in contrast, India and Pakistan worked to *limit* the transfer of population. Inter-dominion conferences were held to assure the minorities of their security. Indian and Pakistani rehabilitation ministers issued a joint declaration in Calcutta in April 1948 in which they expressed a determination 'to take every possible step to discourage such exodus and to create such conditions as would check mass exodus in either direction'.[35] However refugees continued to leave East Bengal despite these assurances. Upper-caste Hindus were particularly affected by status reversal,[36] requisitioning of property and inappropriate behaviour to their women by newly emboldened Muslims.[37] Such anxieties were further intensified at times of communal tension and violence, both within the region and elsewhere in the subcontinent. Indeed, the waves of migration in Bengal can be mapped around these periods. One million Hindus left East Bengal in 1964 at the time of tension arising from the theft of Muslim relics at the Hazratbal shrine in Kashmir. Muslims also migrated from West Bengal on a large scale at such times.[38] The serious riots in 1950 sparked off large-scale migration of Hindus from East Bengal and Muslims from Assam, Bihar and West Bengal, and by mid-April 1950 there were over 800,000 Muslim refugees in East Bengal.

In response to these riots, the Indian and Pakistan prime ministers tried to restore some stability through the Nehru–Liaquat Pact (April 1950). It promised equality of citizenship for minority communities and stated that refugees who returned home by 31 December 1950 would be entitled to the restoration of their houses and land. This stemmed migration for a time and even led to around 1.2 million of refugees returning to East Bengal.[39] Most were able to recover the houses they had abandoned, and the provincial government set aside 700,000 rupees to cover the cost of their rehabilitation.[40] Returning Hindus together with Muslim refugees from West Bengal increased the population of East Bengal by nearly 950,000 by the middle of 1951.[41] However, there was a further outflow

---

[34] *Eastern Times* (Lahore), 16 September 1947.

[35] Cited in Kudaisya, 'Divided Landscapes', p. 109.

[36] A Hindu doctor from a village in Bagura district left East Bengal immediately when one of his Muslim servants tried to become friendly with him. He entered the doctor's bedroom, saying 'Master, in Pakistan we are not inferior to you. So you must not forget to treat us as equals.' See Hiranmoy Bandopadhyay, *Udbastu* (Calcutta: Shaitya Sansad, 1970), p. 15.

[37] See Chatterji, *Spoils of Partition*, p. 111.

[38] Around 800,000 Muslims left for East Bengal at the time of the Hazratbal incident. Chatterji, *Spoils of Partition*, p. 167.

[39] Chaudhuri, *Refugees in West Bengal*, p. 38.   [40] *Dawn* (Karachi) 18 June 1951.

[41] *Dawn* (Karachi) 18 June 1951.

of the Hindu population the following year, when the introduction in October of a passport system created fears that future migration would be more difficult. As a result nearly 2,000 people arrived each day at the Indian border outposts of Bongaon and Ranaghat. The trains on which they travelled were 'dangerously overcrowded with passengers riding on footboards and hanging on to iron beams and rods beneath the carriages'.[42] The authorities opened an interception camp at Ambagaon less than half a mile from Bongaon railway station, but many preferred to sleep on the platform or under railway wagons. Eventually special trains took them to Sealdah Station Calcutta which itself soon presented 'a scene of indescribable confusion'. 'A fog of blue smoke' from countless cooking fires, a correspondent for the *Statesman* newspaper recorded, 'hangs over the listless grey brown mass of humanity'.[43] Many of the refugees were from poorer lowercaste communities in the East Bengal hinterland. They were eventually dispersed to transit camps on the outskirts of the city or forced to fend for themselves in the crowded and squalid squatter colonies which had sprung up in Calcutta.

Finally, it also is important to recognise that Partition led to large-scale migration *within* the borders of West Bengal. Muslims who felt insecure, or whose property was seized by incoming refugees, clustered in safer enclaves. South Calcutta, once the location of considerable Muslim settlements, became dominated by East Bengali refugees.[44] Muslims were also forced out from the Nadia district by Namasudra refugees who had been displaced by the 1950 Jessore riots in East Bengal. Chatterji has noted that a virtual exchange of population took place in Nadia which bore some similarities with the earlier situation in the Punjab.[45] In many instances Muslim populations increasingly gravitated to northern districts of West Bengal such as Malda, and Murshidabad, where they formed majority enclaves along the border with East Bengal.[46] Partition is usually seen as dramatically changing population profile because of cross-border migration. But in the case of West Bengal it transformed the communal landscape by a series of local upheavals.

---

[42] *Statesman Weekly* (Calcutta) 11 October 1952.
[43] *Statesman Weekly* (Calcutta) 18 October 1952.
[44] The Muslim population of Calcutta declined by nearly 200,000 between the 1951 and 1961 Census.
[45] Joya Chatterji, 'Of Graveyards and Ghettos. Muslims in Partitioned West Bengal, 1947–1967', in Mushirul Hasan and Asim Roy (eds), *Living Together Separately: Cultural India in History and Politics* (New Delhi: Oxford University Press, 2005), p. 243.
[46] The Muslim population in Malda and Murshidabad grew by 63 and 35 per cent respectively in the decade 1951–1961. Chatterji, *Spoils of Partition*, p. 186.

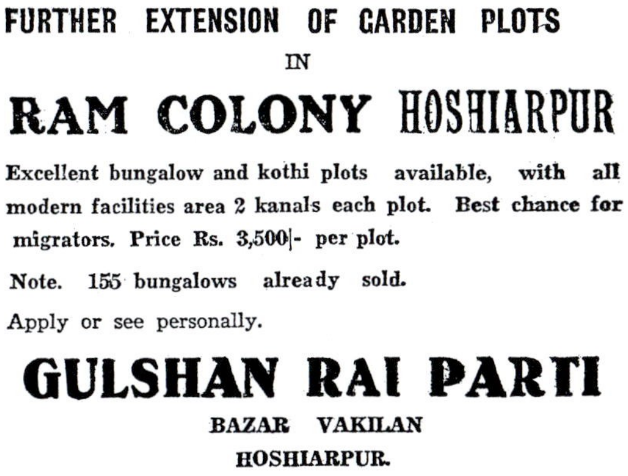

FURTHER EXTENSION OF GARDEN PLOTS

IN

RAM COLONY HOSHIARPUR

Excellent bungalow and kothi plots available, with all
modern facilities area 2 kanals each plot. Best chance for
migrators. Price Rs. 3,500|- per plot.

Note. 155 bungalows already sold.

Apply or see personally.

GULSHAN RAI PARTI

BAZAR   VAKILAN

HOSHIARPUR.

Figure 2 Migrators' Advertisements *Tribune* 9 July 1947.

Class, gender, caste and community experiences
of migration and rehabilitation

In many ways the standardised refugee experience in Punjab has tended to
overlook the enormous variations that occurred as result of class, gender,
caste and community. These accounts, for example, seldom mention the
anticipatory migration by wealthy Punjabi Hindus.[47] Ravinder Kaur writing
on Delhi notes that political connections along with wealth could not only
secure a safe migration passage, sometimes even by air, but could also enable
return visits to secure personal belongings. Khosla recalls, for example, that
he returned to Lahore from Simla in November 1947 with an armed Gurkha
escort and removed two truckloads of personal belongings that had been
stored in the garage of the Lahore High Court. His father-in-law and his
friend, Dr Nihal Chand Sikri, had also secured two trucks each for trans-
porting their belongings.[48] The resulting fracas in Rawalpindi when Qurban
Ali, Inspector General of Police in West Punjab assisted his personal friend
Sirdar Sohan Singh in removing his belongings, even came in for discussion
at Indian Cabinet level.[49] A number of allegations surrounded the misuse of
army vehicles by Nathu Ram, India's Chief Liaison Officer in Lahore. He
was said to have deployed these to remove the household goods of Diwan
Ram Lal, the newly appointed Chief Justice of the East Punjab High Court.[50]

---

[47] Ravinder Kaur, *Since 1947: Partition Narratives among Punjabi Migrants of Delhi* (New
Delhi: Oxford University Press, 2007), pp. 67–8.

[48] Khosla, *Memory's Gay Chariot*, pp. 164–8.

[49] Report of K. L. Panjabi 29 December 1947. Circulated to the Cabinet Meeting of 30
December 1947. MB1/D278, University of Southampton.

[50] Raghuvendra Tanwar, *Reporting the Partition of Punjab 1947: Press, Public and Other
Opinions* (New Delhi: Manohar, 2006), p. 433.

The wealthy could also bypass the cumbersome state processes of compensation, by arranging, through agencies, international exchange of properties. Politicians who carved out new careers as refugee spokesmen, in many instances, were able to avoid or mitigate the indignities and economic losses of the majority of those they represented. It is a little-remarked fact of Partition migration history that the British Overseas Airways Corporation transported 28,000 people from Pakistan and 18,000 from India in the period 15 September to 7 December 1947. This was in addition to the twice-daily service from Lahore to Amritsar and the daily service from Delhi to Rawalpindi run by Indian National Airways.[51] Such passengers could look down on the burning villages and ant-like refugee columns traversing the Punjab's killing fields. On the rare occasions that the elite travellers were inconvenienced, it could reach even Cabinet-level discussion. Nehru noted with displeasure, for example, early in October an incident when a flight direct from Peshawar to Delhi had to set down at Lahore because of slight engine trouble and its 'occupants had been stripped of all their belongings'.[52]

The wealthy and the elite were also the groups who in the early years after Partition articulated the cultural senses of loss and the refashioning of new identities. These groups were most sensitive to decline in status or in exercising a sense of cultural superiority over the community in which they were resettled. The East Bengal *bhadralok* resettled in Calcutta and the UP *mohajir* elite of Karachi were perhaps most acutely influenced by a sense of loss. There is an elegiac quality about their memory of the idyllic villages of 'Golden Bengal' and the small towns of eastern UP.[53] Accounts such as those compiled in *Chhere asha gram* (The Abandoned Village) focused on memories of public holidays at the time of the major religious festivals, boat races, the abundance and beauty of the East Bengal countryside, harmonious social relations and the 'respect' for elders and women.[54] One of the Bengali words for refugee, *udvastu* (outside of home), attested to this painful separation from ancestral roots.

---

[51] Kaur, *Since 1947*, p. 79.

[52] Extract from Emergency Committee 20th Meeting, 3 October 1947 MB1/D275, University of Southampton.

[53] The latter is the setting for the famous Urdu writer Intizar Husain's short story 'Akhri Mom Batti' which explores the theme of Partition loss. See I. Talbot, *Freedom's Cry: The Popular Dimension in the Pakistan Movement and Partition Experience in North-West India* (Karachi: Oxford University Press, 1996), pp. 142–3. Nostalgia for East Bengal is seen in such poems as Taslima Nasreen's 'Broken Bengal', which has been translated into English by Subhoranjan Dasgupta from the selection, *Behula eka bhasiyechilo bhela*.

[54] See Dipesh Chakrabarty, 'Remembered Villages: Representations of Hindu–Bengali Memories in the Aftermath of Partition', in Low and Brasted (eds), *Freedom, Trauma, Continuities*, pp. 133–53.

Plate 10 Mridula Sarabhai with refugees in West Punjab.

Equally members of the prosperous Punjabi migrant community in Delhi have kept alive a strong nostalgic attachment to the pre-Partition Lahore of their youth.[55] For this group, post-1947 Indian Punjab has become too Sikh-centred to act as a cultural referent for a community which has otherwise submerged its identity into a national Indian one. Significantly, both Punjabi and Bengali Hindu identification of Partition with loss was able to sit more comfortably with the nationalist discourse than the ambiguous relationship of the migrant UP elite within Pakistan.

The gendered dimension of migration has been the focus of much recent work, especially with respect to the recovery of abducted women.[56] Women were seized by war bands and *jathas* during attacks on villages and refugee columns; they were also abducted from refugee transit camps.[57] Recovery offices and transit camps were established in both India and

[55] This is reflected in such works as: Anand, *Lahore: Portrait of a Lost City*; Pran Nevile, *Lahore: A Sentimental Journey* (New Delhi: Allied Publishers, 1993); Sahdev Vohra, *Lahore, Loved, Lost and Thereafter* (Delhi: Indian Publishers' Distributors, 2004).

[56] See Ritu Menon and Kamla Bhasin, *Borders and Boundaries: Women in India's Partition* (New Brunswick, NJ: Rutgers University Press, 1998).

[57] See Andrew Major, '"The Chief Sufferers": Abduction of Women during the Partition of India', *South Asia* XVIII, Special Issue (1995), pp. 57–72.

Pakistan, following agreement in November 1948. By October 1952, just over 8,000 women and children had been rehabilitated from Pakistan. Twice this number had been recovered from India. The human misery and physical and psychological scars arising from abduction is of course hidden by such bald statistics. Amrita Pritam's novel *Pinjer* has brilliantly portrayed the horror and pathos arising from abduction.[58] The theme also inspired a number of short stories, notably, Rajinder Singh Bedi's *Lajwanti* and Saadat Hasan Manto's *Xuda ki Qasam* (I Swear by God). Such scholars as Urvashi Butalia, Ritu Menon and Kamla Bhasin have revealed how women were often doubly victimised: firstly by their abductors, and then by the recovery machinery which forced them to leave families they had established to return to uncertain futures in their own homeland. Much less has been written about the abuses women suffered after they had migrated. Qudrat Ullah Shahab's short story *Ya Khuda* (O God) touches on this sensitive theme through the main character of Dilshad who is assaulted by a would-be benefactor, Mustafa Khan. According to a report by a Communist Party activist, writing in December 1947, the pretext of distributing clothes among refugees was frequently adopted to 'entice away young girls for immoral purposes'. The same writer claimed that prostitution had grown tenfold in such towns and cities as Lahore, Gujranwala and Lyallpur.[59]

The post-colonial states attempted to uphold traditional gender roles in their treatment of refugees. In Lahore the state's guardianship role with respect to young female orphans extended to their arranged early marriage, thereby like a family patriarch establishing control over female sexuality. Social stigmas attached to widowhood were reflected in the establishment in Delhi, for example, of a separate refugee colony for young widows; again the state closely monitored and controlled social behaviour by ensuring that the colony's inhabitants did not go outside its boundaries without the permission of the female social workers.[60]

The Punjab bias in the literature may have distorted historical understanding of women refugees' experience. Its focus on abduction and restoration has fixed a stereotype of women as 'victims' in the upheaval. Recent work on Bengal however reveals important changes in the social status of Hindu middle-class women arising from the refugee experience. Old extended families because of space constraints were replaced by nuclear

---

[58] The Punjabi novel was published in English translation by Khushwant Singh in 1973, entitled *The Skeleton*.

[59] 'Refugees in landlord-ridden West Punjab facing death from cold and hunger', Lahore 26 December 1947 Mian Iftikharuddin Papers.

[60] Kaur, *Since 1947*, p. 252.

families. Displaced families turned to matrilineal ties for shelter, overturn-
ing traditional emphasis on patrilineal relationships. Educated women
joined the paid workforce giving rise to the new phenomenon of the working *bhadramahila* (gentlewoman). Chatterji rightly regards such changes as
falling short of emancipation or empowerment. But they nonetheless represented greater opportunity and a widening of female horizons from the
seclusion of the *antahpur* (inner chambers of the household).[61]

The processes of rehabilitation were extremely variegated. Whereas
official accounts emphasised the range of state provisions – grants,
loans, training and the administration of evacuee moveable and immoveable property – that helped smooth settlement, oral testimonies of Punjabi
migrants in localities such as Lahore, Amritsar and Delhi rarely acknowledged this role. Instead individual self-reliance was trumpeted[62] with
political parties, communal organisations and individual philanthropists
singled out for special praise. Naturally amidst the communal carnage the
state was often seen as the source of people's miseries rather than their
protector, and given the magnitude of the calamity that most people had
suffered, the support given, however generous, was often viewed as charity
rather than a blessing. Certainly oral testimonies have demonstrated a
huge gap between 'official' and 'people's' discourses and the fact that, for
many, rehabilitation was a drawn-out process.[63]

Rehabilitation also created huge risks as well as new opportunities.
Well-off families, for example, could be brought to their knees through
the mischance of abduction, illness or the failure of compensation claims.
The naturally enterprising, on the other hand, exploited the mayhem to
illegally seize property and goods, especially in fashionable areas. But in
the main the ability to recover from the trauma of displacement was
determined by the migrants' social and economic capital: Sylheti upper-
caste Hindu refugees, for instance, were quickly absorbed into Assam
because of their education and long-standing economic contacts with the
Brahmaputra Valley and Cachar region.

Pre-existing social class distinctions were institutionalised by the Indian
and Pakistani states' response to relief and resettlement. Whether refugees
could afford their own food rations, for example, determined if refugees in
Delhi would be directed to a life under canvas in the Edward and Outram
Lines of the Kingsway camp, or to be accommodated in concrete barracks
at the Hudson and Reeds Lines.[64] Both Indian and Pakistani satellite

---

[61] Chatterji, *Spoils of Partition*, pp. 153–4.
[62] See Talbot, *Divided Cities*; Talbot, *Epicentre of Violence*; Kaur, *Since 1947*.
[63] See for example the interviews with Sardar Mohan Singh, Sardar Tirath Singh and Sardar
Dalip Singh in Talbot, *Epicentre of Violence*.
[64] Kaur, *Since 1947*, p. 99.

towns and refugee housing colonies had varieties of house plot sizes, streets and availability of services to suit the different classes of refugee. 'The class differences visible during the population movement', Ravinder Kaur has observed, 'became further entrenched when permanent housing projects were undertaken on such basis. This ensured that refugees were reinvented in their old class of social stratification.'[65] Perhaps the clearest illustration of this was the Indian state's provision of separate colonies and camp accommodation for Untouchables.

Regional social biases also failed to be erased by common cultural boundaries. Bengali-speaking refugees from the East were derisively referred to as *Bangaals* (country bumpkins) by the West Bengal population which regarded itself as more sophisticated.[66] Bihari refugees found it more difficult to settle in East Bengal than did Muslims from West Bengal. They complained to the newspapers and the Muslim League authorities that they were being victimised and harassed in East Bengal's towns 'simply because they happened to be up-country Muslims'.[67] Refugee rehabilitation for West Bengali Muslim migrants was, on the other hand, somewhat easier than for both the Biharis and their East Bengali Hindu counterparts. Much smaller numbers were involved and they were dispersed to Dhaka, Narayanganj, Kulna and Chittagong. In contrast with the greater Calcutta area, where the bulk of urban refugees in West Bengal congregated, there was no shortage of evacuee property in the East Pakistan towns[68] and the countryside was also better able to accommodate new arrivals than West Bengal.

Agriculturalists faced fewer difficulties in Pakistan than in the Indian Punjab. Significantly, much more land had been abandoned by outgoing migrants and it was also more fertile. Hindu and Sikh refugees vacated 9.6 million acres of land in Pakistan, while Muslims left behind 5.5 million acres of land in India.[69] Punjabi Sikh farmers had to make do with both fewer irrigated tracts of land and smaller holdings under the system of 'graded cuts', or were allotted lands in Rajasthan, Haryana or Western UP.[70] Muslim cultivators from the East Punjab, in contrast, took over the

---

[65] Kaur, 'Narratives of Resettlement', p. 166.

[66] West Bengal inhabitants referred to themselves as Ghotis.

[67] Ghosh, *Partition and the South Asian Diaspora*, p. 19.

[68] T. Y. Tan and Gyanesh Kudaisya, *The Aftermath of Partition in South Asia* (London: Routledge, 2000), p. 169.

[69] See, J. B. Schechtman, 'Evacuee Property in India and Pakistan', *Pacific Affairs* 24 (1951), pp. 411–12.

[70] In one important respect, however, Sikh cultivators from West Punjab were better off than their peasant brethren who migrated from Sindh, the Frontier and Balochistan, in that there was an exchange of land-revenue records between the two Punjabs, unlike these other areas. This meant claims could be verified much more smoothly with allotments becoming quasi-permanent. They only became permanent after the 1954 Displaced Persons Act.

most fertile tracts of land in the Canal Colony areas abandoned by Sikh farmers. Yet rural resettlement in West Punjab was not without its diffi-culties. Muslim landlords continued to demand their share of the crop *batai* (rent in kind) from refugees. Their long-standing tenants in such districts as Multan, Montgomery and Shahpur feared that their rights would be undercut by the incoming refugees. Despite being allotted houses, some refugees were forced to live in the fields because of clashes with existing inhabitants who had appropriated buildings as well as crops and cattle abandoned by Hindus and Sikhs. There were also delays in making permanent allotments of land to refugees because of the time it took to exchange land settlement records; refugees were even ejected from land they had been semi-permanently allotted.[71] In some instances this was because corrupt officials wished to rehabilitate their refugee relatives on this land.

The towns of the West Punjab were favoured destinations for urban Punjabi refugees who were able to fill some of the entrepreneurial and commercial niches abandoned by Hindus. Even so, the competition for abandoned property could cause conflicts as in Gujranwala where refu-gees from Amritsar and the old inhabitants came to blows over the allot-ment of shops. Urban migration was on a smaller scale in the Indian Punjab, although Jullundur and Ludhiana were to experience rapid post-Partition growth. The former commercial and industrial centre of Amritsar suffered badly with the loss of markets, labour and the vulnerable border situation. A significant proportion of the former West Punjab Hindu capitalist class was to abandon Punjab altogether and relocate to Delhi and Bombay.

While the differences in the size and amount of landed and urban property available for migrant resettlement in East and West Punjab and East and West Bengal led to allegations of unfair treatment,[72] there were considerable variations in the response of regional governments to the crisis. In Punjab, the governments of East and West Punjab agreed on a response to the problem of abandoned property as early as September 1947. Arrangements were made for the exchange of property and com-pensation for abandoned property. At the same time, the two govern-ments, through refugee taxes and disbursements from the Centre, set aside large sums for resettlement. The East Punjab government attempted to ease the resettlement of West Punjab cultivators by establishing rural

---

[71] *Statesman Weekly* (Calcutta) 31 May 1952.
[72] Prafulla Chakrabarti, *The Marginal Men: The Refugees and the Left Political Syndrome in West Bengal* (Calcutta: Naya Udyog, 1999), pp. 250–2.

housing schemes. Model villages were constructed on the sites of evacuee villages which had been demolished during the violence. According to Randhawa, there were some 1,800 East Punjab villages where 90 per cent of the houses were demolished.[73] Before refugees were permanently allotted land they were given loans for food and for fodder. Large sums of money were also set aside for the purchase of bullocks, seed and the reconstruction of houses and wells. When land was permanently allotted in 1950, loans were provided for agricultural modernisation such as water pumps, tractors and tube-wells. Tractor loans, for example, amounted to 3.2 million rupees.[74] Between September 1947 and March 1951, 40 million rupees was disbursed to displaced cultivators.[75] These measures were to lay the foundations of the 'Green Revolution' two decades later.

The East Punjab government addressed the needs of urban refugees by the building of new satellite towns such as Faridabad and Rajpura, as well as the provision of training and funding for refugees to set up their own businesses. The development at Rajpura on the Grand Trunk Road, fifteen miles west of Ambala, cost 20 million rupees. It was termed 'one of the biggest experiments of the Government of India in building a well planned and simple yet dignified home for refugees'.[76] This type of support as much as the famed Punjabi self-reliance was crucial in the successful resettlement, though official efforts were significantly supplemented by charitable donations from individuals and community organisations.

In West Bengal the government established 'Transit Camps', 'Worksite Camps' and 'Permanent Liability Camps' to feed and shelter the refugees. They were kept open for many more years than those in Punjab due to the refugee flows and fewer opportunities for self-resettlement. Overcrowded, insanitary and disease-ridden, they were rudimentary to the core.[77] The West Bengal government, however, did little more than provide this basic immediate relief as Delhi's financial support was much less generous than to Punjab. As a result fewer townships and houses were constructed and much less employment was generated. In the circumstances, the provincial government's solution to the refugee problem was to disperse refugees to outlying districts such as Bankura and Midnapore and to neighbouring states. This dispersal policy became politically controversial not only within the state, but also in neighbouring provinces such as Assam which were reluctant to receive more refugees. Eventually a

---

[73] Randhawa, *Out of the Ashes*, p. 153.   [74] Randhawa, *Out of the Ashes*, p. 167.
[75] Randhawa, *Out of the Ashes*, p. 162.   [76] *Statesman* (Calcutta) 28 May 1949.
[77] Chakrabarti, *The Marginal Men*, p. 223.

large dispersal centre was established at Bettiah in the Champaran district of Bihar. The most ambitious and controversial settlement scheme involved moving over 25,000 families to the 270,000 cleared acres of forest at Dandakaranya in Orissa and Madhya Pradesh.[78] Many refugees saw this as deportation, rather than rehabilitation, and claimed they were being exiled to the 'dark forest' like Lord Rama in the *Ramayana*. By 1978 over 11,000 families had deserted the settlement.

In the early 1960s, Untouchables from East Bengal were also resettled in the remote Sunderbans region. This scheme was better thought through than that at Dandakaranya in that the cultivators who were sent there originated from the Khulna and Barisal districts and as such had experience of agricultural conditions. They were provided with three acres of land each and loans to build houses and purchase agriculture equipment. Nevertheless, a survey of the settlement a decade later found the bulk of the inhabitants mired in poverty: at least 25 per cent of the cultivators were living in distress and barely 58 per cent at subsistence level.[79] Government cash support had ceased and agricultural productivity remained low and was hindered by poor communications. As the investigators concluded, much poverty was the result of the 'lack of far-sightedness of the Government department responsible for planning the project'.[80]

The West Bengal government's limited success in addressing the refugee 'problem' was in part the result of disputes with the Centre over funding and in part reflected the sense of being overburdened because of its weak economy[81] and population density. Economic reconstruction and refugee rehabilitation were further hindered by the state's declining share in the national distribution of excise duties and income tax.[82] The government of India, most importantly of all, did not see refugee migration in the east as a permanent phenomenon, unlike in the west. It refused to extend evacuee legislation to either West Bengal or Assam on the grounds that migration was temporary and transfers of population should be discouraged. Indeed, later waves of refugees were designated as 'economic migrants' rather than as victims of Partition. At the same time the West Bengal government was reluctant to raise its own resources to tackle the problem. Significantly, unlike East Bengal or East and West Punjab, it

---

[78] See Kudaisya, 'Divided Landscapes', pp. 115–16.

[79] S. L. De and A. K. Bhattacharjee, *The Refugee Settlement in the Sunderbans, West Bengal: A Socio-economic Study* (Calcutta: 1972), p. 47.

[80] De and Bhattacharjee, *Refugee Settlement*, p. 50.

[81] Partition badly hit its largest industry, the jute industry, and also undermined its tea and paper industries, by cutting off raw material supplies and disrupting the railway network.

[82] Chatterji, *Spoils of Partition*, pp. 256–9.

did not levy a 'refugee tax'.[83] It was thus dependent on funding from the Centre which eventually flowed in large sums but neither as easy to spend, because of bureaucratic delays, nor as well utilised as it might have been. The findings of the Statistical Bureau published in February 1952 represented a grave indictment of the government's policy: 72 per cent of the refugees were unemployed and 12 per cent of the 2.14 million refugees were living on land on which they had trespassed.[84] The forcible occupation of public lands began with the colonisation of deserted army barracks in the Jadavpur area of south-east Calcutta. By 1950, there were over 145 squatter colonies in the Calcutta Metropolitan District alone. In sum, squatter colonies were the Bengali refugees' response to politicians' call for self-rehabilitation.

The East Bengal government also took effective measures to address a refugee problem whose scale has not always been acknowledged by historians. It is little remembered that within six weeks of the February–March 1950 violence in Calcutta and Assam, 1.1 million Muslims had entered Pakistan's eastern wing.[85] The government early in 1950 established refugee camps on the outskirts of Dacca and Chittagong to relieve congestion, and around 1,000 people were accommodated in specially constructed barracks at Samair in the Kurmitola area of Dacca.[86] An additional 8,000 refugees were rehabilitated in the Bogra district of East Bengal where they were allotted between three and six acres of land.[87] Such short-term measures were accompanied by longer-term rehabilitation efforts coordinated by a new East Bengal Relief Commissioner N. M. Khan. He reported early in June 1950 that 5 million rupees had already been spent on provision of stalls for shopkeepers and the distribution of sewing machines and looms.[88] His Employment Bureau claimed to have placed 45,000 persons in various jobs by September 1950.[89] A month earlier, the Pakistan government had announced that it was advancing 12 million rupees to the East Bengal authorities for rehabilitation purposes, a grant that enabled an ambitious urban and rural rehabilitation scheme to be planned. The former involved the construction of five satellite townships near Dacca, Chittagong, Sylhet, Jessore and Rangpur at the cost of 1 million rupees. They were designed to house over 100,000 refugees.

[83] The East Bengal Government' levied a tax on the licences which were required for the export of raw jute.
[84] *Statesman* (Calcutta) 16 February 1952.
[85] *Civil and Military Gazette* (Lahore) 26 May 1950.
[86] *Civil and Military Gazette* (Lahore) 5 April 1950.
[87] *Civil and Military Gazette* (Lahore) 20 April 1950.
[88] *Civil and Military Gazette* (Lahore) 7 June 1950.
[89] *Civil and Military Gazette* (Lahore) 22 September 1950.

Three million rupees were set aside for a rural rehabilitation scheme in which families were to receive five acres of land along with a maintenance allowance of 50 rupees per family until their first harvest.[90] In June 1951, the government finalised a scheme for a 10,000-acre refugee colony at Aflong in Sylhet.[91] It simultaneously gave 250 houses free of charge to refugee families in the Mirpur colony, Dacca.[92]

Although overwhelmingly the majority of the Partition refugees were of rural background, the most visible impact of refugee settlement was in the towns and cities. We conclude this chapter by presenting a brief survey of the impact of refugee migration on Calcutta, Dacca, Delhi, Karachi and Lahore.

Calcutta

Partition transformed both Calcutta's physical and political landscape. In 1951 the city's population was nearly 20 per cent higher than it had been just five years before; by 1973, the number of refugees was just under 2 million and represented around two thirds of West Bengal's urban refugee population and one third of the state's total.[93] A quarter of Calcutta's inhabitants were refugees and seven out of every ten migrants from East Pakistan had found their way to the city. Given the relatively little empty property available, accommodating these numbers was a Herculean task. Despite government attempts to disperse refugees and discourage their concentration in the city, Calcutta continued to attract migrants because of its employment attractions.

Naturally the first wave of refugees was the most favoured. Around 60 per cent of the early refugees were upper- and middle-class Hindus who often had pre-existing professional and kinship ties in the city and enough capital to buy up what property was available. Even less affluent members of the first wave[94] were better off than their successors in that they could occupy vacant land near to the city centre, in many instances close to its affluent southern neighbourhoods. These settlements gave birth to the Netaji and Vidyasagar colonies. In the Tolleygunge area alone, before 1950, there were 63 squatters' colonies. The area's population stood 141 per cent higher in 1951 than it had a decade earlier. There was a further heavy concentration in the Dum Dum area[95] as south Dum Dum's

---

[90] *Civil and Military Gazette* (Lahore) 6 August 1950.
[91] *Civil and Military Gazette* (Lahore) 6 June 1951.   [92] *Dawn* (Karachi) 18 June 1951.
[93] Pranati Chaudhuri, *Refugees in West Bengal*, Table One, p. 38.
[94] They included skilled artisans who followed the patrons who had provided their livelihoods.
[95] Chaudhuri, *Refugees in West Bengal*, p. 20.

population increased by 119 per cent.[96] Only around 150,000 of the 1.3 million refugees who had arrived by December 1949 sought admission to relief camps.[97] The very poor eked out an existence on the pavements and the platforms at Sealdah Station. Protests at its terrible overcrowding and squalid conditions led to clashes with the police in January 1949 in which nine people were killed.[98]

Squatter colonies emerged overnight as thatched huts were constructed under the cover of darkness on vacant land. Most were eventually to be regularised as the government compensated the landowners, and were well managed with committees which raised subscriptions and labour for the construction of drains, roads and water supplies – giving a lie to the myth of East Bengali refugee dependency and indolence. They also contrasted starkly with the government's own feeble efforts which sponsored only 156 colonies in the Calcutta Metropolitan District out of a total of 268. A further 77 private colonies were established through the legal purchase of land.[99]

Later migrants drawn from the poorer agricultural classes of eastern Bengal swelled Calcutta's underclass throughout the 1950s. They were 'acute migrants' and unlike the wealthier classes lacked the skills and the connections which could help smooth the migration process. The poorest of all tended to leave Pakistan only in extreme situations. Invariably resettlement was to prove a more troubled process for these groups than the middle-class Bengalis, or their more favoured Punjabi rural brethren. Many peasant refugees settled not in urban areas, but on poorly drained and infertile tracts of land along the border.[100]

Within Calcutta, refugees were accommodated in tented camps, empty warehouses and even on steamers. The most fortunate sought shelter in private or government-sponsored colonies but many illegally squatted in the colonies that sprang up after 1950 on the west bank of the Hooghly river between Magra and Uluberia. Poverty and shortage of land consigned large numbers of agriculturalist refugees to prolonged residence in refugee camps in Calcutta and elsewhere in West Bengal. In 1958, the camp population stood at 800,000; one third of their inhabitants had spent anything from 6 to 10 years living in squalid conditions.[101]

---

[96] Omkar Goswami, 'Calcutta's Economy 1918–1970: The Fall from Grace', in Sukanta Chaudhuri, *Calcutta: The Living City*, vol. 2, *The Present and the Future* (New Delhi: Oxford University Press, 1999), p. 92.

[97] N. Chatterjee, 'The East Bengal Refugees: A Lesson in Survival', in Sukanta Chaudhuri, *Calcutta*, p. 72.

[98] Chatterji, *Spoils of Partition*, p. 132.

[99] Pranati Chaudhuri, *Refugees in West Bengal*, p. 31.

[100] Chatterji, *Spoils of Partition*, pp. 123–4.

[101] N. Chatterjee, 'The East Bengal Refugees', p. 74.

Calcutta's landscape was also radically transformed. A large pavement-dwelling population, overcrowding, poor infrastructure and cholera epidemics came to symbolise the metropolis, earning it the epithet of a 'dying city'. Its expansion in the north and south direction became uncontrollable. In the east reclaimed marshland was to found the settlement in the Salt Lake area. 'The migration of the refugee population', as Chaudhuri observes, 'played a key role in forging of ... the metropolitan district.' In more ways than one the refugee population extended the 'horizon of metropolitan living beyond the limits of existing settlement'.[102]

Equally Calcutta's politics were also irrevocably changed as Congress's hegemony was gradually eroded by the Communist Party of India (CPI). Struggle for survival in the squatter colonies quickly politicised the refugees who were frequently drawn into violent confrontations with landlords' *goondas*; and this process intensified after the West Bengal Eviction Act (1951) which restricted the regularisation to those colonies established before 31 December 1950. As there were large numbers of 'illegal' post-1950 colonies, especially in the Bally and Howrah municipalities, the CPI began to recruit in these localities, thus laying the foundations of its growth and subsequent success in the state. Its rise was also assisted by the anti-*Bangaal* attitudes of the West Bengal Congress. The dominant Hooghly faction disenfranchised East Bengal leaders and stirred anti-refugee sentiment.[103] The Hooghly group turned to patronage to secure political allies and looked to the influence of the previously marginal but wealthy Marwari traders. It even flirted with the Muslims. This shift in approach and the general atmosphere of corruption and decay disillusioned the Congress's traditional *bhadralok* supporters. The ground was being prepared for its post-1967 wilderness years after which Congress became increasingly a marginal force in the state.

Dacca

Despite its historical heritage as an important outpost of the Mughal Empire, Dacca had been in decline even before the East India Company established the centre of its Bengal activities in Calcutta. Nineteenth-century travellers termed it 'the city of the great sleep'. Those fortunes which were to be made were accumulated by Hindu merchants who ran Dacca's shops, bazaars and the handful of industries and controlled as much as 85 per cent of the immoveable properties in the city and

---

[102] Pranati Chaudhuri, *Refugees in West Bengal*, p. 35.
[103] For details, see Chatterji, *Spoils of Partition*, pp. 221–2.

58 per cent of the population, despite the Muslim preponderance in its hinterland.[104] Colonial Dacca was more a Hindu than a Muslim city.

Large-scale Hindu out-migration occurred after 1947 mainly as result of economic losses. Soon after the creation of Pakistan, the East Bengal government began requisitioning private properties to accommodate civil servants. Between August 1947 and March 1948 over 1,100 houses were taken over in this way. Muslim refugees from Bihar, East UP and Orissa also forcibly occupied premises of wealthy Hindus who began to flee to West Bengal. Eventually their proportion of the population was to decline to just 4.6 per cent.[105] According to a survey of Hindu neighbourhoods in December 1950, Muslims controlled 6,255 out of 7,175 properties previously owned by Hindus.[106] A large influx of Muslims entered the city following the riots in Calcutta in February and March 1950. Contemporary press reports stated that Dacca was 'overflowing with refugees'.[107] Camps were established on its outskirts to relieve the congestion. Little has been written about the refugee impact on Dacca which was an important reception area. By early 1950 it had about a dozen refugee camps, and colonies were established nearby at Mirpur with cheap housing.[108] Better-off refugees were directed to private dwellings.

Dacca's spatial dimensions changed further as it emerged as Pakistan's 'second capital'. Much of this work was undertaken during the Ayub regime in the 1960s when a new assembly building, supreme court, the largest mosque in East Pakistan (the Al-Baitul Mukarram) and a fourteen-square-mile cantonment area were constructed. These new public buildings were set in a complex some seven miles from the old city that covered a thousand acres. The city underwent further transformation following the 'second Partition' and the emergence of independent Bangladesh in 1971. As we have already noted, one consequence was the establishment of refugee camps for 'stateless' Biharis; these 'Geneva Camps' numbered 66 in all and housed around 238,000 people.

Delhi

It is now almost a cliché that Partition transformed Delhi from a Mughal to a Punjabi city. The bitter experiences of the refugees encouraged them

[104] Tan and Kudaisya, *The Aftermath of Partition*, p. 168.
[105] Tan and Kudaisya, *The Aftermath of Partition*, p. 169.
[106] Tan and Kudaisya, *The Aftermath of Partition*, p. 168.
[107] *Civil and Military Gazette* (Lahore) 18 March 1950.
[108] Ghosh, *Partition and the South Asia Diaspora*, p. 17.

to support right-wing Hindu parties.[109] Delhi, unlike Calcutta and Dacca, as we have seen, suffered violence at the time of the transfer of power and as a result its demographic changes were hastened. Trouble began in September after the arrival of refugees from Pakistan who were determined on revenge and driving Muslims out of properties which they could then occupy. Gandhi in his prayer sessions at Birla House denounced the 'crooked and ungentlemanly' squeezing out of Muslims.[110] Despite these exhortations, two thirds of the city's Muslims were eventually to abandon India's capital. By 1951, their proportion of the city's population had declined from 40.5 per cent (1941) to 6.6 per cent. Conversely, the Hindu proportion increased from 53.2 per cent (1941) to 82.1 per cent.

Violence occurred not only in Old Delhi but also the elegant colonnaded shopping arcade of Connaught Circus. Muslims were driven to take sanctuary in refugee camps at Jama Masjid, Purana Qila and Humayan's Tomb. The latter camp was still bulging with over 30,000 refugees in December 1947.[111] Shahid Ahmad, the publisher and progressive writer, has provided a harrowing account of its desperate conditions in his autobiographical work *Dilhi ki Bipta*.[112] The cross-border migrations should not obscure the fact that large numbers of Muslims were displaced within the city itself. There was a movement overseen by the state from 'mixed localities' to 'Muslim zones'.[113] This was designed to provide security. The Muslims who moved found however that far from being a temporary measure, they became permanently housed in the new enclaves. They thus became refugees in their own city. In Zamindar's telling phrase, 'Muslim zones, rather than serving as a refuge for Muslims, became part of a contested and fearful urban geography, in which institutions of the state were complicit in unsettling Muslims.'[114]

Despite the departure of around 300,000 Muslims, Delhi's population grew by 1.1 million in the period 1941–1951, an increase of 106 per cent fuelled by Partition migrants.[115] These came predominantly from the Hindu and Sikh Khatri and Arora commercial castes of the West Punjab's towns and cities. Most were drawn by the economic opportunities afforded by India's new capital and many already had professional,

[109] See C. Jaffrelot, 'The Hindu Nationalist Movement in Delhi: From 'Locals' to Refugees and towards Peripheral Groups?', in V. Dupont, E. Tarlo and D. Vidal (eds), *Delhi: Urban Space and Human Destinies* (New Delhi: Manohar, 2000), pp. 181–203.

[110] Tan and Kudaisya, *The Aftermath of Partition*, p. 198.

[111] Report of A. S. Bhatnagar, Secretary to the Chief Commissioner Delhi, 4 December 1947. MB1/D276, Mountbatten Papers, University of Southampton.

[112] Shahid Ahmad, 'Dilhi ki Bipta', in M. Shirin (ed.), *Zulmat-e-Neem Roze* (Karachi: no pub., 1990), pp. 145–7.

[113] Zamindar, *The Long Partition*, pp. 28–32.   [114] Zamindar, *The Long Partition*, p. 33.

[115] Kaur, 'Narratives of Resettlement', pp. 34–5.

commercial and kinship ties in the city which had seen its Punjabi community grow from the late nineteenth century. Temporary refugee accommodations were located in north and central Delhi. A large refugee camp was established in the north of the city at Kingsway on the site of former British barracks. At one stage it housed 30,000 refugees. Large refugee housing projects were also constructed in the 1950s in the south of the city at such places as Lajpat Nagar. This area comprised of compact two-storey flats. Similar basic facilities were provided in other projects which housed refugees in localities whose names celebrated heroes of the freedom movement.[116] Important refugee commercial areas grew up in former Muslim areas such as Karol Bagh, with businesses proclaiming their owners' place of origin in West Punjab – a feature to be found throughout north Indian cities. Adjacent to Karol Bagh is one of the oldest refugee colonies, Rajinder Nagar which grew out of a campsite.[117] As in Calcutta, the city's expansion in the 1950s and 1960s owed much to rehousing the new arrivals and housing construction in east, west and south Delhi was undertaken by the state in order to meet these needs. A city of 170 square kilometres in 1941, Delhi grew to 280 square kilometres by 1956.

Karachi

The conventional wisdom is that Partition transformed the sleepy backwater of Karachi into a sprawling metropolis, but this overlooks the fact that the city had undergone considerable commercial development in the late colonial era. By the 1940s, for example, it had overtaken Bombay as the main port for exporting raw cotton. It was also fast developing as an air-transportation hub and its population had by this time increased to around 400,000, with migration from the Kathiarwar coast. Instead of native Sindhis, Gujarati-speaking Hindus dominated the city's financial and commercial life. Sindhi Lohanas were important as cotton brokers, while Parsis had major interests in shipping export companies. In all, Hindus owned just over 28,000 properties in Karachi.[118] Like Dacca, Karachi was a Hindu-majority city surrounded by a predominantly Muslim-populated hinterland. In 1941 Muslims formed 42 per cent of

---

[116] Lajpat Nagar was named after the Punjabi Hindu leader Lala Lajpat Rai. Similarly named refugee housing developments included Tilak Nagar and Patel Nagar. Housing conditions vary greatly in quality between East and West Patel Nagar. See Kaur, *Since 1947*, p. 111.

[117] Kaur, *Since 1947*, p. 129.

[118] Cited in K. R. Sipe, 'Karachi's Refugee Crisis: The Political, Economic and Social Consequences of Partition-Related Migration', unpublished PhD thesis, Duke University, 1976, p. 67.

the population while caste and scheduled-caste Hindus together comprised 50.9 per cent.[119]

Karachi did not experience the violence which had become endemic in many northern India cities during 1946–1947. Its wealthy Hindu population, nevertheless, moved out large amounts of capital to banks in Delhi and Bombay in the weeks leading up to Independence.[120] Muslim politicians were anxious to stem this flood and to ensure that the wealthy Hindu elite retained their role in the city's and province's economic life, but reports of violence in Punjab in the weeks after partition unnerved many; and by mid-September around 1,000 persons a day were departing by boat for Bombay and the Kathiawar. This rush to depart was seen by some as part of the wider conspiracy to 'strangle Pakistan at birth'.[121] It tended to be the Gujarati Hindus rather than their Sindhi brethren who jumped the gun with respect to migration. As in much of north India, it was the refugee presence that heightened tensions, resulting, as we have seen in chapter three, in the total exodus of Hindus which gathered pace in January 1948. Its short-term effect was to cripple much of the city's banking activity.

Between 1947 and 1953 Karachi's population increased from 400,000 to 1.3 million. The former Hindu-majority city become dominated by refugees who accounted for just under 60 per cent of the population in 1951 while the Hindu presence slumped to 0.5 per cent. The city's rapid growth severely strained its housing and infrastructure as the mismatch between housing availability and demand resembled the situation in Calcutta. In fact Karachi had two other similarities with the West Bengal capital: refugees continued to arrive in waves in the 1950s and as Pakistan's capital it became an attraction for up-country migrants who competed with the refugees for scarce resources.

A quarter of a million refugees flooded into Sindh from UP in mid-1950 during the period of communal disturbances. They came via the Khokrapar border railway station. Despite attempts to disperse them, this influx added a further 80,000 people to Karachi's overcrowded environs. By the end of May 1950, the authorities had withdrawn all refugee assistance at the border to attempt to stem the tide. There were even allegations that Sindh's inspector general of police had requested permission for his officers to open fire on the refugees should the need arise.[122] Nor was

---

[119] Sipe, 'Karachi's Refugee Crisis', p. 132.
[120] By early July, an estimated 200–300 million rupees had been shifted in this way. See Ansari, *Life after Partition*, p. 48.
[121] See *Dawn* (Karachi) 19 September and 5 November 1947.
[122] Ansari, *Life after Partition*, p. 130.

this the final wave of migration. As late as 1954, refugees were still enter-
ing Karachi from India.[123]

On arrival, where possible, refugees seized vacant property, although
this was not on the scale of the land-grabbing movement in Calcutta. As in
Calcutta, many were kept in 'improvised dwellings'. A census undertaken
in Karachi in 1955 revealed that an estimated 800,000 people were still
living on the city's pavements, or in underdeveloped housing colonies,[124]
creating 'eyesores' that alienated government spokesmen and local inhabitants alike who often described their occupants as 'idlers' and 'misfits'.[125]

Karachi's rehabilitation and resettlement reflected the experience of
other regions and cities. The wealthiest refugees acquired the property
abandoned by the Hindu elite in such localities as Clifton, Victoria Road
and Mcleod Road. Almost as favoured were those refugees accommodated in Co-operative Housing Schemes, such as the Central Pakistan
Government Employees' Co-operative Housing Society (PECHS). The
eastern part of the city became the favoured location for better-off refugees
and senior government.

Colonies and Co-operative Housing Societies were often very clearly
demarcated on ethnic and geographical lines. Memon colonies had their
street signs in Gujarati; Biharis had their own cooperative societies.
Wealth nevertheless cross-cut these ethnically and regionally defined
neighbourhoods. Middle-class refugees from central India lived from
the early 1950s in the Hyderabad Colony where the houses were concrete
and the streets paved. Poorer Hyderabadis resided in Usmania Mohajir
Colony which had begun life as a slum with no permanent dwellings. And
the wealthiest Hyderabadis lived a mile away in a locality called
Bahadurabad.[126]

Official schemes to house the refugees took many years to complete.
There were numerous complaints about the conditions which faced their
inhabitants in the distant Drigh Road and Lalukhet colonies. The former,
which housed around 50,000 by the mid-1950s, was vulnerable both to
flooding and sandstorms.[127] Lalukhet, by the mid-1950s, contained a
population of around 100,000 clustered into distinctive satellite settlements.[128] The whole of the Lalukhet area suffered from a lack of drainage,
water supplies, adequate sanitation and roads. Once proud locksmiths

---

[123] Ansari, *Life after Partition*, p. 122.   [124] Ansari, *Life after Partition*, p. 155.
[125] Ansari, *Life after Partition*, p. 155.   [126] Sipe, 'Karachi's Refugee Crisis', p. 241.
[127] See *Dawn* (Karachi) 19 February 1954; 15 March 1956.
[128] See the special report entitled 'This Is Lalukhet' by Asghar Ahmed Khan in *Dawn*
(Karachi) 22 January 1956.

from Aligarh, carpet-makers from Bareilly and utensil-makers from Moradabad struggled to earn their living as rickshaw pullers.[129]

Lahore

Hindu commercial classes dominated the economic life of Lahore just as much as they did that of Dacca and Karachi. Non-Muslims paid 70 per cent of the urban property tax, owned 67 per cent of the shops and 80 per cent of registered factories.[130] The city, however, had a two-thirds Muslim majority and was awarded to Pakistan. The British departure saw the final round of violence in the city and the exodus of its Hindu and Sikh inhabitants. A tiny Hindu population stayed on to play crucial roles in the banking system, but the demographic transformation was as dramatic as that in Dacca and Karachi.

The availability of large amounts of evacuee property meant that the resettlement of Muslim refugees did not present the problems which arose from the refugee influx in Calcutta or Karachi. There was also the added advantage that many of the migrants had pre-existing family or commercial links which eased their integration. This was most clearly the case with respect to members of the Kashmiri and Arain communities who migrated from neighbouring Amritsar and other East Punjab towns. The Pakistan government also invested heavily in industrial training to help refugees fill the economic niches left by the departing Hindus and Sikhs. Despite the city's border location, there was no flight of industry as in Amritsar; rather, Lahore emerged as a major centre of manufacturing.

While many refugees suffered individual hardship and trauma, there was no period of prolonged dislocation of the kind witnessed in some areas of north India. Most were sympathetically received and their common Punjabi culture – despite differences in dialect and cuisine – helped to accelerate the process of resettlement, though in such areas as marriage, locals were reluctant to enter into alliances with new arrivals. Oral testimonies highlight the fabled Punjabi spirit of enterprise. 'Since there was no woollen factory in Pakistan, at the time', Khawaja Zubair, a refugee from Amritsar to Lahore has recalled, 'My father went to Landa Bazaar and purchased a few woollen sweaters there. My mother unwove them to get the woollen thread. By using cauldrons at home we dyed the thread. And that's how the first carpet of Pakistan was manufactured.'[131] However, both the state and community organisations played a critical role in mitigating the pain of uprooting and were crucial in creating the

---

[129] Khan, 'This Is Lalukhet'.   [130] Tan and Kudaisya, *The Aftermath of Partition*, p. 176.
[131] Talbot, *Divided Cities*, p. 97.

Plate 11 Refugees with Lady Mountbatten at Lahore.

circumstances in which refugees could display initiative, by arranging loans, training and enabling the exchange of moveable and non-moveable assets.

Refugees were resettled in areas previously inhabited by non-Muslims which included such suburbs as Krishan Nagar and Sant Nagar, the inner-city areas of Shah Almi and the areas outside the walls such as Gowal Mandi and Nisbett Road. The latter area became home to the large number of Kashmiri refugees. In contrast to many other cities, there were few newly built refugee colonies or satellite towns. Indeed, many of Lahore's housing developments of the 1950s catered for locals or the incoming administrative elites rather than refugees. In this sense Lahore was much less a refugee city. Similarly, its spatial development owed more to the city's rapid growth and in-migration from elsewhere in Pakistan than the need to accommodate Partition arrivals. After 1947 Lahore was to become a magnet commercial and industrial development when the city's importance increased as the capital of West Punjab and of the West Pakistan province during the period of One Unit (1955–1971).

Conclusion

Clearly the conventional accounts of Partition-related migration and rehabilitation, such as *Millions on the Move*,[132] tended to universalise the Punjab experience which itself was highly distorted by official constructions. It is true that the patterns of migration in Bengal and Punjab were very different: Punjab's two-way chaotic flight was virtually complete by the end of December while East and West Bengal were to receive waves of migrants for several decades after 1947. But such broad generalisation overlooked the specific experience of different classes, castes, communities and genders. New research over the decades and oral testimonies of those affected reveals a highly differentiated process in which all the social inequalities of the South Asian formation played a critical role. In Punjab and East Bengal, for instance, there is considerable evidence of anticipatory Hindu migration before August 1947 which involved the moving of capital, exchange of property and sending women and children to areas 'safely' within a future Indian boundary. Inevitably it was the poorer or politically less connected communities that were taken by surprise by the unfolding drama of Partition. And this was also reflected in West Bengal where the dominance of *bhadralok* refugee narratives tells us little about the movement of non-elite groups such as Santhals to Tripura or the largely

---

[132] Government of India, *Millions on the Move* (Delhi: Ministry of Information and Broadcasting, 1948).

untold history of Muslim migrants from West Bengal, Assam, Tripura, Bihar and Uttar Pradesh to East Bengal.

Equally rehabilitation and resettlement were long and drawn-out processes. Although official histories homogenised resettlement narratives, with the relative 'success' of Indian and Pakistani Punjab being trumpeted as landmarks in nation-building, in reality pre-existing social capital was as important as government initiatives. In West and East Punjab, Karachi and West and East Bengal, community and religious organisations played a crucial role – an area that has so far received little attention from historians.[133] Indeed, ethnic and community initiatives were to transform regions, cities and localities into ethnic enclaves. The gradual transformation of the major cities of the Indian subcontinent into new migrant homes was to have a lasting impact on the social and political life of modern India and Pakistan. Perhaps more significantly, the Partition and the migration were to leave an enduring legacy of religious and ethnic nationalisms that would continue to pose a permanent challenge to the Partition settlement itself.

---

[133] For the roles of the Arya Samaj, Pingawala and the Chief Khalsa Diwan in refugee rehabilitation in Amritsar, for example, see Talbot, *Divided Cities*, pp. 168–72.

5   Partition legacies: ethnic and religious nationalism

Partition is often portrayed as a clinical act, the final solution to irreconcilable differences between the Congress and the Muslim League that could not be accommodated within one state.[1] Yet it bequeathed troublesome, if not enduring, legacies for the successor states. One such permanent legacy was the creation of an Indo-Pakistan rivalry centred on Jammu and Kashmir, the so-called 'unfinished business of Partition', which is discussed at length in the next chapter. In this chapter we focus on ethnic and religious nationalisms that have their roots in the 1947 divide and have fundamentally shaped the fortunes of the successor states of India, Pakistan and, later, Bangladesh.[2] We examine how the large movements of people occasioned by the Partition laid the bases of future ethnic conflicts within India and Pakistan, and do so by highlighting two interrelated processes: the new patterns of ethnic consolidation which followed refugee resettlement and the post-1947 projects of nation- and state-building that led to the creation of highly centralised states, not least in order to prevent further separation or secession.

The remainder of the chapter outlines how Partition increased ethnic consolidation among some of the displaced groups, while for others it involved the transfer of local and regional loyalties to extreme forms of official, ideological nationalism. These developments will be set against the efforts to construct highly centralised states and the drafting of new rules for managing ethnic and religious conflicts. Finally, the chapter assesses how the new states managed these movements and

---

[1] See S. R. Mehrotra, 'The Congress and the Partition of India', in C. H. Philips and M. D. Wainwright (eds), *The Partition of India* (London: George Allen and Unwin, 1970), pp. 188–221, p. 220.

[2] The distinction between ethnic and religious nationalism is, of course, difficult to sustain in such cases as the Sikhs in Punjab and, arguably, Muslims in Jammu and Kashmir. Religious nationalism here is distinguished from conventional claims on language, caste and region. For further discussions of ethnic and religious nationalism, see Antony D. Smith's *The Ethnic Revival in the Modern World* (Cambridge University Press, 1981) and *Chosen People: Sacred Sources of National Identity* (Oxford University Press, 2003).

the dialectic that has given rise to powerful modes of religious nationalism in both countries.

Partition, refugees and ethnic consolidation

As we saw in chapter four, Partition not only marked a division of colonial India on religious lines, but also furthered ethnic consolidation of some groups and communities. Uprooted and dislocated communities generally sought safety in numbers, or sometimes, as in the case of Punjabi Hindus and Sikhs and Bengali Hindus and Muslims, in their ancestral homes from which they had migrated a long time before. In this way the demographic characters of localities, cities and, indeed, sometimes whole provinces, were dramatically transformed. In East Punjab, for instance, a largely mixed province of Hindus, Muslims and Sikhs before 1947, the central districts and the former Sikh princely states received significant numbers of Sikh refugees. The lack of a majority which had undermined Sikh political claims to a separate statehood was now reversed. The new demographic concentration of the community laid the basis of the subsequent campaign for a Sikh-dominated *Punjabi Suba* (a Punjabi-speaking state).[3]

As well as creating majorities where they did not previously exist, the resettlement of a large number of refugees laid the basis of permanent, long-term conflicts between the new arrivals and the local inhabitants, whether they were urbanites or 'sons of the soil'. Probably the most striking example of this was to be the clash between the Urdu-speaking UP refugees (*mohajirs*) and the native Sindhis that we will discuss in more detail in this chapter.[4] The *mohajirs*, who viewed themselves as the elite vanguard of the Pakistan movement would eventually, as a result of their fraught relations with Sindhis, follow their own path to ethnic separatism. Much lesser, but no less significant conflict was to arise in the south-western districts of Pakistan between native Saraiki-speakers and Punjabi refugees. It continues to simmer to the present day. But perhaps the most notable effects of these post-Partition settlements were to occur in the sparsely populated north-eastern states of India where the influx of new settlers, many well educated and of urban background, was to lay the basis of new ethnic domination of the pastoral native communities, a development that would have profound long-term implications for the management of ethnic relations in Assam, Manipur and Tripura, and embroil the

---

[3] See Gurharpal Singh, *Ethnic Conflict in India: A Case-Study of Punjab* (Basingstoke: Palgrave, 2000), chapter 5.
[4] See Ansari, *Life after Partition*.

Indian security forces in decades-long security operations. But these conflicts, however, were not limited to rural spaces. Their most dramatic manifestation would occur in urban localities that bore the initial brunt of demographic change in response to the shock waves unleashed by 1947. It was the urban centres that gave shelter to both the ideological religious nationalists and the new ethnic entrepreneurs who were to subsequently reap such devastation on the newly independent states.

Yet initially, in both India and Pakistan, the militant urban refugee became the standard bearer of the nation, playing a crucial role in the ideological legitimation of the new states.[5] Refugees' personal hardships and experiences of violence nurtured 'right-wing' visions of the nation. The Jan Sangh in India, for instance, was to rely heavily on the urban Punjabi Hindu refugees for its support base. Its campaign against special constitutional status accorded to Jammu and Kashmir in the early 1950s was very much founded in the urban Hindu refugee constituency, especially in Jammu that had received large number of Hindu settlers from across the border. Lal Krishna Advani, a Sindhi who remained in Pakistan until 1955, was later to become the Bharatiya Janata Party's (BJP) leader, a deputy prime minister and the prime mover of the *Hindutva* movement in the 1980s. The community of prosperous Punjabi urban Hindus who migrated from West Punjab and settled in Delhi, moreover, were to establish a powerful hold on the Indian political establishment, sublimating its own ethnic and religious interests in the support for a strong secular state that would deal firmly with minority communalisms.

In Pakistan, the early debate about the position of Islam in public life was greatly influenced by the arrival from India of Maulana Nadvi from the Nadwat-ul-Ulama of Lucknow and Maulana Maududi, a journalist and theologian who had founded the Islamist Jamaat-i-Islami (JI) party in 1941. JI had opposed the Muslim League's demand for Pakistan, because of the secularist orientation of the League leadership and the modernist reconciliation of the nation-state concept with Islam. As soon as it shifted its headquarters from East Punjab to Zaildar Park in Lahore, it worked for the Islamisation of the state. Despite their sectarian differences, Nadvi secured JI's support for a conference of the *ulama*, in January 1951 under his leadership in Karachi. It was Maududi however who dominated the

---

[5] The role of the urban refugee with a highly charged communal outlook in fashioning the new nation has been little understood. In India the Hindu urban press, notably in Punjab, became the champion of aggressive anti-Muslim, as well as anti-Sikh sentiment. A parallel development also took place in Karachi where the *mohajirs* developed their own press and publishing outlets to publicise their ideological stake in Pakistan. See Robin Jeffrey, *India's Newspaper Revolution: Capitalism, Politics and the Indian-language Press, 1977–97* (London: C. Hurst, 2000); Ansari, *Life after Partition*, chapter 5.

proceedings and produced twenty-two principles for the establishment of an Islamic state. This was a riposte to Liaquat Ali Khan's attempt to meet the religious leaders' expectations by means of the Objectives Resolution. Liaquat was forced to delay the whole constitution-making process to avoid incorporating the twenty-two principles into the constitution. The issue of the role of Islam in the constitution was overtaken firstly by Liaquat's assassination at Rawalpindi on 16 October 1951 and secondly by the *ulama*'s agitation against the heterodox Ahmadi community.[6] Nevertheless, the stage had been set for continuous debate about the vision for Pakistan. Maududi, until his death in 1979, was to play an important role in undermining the secular understanding of the state espoused by Jinnah and Liaquat.[7]

Nation- and state-building after 1947: Partition as the 'end of history'

It is generally accepted that the Partition was the seminal event of modern South Asian history: independent India and Pakistan began life as nation-building failures. As Brass notes, for most Hindus it was a

Historical scar that not only divided the subcontinent but defied the truth they had fought for as their rightful heritage: the unity of India. Muslims, for their part, fought for another truth invented out of their past in India, namely, that they constituted a separate civilisation distinct from that of the Hindus, that they had always been separate, and would have to remain so in the future.[8]

The tragedy that ensued left a permanent imprint on the national consciousness of both states, the conjoined twins who appeared to be cursed at birth. Even sixty years after the event, it continues to provide a haunting reminder of what divides the two neighbours. In the case of India, as Khilnani has aptly noted, 'Partition is the unspeakable sadness at the heart of the idea of India: a *memento mori* that what made India possible also profoundly diminished the integral value of the idea.'[9] For Pakistan, Partition has become shorthand for Renan's definition of a nation: as a 'daily plebiscite' that is conducted as an everyday ritual at the Wagha border and, above all, in 'Azad Kashmir'.[10]

---

[6] For details see, Talbot, *Pakistan*, p. 141.
[7] S. V. R. Nasr, *Maududi and the Making of Islamic Revivalism* (Oxford University Press, 1996).
[8] Brass, *The Production of Hindu-Muslim Violence*, p. 363.
[9] Sunil Khilnani, *The Idea of India* (New Delhi: Penguin, 1997),pp. 201–2
[10] For the significance of the Wagha ceremony see Gurharpal Singh, 'Beyond Punjabi Romanticism', *Seminar* 513 (November 2006), pp. 17–21.

The starting point for any meaningful understanding of the long-term legacies of Partition is to recognise its construction by Indian and Pakistani elites as the 'end of history'.[11] In this respect Partition was far from just a triumph of hegemonic projects pursued by the Congress and the Muslim League: it marked the beginning of the competing visions of the future that severed, once and for all, the organic connection between community, ethnicity, locality and the past in preference to historicised constructions of these categories. In India this process was eventually to become enshrined in the futurism of the constitution with its determinative principles of socialism, democracy, planning and secularism. In Pakistan, on the other hand, Islamic modernism became the template on which the new nation-state was to be inscribed. Yet for both states the Partition marked a closure, a new beginning in which there would be *no* more partitions.[12]

This objective was pursued by making Partition the national foundational myth: as the permanent reminder of the destructive power of religious nationalism in a multi-ethnic and multi-religious society (India); and as the ultimate principle of self-determination for a self-conscious religious community (Muslims) which was destined to rule (Pakistan). Clearly there could be no competing foundational myths for they would contest, as we shall see below, the political settlement and provide alternative, if not unsettling national narratives. It is for these reasons that the idea of Partition in post-1947 India and Pakistan has acquired an almost incontestable, meta-narrative status. For Indian elites it became synonymous with a 'bad idea' erroneously introduced by the British into a social formation that neither conformed to the hard boundaries required by modern nationalism, nor could sustain such a proposition because of its multiple religious and ethnic identities.[13] For Pakistani elites, on the other hand, while the logic of two-nation theory did not foreclose further partitions or the Balkanisation of India, the culmination of Pakistan was the fulfilment of a historical truth that would brook no challenge, especially from its constituent parts.

Partition and India: nationalism and statecraft

In India one direct consequence of the Partition was to reinforce the pressure for a highly centralised polity. The original intention of the

---

[11] The reference, of course, is to Francis Fukuyama's *The End of History and the Last Man* (Harmondsworth: Penguin, 1992).

[12] See Uday Mehta, 'The Making of the Indian Constitution and Comparative Experience', paper presented to a workshop on 'The Indian Constitution after Fifty Years', School of Oriental and African Studies, 24 November 2000 (unpublished).

[13] See Bhikhu Parekh, 'Ethnocentricity of the Nationalist Discourse', *Nations and Nationalism* 1, 1 (1995), pp. 25–52.

framers of the Indian constitution, as stipulated in the Constituent Assembly Objective Resolution of 1946, was to create a 'loose federation in which the states would retain the status of autonomous units'. This objective soon became meaningless as the Congress and the Muslim League jockeyed for a quick transfer of power. Nineteen forty-seven and its bloody aftermath provided the ideal opportunity to create a centralised state for Nehru and a section of Congress leadership who had long advocated a strong centre with 'a great deal of unitary control'.[14] In the unique conditions following Independence this design encountered little resistance. In fact within four days of the announcement of the 3 June Plan, the Constituent Assembly resolved to construct a constitution that would be 'federal with a strong centre'.[15]

A key element of this strong centre was the need to build an 'inde-structible union' that would be 'both unitary as well as federal according to the requirements of time and circumstances'.[16] Accordingly for the Constituent Assembly the states did not have an entity prior to the union. Rather, the union was 'one integral whole, its people a single people living under a single imperium derived from a single source ... The Drafting Committee thought that it was better to make it clear at the outset rather than leave it to speculation or disputes.'[17] These aims were explicitly enshrined in the legislative, financial and executive para-mountcy of the centre; and when to these provisions was added the residual and emergency powers invested in the centre – and the system of central planning in 1950 – the autonomy of the states was severely circumscribed.[18]

Concern with national unity was also at the root of the Constituent Assembly's reluctance to entertain the call for separate electorates by minorities – Muslims, Sikhs and Christians. For most Congressmen, Pakistan was the outcome of the pernicious politicisation of religion by colonial rule, and, as such, demands based on religion were considered non-negotiable. The only significant concession to religious demands was the Muslim Personal Law, though with a strong qualification that it would be eventually superseded by a unified civil code that would embrace *all* religious communities.

---

[14] Granville Austin, *The Indian Constitution: Cornerstone of a Nation* (Oxford: Clarendon Press, 1966), p. 189.

[15] Austin, *The Indian Constitution*, p. 193.   [16] Austin, *The Indian Constitution*, p. 188.

[17] Government of India, Commission on Centre–State Relations, *Report. Part 1*. (New Delhi: Government of India), p. 9.

[18] Gurharpal Singh, 'Re-examining Centre–State Relations in India since 1947', inaugural lecture, 15 May 2000, University of Hull (unpublished), pp. 1–34.

The framework established by the Constituent Assembly's deliberations consolidated a nationalist discourse in which the territory of India was also naturalised. 'What the partition succeeded in doing', Gupta has concluded, 'was searing the lineaments of India's territorial boundaries deep into the national conscious … [through] the popular sacralisation of territory.'[19] Whereas the popular manifestation of this was often the figure of *Bharat Mata* ('Mother India') as a geographical entity, its political articulation was especially evident in the resolute defence of India's border, even when, as in the case of the boundary with China, Nehru and Indian nationalists 'assumed, without verification, that the large imaginary north-eastern and north-western borders … (mainly defined by the McMahon Line) as determined by the colonial power would hold good in perpetuity'.[20] Borders became coterminous with the body politic, the new metaphor for the nation that had suffered 'vivisection', 'division' and 'amputation'.

Borders, and threats to them from secessionists 'within' and 'without', also became part of the new nationalist discourse marked by binary opposites: national 'unity' and 'integrity', for instance, was regularly contrasted with 'secessionist' and 'fissiparous' tendencies that constantly held out the spectre of further partitions, if not 'Balkanisation'. Similarly, 'secularism', the keystone of the new Indian constitution, had its counterpoint in 'communalism', the political articulation of religious-based interests. Communalism in fact became the ultimate derogatory appellation for undermining and disarticulating movements and demands that appeared to be ostensibly defined by religion, even though they often reflected genuine grievances. Communalists were also frequently identified in popular discourses as 'obscurantist', 'fundamentalists', and 'separatists' – the complete antithesis of the 'secular' ideal that defined the 'national mainstream'.[21] The only way in which communalism could be contained, managed and rendered harmless, it was regularly argued, was by secularism backed by a strong centralised state.[22]

Despite the crystallisation of this nationalist discourse after 1947, which developed a distinctly stigmatised outlook towards religious minorities

---

[19] Dipanker Gupta, *The Context of Ethnicity: Sikh Identity in a Comparative Perspective* (Delhi: Oxford University Press, 1997), p. 23.

[20] T. V. Sathyamurthy, 'The State of Debate on Indian Nationalism', 25th Millennium Anniversary Conference Paper, October 1996 (unpublished), p. 23.

[21] See S. Patel, 'On the Discourse of Communalism', in T. V. Sathyamurthy (ed.), *Nation, Religion, Caste, Gender and Culture in Contemporary India*, vol. 3 (Delhi: Oxford University Press, 1996), pp. 145–79.

[22] See Paul R. Brass, 'India: Democratic Progress and Problems', in Selig S. Harrison, Paul H. Kreisberg and Dennis Kux (eds), *India and Pakistan: The First Fifty Years* (Cambridge University Press, 1999), pp. 23–44.

such as Muslims and Sikhs and their claims for territorial autonomy in Jammu and Kashmir and Punjab, it is generally agreed that Nehru was able to manage the projects of nation- and state-building during India's 'most dangerous decade' with considerable finesse in deflecting the underlying tensions created by Partition. This achievement is normally accredited to his leadership of the 'Congress System', the construction of a dominant one-party system that accommodated regionalism, and Nehru's personal outlook that tempered the pursuit of national unity with a de facto recognition of India as a multinational society.[23] Perhaps the greatest achievement during these years was the linguistic reorganisation of Indian provinces which was achieved against the spectre of Balkanisation and made India unique among post-colonial states in being able to reorganise its internal boundaries successfully. It was in these years that Nehru evolved four rules of managing religious and ethnic conflicts that, though they were not formalised, were largely adhered to. First, no secessionist movements were to be tolerated; where necessary they would be suppressed by force. Second, given the commitment to secularism, 'no demand for political recognition of religious groups would be considered'. Third, 'no capricious concessions would be made to the political demands of any linguistic, regional or other culturally defined group'. Finally, 'no political concessions to cultural groups in conflict would be made unless they had demonstrable support from both sides'.[24]

However, the consistent application of these guidelines, as we shall see below, ran into severe difficulties in the border states in the north-west and the north-east, where Congress organisations were weak. Here a distinction was established between the 'periphery' and the 'mainstream'. In the former, more direct forms of political management were justified because of the perceived threat to national integrity. In Jammu and Kashmir, Punjab and the north-eastern states, a distinctive pattern began to emerge where political accommodation soon gave way to coercion, electoral manipulation and direct administration from New Delhi through President's Rule. Even where the Congress had considerable strength, the blatant subversion of legal and administrative structures was overlooked because of the requirement to manage what were generally described as 'secessionist', 'regionalist' and 'communal' forces.[25]

The distinction between the 'periphery' and the 'mainstream' was often justified because the former regions were hotbeds of active secessionist

[23]   Brass, 'India', p. 38.
[24]   Paul R. Brass, *Ethnicity and Nationalism: Theory and Comparison* (New Delhi: Sage, 1991), p. 168.
[25]   See Singh, *Ethnic Conflict*, chapter 12.

movements and were the sites where the logic of partition unravelled. In Jammu and Kashmir, Punjab and the north-eastern states, the preservation of national unity came across hardened ethno-religious and regional identities that had historically supported the 'third way' (provincial or princely self-determination in opposition to accession to Indian or Pakistani dominions) before 1947. Some of these regions were coerced into the Indian Union or became the battlegrounds of ethnic cleansing associated with Partition. Here Indian nation- and state-building projects frequently had to engage in 'nation-breaking' of regional identities that proved – and continue to prove – difficult. Some writers have suggested that the distinction between the 'periphery' and the 'mainstream' was indicative of a broader division within Indian nationalism characterised by an ethnic democracy with a Hindu core.[26] Whatever the merits of this argument, it is difficult to overlook the view that political construction of India's external boundaries were intimately interlinked and defined by the Partition.[27]

Jammu and Kashmir

This relationship becomes most apparent when we examine the post-1947 history of Jammu and Kashmir. The background to the Jammu and Kashmir dispute, the oldest unresolved conflict before the United Nations, is examined in chapter two, with its importance to the rivalry between India and Pakistan the subject of chapter six. Here we focus on the *internal* developments within the state between 1947 and the present to illustrate how the management of the borderlands have influenced the nationalist debate within India.

The decision of the Hindu ruler of a Muslim-majority kingdom to accede to India in October 1947 resulted in hostilities between India and Pakistan, United Nations' intervention, and a de facto division of the province in January 1949 along the ceasefire line. Jammu and Kashmir's accession to India was secured by concessions to Kashmiri nationalism, most notably Article 370 of the Indian constitution that provided a substantial measure of autonomy, but at the time of United Nations' intervention in the dispute this article was projected as a transitional measure to the exercise of self-determination by Kashmiris. Nehru

---

[26] Singh, *Ethnic Conflict*, chapter 3.
[27] Singh, *Ethnic Conflict*, chapter 12. See also Gurharpal Singh, 'The Partition of India in a Comparative Perspective: A Long-Term View', in Ian Talbot and Gurharpal Singh (eds), *Region and Partition: Bengal, Punjab and the Partition of the Subcontinent* (Karachi: Oxford University Press, 1999), pp. 95–115.

personally gave an open pledge to ensure that the there would be 'no forced unions', and that if the people of Jammu and Kashmir decided 'to part company with us, they can go their way and we shall go ours'.[28] He also accepted the Security Council resolution of April 1948 that the dispute should be 'decided through democratic method of free and impartial plebiscite'.[29] However, this commitment soon waned as Congress first promoted the Kashmiri nationalist National Conference led by Sheikh Abdullah and then, in a *volte face* as result of Hindu nationalist pressure in 1952–1953, Nehru started the piecemeal integration of Jammu and Kashmir into the Indian Union. Abdullah, the 'Lion of Kashmir', was interned for almost two decades while a compliant assembly, established by extensive vote-rigging, voted for the merger with the Indian Union in 1956. Thereafter India's response to the renewed Security Council resolution (March 1957) – for a 'free and impartial plebiscite conducted under the auspices of the United Nations' – was to cloak its integrationist intent under the pretext of the Cold War threat emanating from the US policy of encirclement which included a military alliance with Pakistan.

Three wars (Indo-China [1962], and Indo-Pakistan [1965 and 1971]) and the emergence of India as an atomic power (1974) convinced Abdullah of the limits of the demand for Kashmiri sovereignty. Towards the end of his life he signed an accord with Mrs Gandhi (1975) which recognised that Kashmir was a 'constituent unit of the union of India' in return for the formal survival of Article 370, though its actual provisions were extensively diluted in the application of central powers to the state. The accord enabled Abdullah to nurture a political dynasty, and upon his death (1982), his son Farooq took over. Farooq's tenure was marred by the need to straddle regional nationalism and the limits of autonomy imposed by New Delhi; his efforts to establish an all-India oppositional front for more autonomy resulted, first, in his dismissal, and, then, his return to power in alliance with Congress in the rigged assembly elections of June 1987. It was these elections, and the denial of the growing support of the Muslim United Front, that triggered the uprising in the Kashmir valley from 1987 onwards. Thereafter the separatist groups (Jammu and Kashmir Liberation Front and Hizbul Mujahideen) transformed decades of ethnic oppression into a generalised uprising against the Indian state. Between 1990 and 1995, 25,000 people were killed in Kashmir, almost

---

[28] J. B. Dasgupta, *Jammu and Kashmir* (The Hague: Martinus Nijhoff, 1968), p. 113.
[29] For full text of the resolution see, http://daccessdds.un.org/doc/RESOLUTION/GEN/NR0/047/72/IMG/NR004772.pdf?OpenElement.

two thirds by Indian armed forces; Kashmiris put the figure at 50,000.[30] In addition, 150,000 Kashmiri Hindus fled the valley to settle in the Hindu-majority region of Jammu. In 1991 Amnesty International estimated that 15,000 people were being detained in the state without trial.[31]

The Indian government's response to the Kashmir crisis has been to use violent control which is justified according to four principles: that the insurgency is externally supported and directed by Pakistan; that it is rooted in Islamic fundamentalism which poses a serious threat to Indian state secularism; that the separatist movements have no legitimate claim to independence; and that the insurgency is a threat to India's overall security, territorial integrity and nationhood.[32] In furtherance of these objectives the Indian Army, para-militaries and lumpen counterinsurgents were unleashed against Kashmiri separatists to contain the violence and re-establish control. This strategy was partially successful and paved the way for fresh elections in September 1996, which produced a dismal turnout of less than 30 per cent, and led to the re-election of Farooq.[33] But this 'restoration' was soon undermined by the conflict between India and Pakistan over Kargil (1999) and the mobilisation by both countries in 2002 following the terrorist attack on the Indian parliament that brought the two countries to the brink of a nuclear war.[34] In the fallout and the emerging peace process brokered by the US,[35] new assembly elections in 2002 marked a firm rejection of the dynastic National Conference of Farooq and brought to power a Congress–PDP (People's Democratic Party, a progressive regional party) coalition which has begun a dialogue both with New Delhi and the local militant groups. The outcomes of this process will be determined by the broader peace process with Pakistan, but India's determination not to alter the boundary or 'abandon the people on the other side of Jammu and Kashmir' (that is Azad, Pakistani, Kashmir) in preference for a 'people-centric approach'[36] is

---

[30] K. Balagopal, 'Kashmir: Self-determination, Communal and Democratic Rights', *Economic and Political Weekly* (2 November 1997), pp. 2916–21.

[31] See Amnesty International, *India: Torture, Rape, and Death in Custody* (London: Amnesty International, 1992).

[32] J. N. Dixit, 'Kashmir: The Contemporary Geo-political Implications for India and Religional Stability', paper presented at the School of Oriental and African Studies, London, 8 April 1994 (unpublished), pp. 6–7.

[33] *India Today*, 31 October 1996.

[34] Gurharpal Singh, 'On the Nuclear Precipice: India, Pakistan and the Kashmir Crisis', *OpenDemocracy* (6 August 2002), www.opendemocracy.net/conflict-india_pakistan/article_194.jsp.

[35] Gurharpal Singh, 'The Indo-Pakistan Summit: Hope for Kashmir?', *OpenDemocracy* (16 February 2004), www.opendemocracy.net/conflict-india_pakistan/article_1738.jsp.

[36] Comments of Shyam Saran, prime minister's special envoy on Kashmir, *The Tribune* (Chandigarh) 23 November 2006.

unlikely to provide a new legitimacy for governance in the province or undermine the claims for Kashmir sovereignty and accession to Pakistan.

Punjab and the Sikhs

Although Punjab, unlike Jammu and Kashmir, has never been a disputed territory, the demands of the Sikhs have posed different challenges to dominant beliefs about Indian nationhood and state borders. As we have seen in earlier chapters, the increasing likelihood of Pakistan encouraged Sikh demands for their own state. The call for the division of Punjab was officially made by the SAD in the wake of the Rawalpindi Massacres. The Sikh political leadership's decision to join the Indian Union was qualified by the demand for special guarantees to protect the community's future. After Partition these guarantees failed to be realised with the result that the SAD launched a campaign for a Punjabi-speaking province. Opposition to this campaign was marshalled by Nehru and the Punjab Congress which mobilised the Punjabi Hindu population to declare Hindi as their mother tongue, and thereby undermine the case for a Punjabi province. The 1950s and 1960s saw sustained agitations by the SAD for a Punjabi-speaking state that was eventually conceded (1966) in the backdrop to the Indo-Pakistan war (1965). Linguistic reorganisation however was hemmed in by so many qualifications that it soon led to a new autonomy movement by the SAD around the 1973 Anandpur Sahib Resolution (ASR) which called for the Centre's powers to be limited to currency, communications, defence and external affairs. This agitation eventually climaxed in Operation Blue Star (1984) in which the Indian army stormed the Golden Temple, the Sikhs' holiest shrine.[37]

Coercive measures had been used in the Punjab in the 1950s and 1960s, but what distinguished the 1980s and the early 1990s was the extent to which central government was prepared to use force to crush Sikh separatism, in particular the post-1984 campaign for Khalistan (a Sikh state). By conservative estimates 25,000 people were killed as a result of separatist violence and counterinsurgency operations by the security forces between 1981 and 1993.[38] The number of involuntary disappearances and illegal detainees were estimated to vary between 20,000 and 45,000.[39] At the height of the insurgency in the early 1990s, almost a quarter of

---

[37] Robin Jeffrey, *What's Happening to India? Punjab, Ethnic Conflict, Mrs. Gandhi's Death and the Test for Federalism* (Basingstoke: Macmillan, 1986).

[38] See Singh, *Ethnic Conflict in India*, chapter 10.

[39] Shinder Singh Thandi, 'Counterinsurgency and Political Violence in Punjab', in Gurharpal Singh and Ian Talbot (eds), *Punjabi Identity: Continuity and Change* (New Delhi: Manohar, 1996), p. 165.

a million military and para-military forces were engaged in counterinsurgency operations against Sikh separatists. Nevertheless, these groups were not without significant support. In the 1989 Lok Sabha elections (national parliamentary elections), their representatives won 10 of the 13 parliamentary seats from Punjab and gained a majority of the popular support; and in June 1991, if the newly elected national Congress government had not postponed the poll, the militants would certainly have won the assembly elections scheduled at the time.[40] In the event, Congress aborted these polls and held Khaki elections in February 1992 which were boycotted by the militants and moderate SAD, resulting in a Congress landslide (with a turnout of 24 per cent) that was used as pretext to intensify the campaign against separatism. By the end of 1993, most leading militants and their organisations had been eliminated, the moderates had been muzzled, and Punjab was hailed as a 'model' of combating separatism.[41]

The end of Sikh militancy highlighted the limits of Sikh ethno-religious nationalism and the resolute determination of the Indian state to defeat it. 'Normalcy' returned to the province with the election of a SAD government (1997) and the return of Congress to power in the state in 2002 – the first time since 1980 – but the 'strange death' of militant Sikh ethno-religious nationalism has belied the continued persistence of demands rooted in the ASR. Efforts by both the SAD and Congress leadership to manage the 'Sikh question' by symbolism and economic development have seriously failed to address the cultural and religious demands of Sikhs, thus retaining a potential for 're-imaging Punjab' beyond the borders defined by the partition.[42]

The north-east

In the north-eastern states, Indian nation- and state-building has always been bitterly contested since Partition. After sixty years of independence the region is still tormented by separatist insurrection, guerrilla warfare and terrorism with some of the movements campaigning for independence from before 1947. The original inhabitants of the region, nearly a half of whom are from aboriginal tribes, are uncertain of their place, whether within India or outside it. In a visit to the area in 1996, the then Prime

---

[40] Singh, *Ethnic Conflict in India*, chapters 8 and 9.
[41] Singh, *Ethnic Conflict in India*, chapter 10.
[42] See special issues of *Seminar* (November 2006) 567 on 'Re-imagining Punjab' and *Sikh Formations: Religion, Culture, Theory* 2:1 (June 2006), on 'Memory and Trauma in Recent Sikh and Punjabi Experience'.

Minister, H. D. Deve Gowda, acknowledged that people in the north-east feel that New Delhi treats them like a stepmother.

In August 1947 Nehru's response to self-determination movements in the region was blunt: 'We can give you complete autonomy but never independence. No state, big or small in India will be allowed to remain independent. We will use all our influence and power to suppress such tendencies.'[43] Thereafter the strategic importance of this area led to state-building and 'nation-destroying' as the inaccessible regions were brought under New Delhi's rule. When economic exploitation of the region's vast natural resources resulted in indigenous opposition to migration from the Indian heartland, and Partition refugees from East Pakistan, or, still, refugees following the creation of Bangladesh, a variety of administrative and constitutional provisions were adopted to placate tribal sentiment – the creation of tribal zones, of autonomous districts, union territories and, eventually, new states. According to one commentator, state-building in the face of separatist pressure has followed three strategies: 'to fight the insurgency with military force for some time; then, when the rebels seem to be tiring, offer negotiations; and finally, when the rebels are convinced that no matter what the casualties are on either side, they are not going to be able to secede, win them over with constitutional sops, invariably resulting in power being given to them in the resulting elections'.[44] Quite frequently these 'sops' have been followed by renewed struggles, violence and endemic terrorism. Since the 1950s the history of Assam, Mizoram, Nagaland, Tripura and Manipur is littered with accords signed by New Delhi with separatists. In Assam, as in Punjab, much of the resentment that fuelled the separatist movement was the failure of New Delhi to deliver on the regional accord agreed in August 1985. This failure revived the fortunes of the United Liberation Front of Assam, resulting in the repeated deployment of the army to crush the movement.

Unlike Jammu and Kashmir or Punjab, coercion tempered with minimal consent has been the main strategy by which India has maintained its hold on the north-eastern states. In this sparsely populated region what is surprising is the determination of separatists to sustain opposition to the Indian state for so long. Contemporary developments suggest that these states have been far from pacified, or politically integrated into the Indian Union, and the emergences of a first generation of educated youth among these communities combined with the growing realisation by them of

---

[43] Neville Maxwell, *India, Nagas and the North-East* (London: Minority Rights Group, 1980), p. 4.

[44] S. Gupta, *India Redefines Its Role* (Oxford: Oxford University Press and IISS, 1995), p. 25.

'internal colonialism' (Assam produces 70 per cent of India's oil) have further strengthened the resources for separatism.

Partition and Pakistan: nationalism and statecraft

Pakistan's creation against heavy odds marked the successful culmination of the two-nation theory, but it also became the nation's chosen trauma,[45] the epic struggle that has served ever since as an ideological resource for all regimes. However, the emergence of the military–bureaucratic combine that has dominated the Pakistan polity since the mid-1950s has laid bare the fundamental contradiction at the heart of the idea of Pakistan: its negative nationalism and, until 1971, unpromising state boundaries that arose from its initial vision as a loose, subcontinental federation. Ironically, transforming the Pakistan movement into a nation and a state was to result in the neat reversal of the Lahore Resolution (1940): the creation of an authoritarian centralised state that shared many of the characteristics of other South Asian states.[46] At the same time this reversal was accompanied by a determination that there would be no secessions from Pakistan of recalcitrant nationalities, and an external politics of 'wrongsizing' in which Kashmir became the permanent *casus belli*.[47]

Conventional wisdom about the emergence of the peculiar nature of Pakistan's polity is that it is the product of the manifold crises that afflicted the new nation at birth – the massive dislocation caused by the large influx of refugees and the exodus of Hindu and Sikhs, the monumental task of building a state where one existed only in provincial form, the external threat from India heightened by the Jammu and Kashmir conflict, and the eventual securitisation as domestic and foreign policy became inextricably linked with Pakistan's entry into the US-led Middle Eastern alliance system during the Cold War.[48] While these events certainly hastened the emergence of the military–bureaucratic combine, its roots can also be traced to the competing visions of the idea of Pakistan itself, and how the set of circumstances identified above led to the deliberate crafting of a centralised polity that was able to ward off a challenge from provincial political elites, especially in Bengal, and laid the foundations for the state's

---

[45] On the importance of chosen traumas in nation-building see Catrina Kinnvall, 'Nationalism, Religion and the Search for Chosen Traumas: Comparing Sikh and Hindu Identity Construction', *Ethnicities* 2:1 (March 2002), pp. 79–106.

[46] See Ayasha Jalal, *Democracy and Authoritarianism in South Asia* (Cambridge University Press, 1995).

[47] Singh, 'Partition of India'.

[48] Khalid bin Sayeed, *Pakistan: The Formative Phase* (Karachi: Pakistan Publishing House, 1968).

domination of society.[49] By the early 1950s the constitution-making process had reached a serious impasse, and as power passed incrementally from the politicians to the bureaucracy and the military, a mode of 'institutional path dependency' emerged that stymied any genuine efforts at building national and provincial administrations that would be account-able and democratic.[50] The high-water mark of these developments was the summary dismissal of the Constituent Assembly in October 1954 by the Governor-General Ghulam Mohammad and the creation of the One Unit scheme in 1955 which established a unified West Pakistan province by dissolving the historic provinces 'in order to preempt any possibility of a Bengali controlled centre'.[51] Thereafter the mould was set for an author-itarian military–bureaucratic polity in which nation-building was to be imposed rather than evolve and where Islam would function as a surrogate for political legitimacy. In sum, Pakistan was predestined for a collision course between 'state consolidation and construction' and 'the social dynamics underlying [its] political processes'.[52]

Punjab

One major reason why the military–bureaucratic combine was able to succeed was the emergence of Punjab as the core of the new state. Before 1947 Punjabi political leadership had been quintessentially pro-vincialist arguing against a unitary post-colonial India. However, after 1947, as the new state was increasingly fashioned in the image of 'Punjabistan',[53] this leadership comprising large landowners and *biraderi* (kinship network) heads willingly acceded to the centrist design of the military and the bureaucracy in return for Punjabi hegemony. Such a turnabout was accomplished not only because of the demographic, mili-tary and strategic importance that Punjab now occupied and the establish-ment leanings of the traditional landowning elites; it was also the direct consequence of the division of the province itself which set in motion a

---

[49] Yunas Samad, *A Nation in Turmoil: Nationalism and Ethnicity in Pakistan, 1937–1958* (New Delhi: Sage, 1995).

[50] For new insights into how 'path dependency' eventually institutionalised the military's presence in Pakistan politics, see Mazhar Aziz, 'The Parallel State: Understanding Military Control in Pakistan', unpublished Ph.D. dissertation, University of Nottingham, 2006.

[51] Jalal, *The State of Martial Rule*, p. 198.

[52] Jalal, *The State of Martial Rule*, p. 1.

[53] Yunus Samad, 'Pakistan or Punjabistan: Crisis of National Identity', in Gurharpal Singh and Ian Talbot (eds), *Punjabi Identity: Continuity and Change* (New Delhi: Manohar, 1996), pp. 61–87.

certain dynamic by which its fortunes became intimately tied to the ideological survival of the state.

To appreciate this it is necessary to recognise that the division of Punjab itself was accompanied by levels and intensity of violence that forever coloured the imagination of most refugees from India, almost 73 per cent of whom arrived across the Wagha border.[54] This violence, which we have examined in chapter three, moreover, was especially virulent in some Muslim-majority districts (e.g. Gurdaspur, Ferozepore) that were expected to become part of Pakistan. Their exclusion from Pakistan, which provided an Indian land route to Jammu and Kashmir, created a deep sense of injustice about the fairness of the Radcliffe Award. In this sense Punjab was the epicentre of Pakistan's nation- and state-building endeavours from the very start, a development that was also reinforced by the need to accommodate 5.3 million refugees, most of whom were from East Punjab or northern India.[55] But in contrast to other provinces (see Sindh below), the assimilation of these refugees was largely an untroubled affair because culturally and linguistically they shared a common heritage and eventually settled in areas of the economy where direct competition with indigenous inhabitants was avoided.[56] Cooperation between East and West Punjab authorities, moreover, in the patterns of settlement enabled whole communities to relocate together in re-establishing the familiar bonds of *biraderi*. However, while the refugees were easily assimilated into broader Punjabi society, their revanchist outlook made them a 'safe constituency for martial law governments, or as a lobby for right wing parties in pursuit of anti-India or Pan-Islamic parties'.[57] The Kashmiri element of refugees settled in Sialkot and Lahore were especially committed to the Pakistan state's approach to the dispute with India. East Punjab refugees generally because of their experiences during Partition were sympathetic to the Kashmir cause.

The gradual melding of Pakistan and Punjab identities had its roots in the colonial state's decision to make Urdu rather than Punjabi the official language of government.[58] Attitudes in contemporary Pakistan, aside from language activists, mirror Orientalist caricatures of Punjabi as a

---

[54] Mohammad Waseem, 'Partition, Migration, Assimilation: A Comparative Study of Pakistani Punjab', in Talbot and Singh, *Region and Partition*, p. 203.

[55] Waseem, 'Partition, Migration, Assimilation', pp. 203–28, p. 211

[56] For the impact on locals' attitudes to refugees in the Punjab in circumstances where refugees were economic assets rather than competitors, see Talbot, *Divided Cities*, chapter 6.

[57] Waseem, 'Partition, Migration, Assimilation', p. 216.

[58] See Tariq Rahman, *Language and Politics in Pakistan* (Karachi: Oxford University Press, 1996), chapter 11.

'rustic' language suitable only for use in the home. The process was thus set before the refugee influx for a neutralisation of a potential Punjabi ethnic question in Pakistan. At the same time, growing Punjabi dominance of the new state as result of the military interventions pitched 'minority' ethnic groups against a perceived 'Punjabisation' of Pakistan.[59] This dominance was characterised, above all, in Punjabi representation in the army (80 per cent) and the federal bureaucracy (55 per cent).[60] And given that the expenditure on the army amounted to almost one third of the federal budget, a pattern was established for a praetorian 'Punjabistan' that had all the hallmarks of colonial engineering.[61] Not surprisingly the most sustained resistance to this polity was to come from ethnic mobilisations in provinces excluded from the new power structure.

Sindh

If by the mid-1950s Punjabi identity was sublimated into the construction of greater Pakistan, then it was the Sindhis who in the long term would become the excluded and marginalised nationality. Sindh in fact was to become the test case of the Partition's failure to successfully integrate the local population and refugees, giving birth to the ethnogenesis of a new community centred on the *mohajirs* and a pattern of national and regional power politics in which the Sindhis would continuously be pitted against the former by the military–bureaucratic combine.

Although the Sindh Muslim League was at the forefront of pledging its commitment to the Pakistan cause, it did so in the knowledge that 'sense of a uniquely Sindhi Muslim identity [lay] uneasily beneath the surface' of support for the struggle for Pakistan.[62] This identity had evolved in the context of plural social and religious milieus and economic development from the late nineteenth century which had seen an increasingly large number of Punjabi cultivators settling in the province as a result of irrigation. Local Sindhi resentment against Punjabi settlers had been simmering since the 1930s, but Partition, with its introduction of Urdu-speaking refugees, intensified Sindhi hostility to outsiders. The fundamental cleavages became the source of the great divide: whereas the

[59] See Samad, 'Pakistan or Punjabistan'.
[60] S. P. Cohen, 'State building in Pakistan', in A. Banuaziz and M. Weiner (eds), *The State, Religion, and Ethnic Politics: Pakistan, Iran, and Afghanistan* (Lahore: Vanguard Books, 1987), p. 318; and C. H. Kennedy, *Bureaucracy in Pakistan* (Karachi: Oxford University Press, 1987), p. 194.
[61] See Clive Dewey, 'The Rural Roots of Pakistani Militarism', in D. A. Low (ed.), *The Political Inheritance of Pakistan* (Basingstoke: Macmillan, 1991), pp. 255–83.
[62] Ian Talbot, quoted in Ansari, *Life after Partition*, p. 40.

Sindhis were largely rural, poorly educated, championed Sindhi, were under the sway of traditional Sufi pirs, and had a well-developed sense of provincial political interest, the refugees, in contrast, tended to be urban, well-educated, vociferous advocates of Urdu as a national language, adherents of scriptural Islam, and looked towards the national government as the guarantor of their interests as well as their 'investment' in Pakistan.[63] Nowhere was this divide more evident than in the transformation of Karachi as a *mohajir* 'refugee city' that was administratively separated from Sindh.[64]

Sindhi opposition to refuges after 1947 was quick to surface. At a time when the national requirements of rehabilitation necessitated a positive response, the spectre of provincial transformation created a deep-seated resentment among the Sindhi elite. Karachi's conversion into federal territory was bitterly opposed. The exodus of non-Muslims, especially from Karachi, was recognised as a potential calamity for the province's economy and the Sindh government sought to limit the number of refugees arriving in the city, much to the chagrin of the national administration. Tensions between refugees and locals occasionally turned violent. These differences intensified as Punjabi dominance in West Pakistan was further strengthened by the One Unit plan. Martial law from 1958 onwards only increased Sindhi marginalisation. The fears expressed during the freedom struggle by the Sindhi politician G. M. Syed that the creation of Pakistan would entail Punjabi domination appeared to be coming true.

If Sindhi ethnic assertion against the state was a predictable outcome of partition, *mohajir* disaffection was unexpected. Indeed in the post-Partition decade, *mohajirs* appeared well satisfied with their sacrifices for Pakistan. They held a significant position in the bureaucracy and dominated the commercial life of Karachi. The *mohajirs'* decline is usually attributed to the Ayub Khan martial law regime, as the shift in power from Sindh to Punjab was symbolised by the move of the capital from Karachi to the newly constructed city of Islamabad in the Margalla foothills. Zulfiqar Ali Bhutto's rise to power signalled a further decline of *mohajir* influence, this time in favour of his fellow Sindhis who benefited from affirmative action policies in education and employment. The ethno-nationalist Mohajir Qaumi Mahaz (MQM) was to significantly emerge in March 1984 from the cadres of the All-Pakistan Mohajir Students Organisation which protested against educational reservations.

---

[63] Ansari, *Life after Partition*, chapter 4.
[64] By 1951, 66 per cent of its population was *mohajir*. Ishtiaq Ahmed, *State, Nation and Ethnicity in Contemporary South Asia* (London: Pinter, 1996), p. 191.

The MQM established a *mohajir* 'new ethnicity' to the backdrop of a flood of Pushtun labourers into Karachi and a further acceleration of Punjabi migration. Drugs, guns and 'new wealth' flooded the city which rapidly became an ethnic battlefield. By 1981, *mohajirs* constituted only 56.3 per cent of the city's population. The *mohajir* community had been a mainstay of an Islamically tinged Pakistani identity since 1947 and had traditionally voted for the Jamaat-i-Islami. By the time of the 1985 'partyless' elections, ethnicity had become the main identity marker. The MQM's youthful leader Altaf Hussain demanded that *mohajirs* should be recognised as the 'fifth nationality of Pakistan'. As the MQM leadership formed tactical alliances with the military to undercut the support of the Pakistan People's Party (PPP) in Sindh, Karachi became a simmering cauldron of ethnic tensions.[65] Towards 'the end of the 1990s, ethnic and sectarian conflict had become an ugly and more-or-less permanent feature of city life'; in 1998, factional in-fighting among the MQM alone left more than 700 people dead.[66] These developments – and MQM's contribution to them – led Altaf Hussain to describe the Partition of the subcontinent as 'the biggest blunder in the history of mankind'.[67]

East Bengal

Bengal's political elite from the very inception of the Pakistan idea had been opposed to a centralised polity, championing instead a loose confederal arrangement that was considered more akin to the spirit of the Lahore Resolution. However, the failure of the constitution-making process between 1947 and 1956 resulted in the permanent exclusion of the Bengali provincial political elite in the new emerging polity that was defined by the bureaucracy and the military. In the event, this clash of competing visions over nation-building culminated in the creation of Bangladesh amidst the human tragedy of civil war. It marked the death-knell of the two-nation theory which had legitimised the demand for Pakistan.

The 'geographical absurdity' of the separation of the western and eastern wings of Pakistan and the existence of a strongly defined Bengali collective consciousness ensured that the major post-Partition challenge to a highly centralised Pakistani polity would come from Bengal. The Bengalis who comprised over 55 per cent of the new state's population

---

[65] Ahmed, *State, Nation*, p196.   [66] Ansari, *Life after Partition*, p. 213.
[67] Ansari, *Life after Partition*, p. 220.

threatened to overwhelm it with their own agenda which conflicted with the interests of the ruling army, landlord and bureaucratic elites. The Pakistan state therefore chose to squash rather than co-opt Bengali provincialist demands. A united Pakistan could have survived, but it would have been a very different entity from the state conceived by the West Pakistan power holders.

There are a number of key landmarks in the clash between Bengali ethno-nationalism and Pakistan centralism: the 1952 language riots in Dacca which provided the first martyrs for the Bengali separatist cause; the April 1954 provincial elections in which the ruling Muslim League was routed by the Awami League and its nationalist allies which together won 223 seats, leaving the Muslim League with only 10 seats;[68] the dismissal, after just three months in power, of the newly formed United Front government; the introduction of martial law throughout Pakistan in October 1958 which marginalised the Bengali voice in politics; the inability of the Pakistan People's Party to share power with the Awami League following the first national elections in 1970; and finally, the fateful decision to launch a military crackdown in East Pakistan on 25 March 1971.

Common to these events was Bengali marginalisation and the Centre's refusal to accord legitimacy to Bengali demands for fear of another partition. Ironically, the Pakistan establishment's response not only precipitated the events it most feared, but it undermined any chances of democratic consolidation in the western wing of the country. Remarkably the creation of the One Unit (in which East and West Pakistan were designated as One Units), the emasculation of constitution-making, and Ayub's October 1958 'pre-emptive coup' were all prompted by the need to counter Bengali influence.

The story of East Pakistan's gradual drift into a campaign for autonomy, and then eventual secession in 1971, is a familiar narrative,[69] but it is important to remember that this process was by no means inevitable.[70] It was hastened by the elitist model of nation-building in which the imposition of Urdu as the national language was also accompanied by politics of control in which Bengali representation in state structures, including the armed forces and the bureaucracy, and the management of the economy, was negligible. Throughout the 1950s and 1960s, East Pakistan was the West Pakistan's premier 'colony', providing major sources of tax revenues

---

[68] Ahmed, *State, Nation*, p. 221.
[69] T. Maniruzzaman, *The Bangladesh Revolution and Its Aftermath* (Dhaka: Bangladesh Books International, 1980).
[70] The geo-politics of the birth of Bangladesh are discussed in chapter six.

and foreign exchange through the export of jute.[71] It was this kind of brazen economic exploitation that, combined with political and social exclusion turned the autonomy campaign centred around the Awami League's Six Points (1966 onwards) into the Magna Carta for Bangladesh.

Although the background to the creation of Bangladesh has been well researched, in terms of the legacies of Partition it is noteworthy that the West Pakistani political elite – both civilian and military – sought to reapply the lessons of 1947 in order to frustrate East Pakistan's secession against the rising tide of internal insurgency and external Indian pressure. Following the first national elections in Pakistan in December 1970 – against the mounting discontent with the military administration of General Yahya Khan – the Awami League, which had led the autonomy campaign, won 160 of the 162 seats for East Pakistan in the 300-member Pakistan National Assembly. The re-emergence of the spectre of Bengali democratic hegemony – as in the early 1950s – was too radical for the West Pakistanis to contemplate, and both the military and civilian leadership sought to undo this result. In mid-1971, as the Awami League leadership was ensnared in futile political negotiations, a military strategy was adopted to crush the secessionists in East Pakistan by undermining the Awami League's power base. This included systematic ethnic cleansing of the Hindu population by Islamist *razakhar* (volunteers) and a general crackdown by the military against the regime's opponents. Following a visit to Dhaka, the US ambassador, Joseph Farland concluded that army 'officials and soldiers give every sign of believing they are now embarked on a *jihad* against Hindu-corrupted Bengalis'.[72] According to one senior Karachi-based journalist this strategy consisted of three elements: that the Bengalis had 'proved themselves unreliable', that they had to 're-educate along proper Islamic lines', and that once the ethnic cleansing of Hindus had been effected, their property would be used as a 'golden carrot to win over the under-privileged Muslim middle-class'.[73] In the event, this policy led to 10 million refugees crossing the border to India and ultimately a decision by India's prime minister, Indira Gandhi, to militarily intervene in East Pakistan in December 1971 in a short-lived Indo-Pakistan war. It climaxed in the unconditional surrender of 93,000 Pakistani troops and the birth of Bangladesh. The

---

[71] Tariq Ali, *Can Pakistan Survive? The Death of a State* (Harmondsworth: Penguin, 1983), p. 48.
[72] Quoted in Husain Haqqani, *Pakistan: Between Mosque and Military* (Washington, DC: Carnegie Endowment for International Peace, 2005), p. 80.
[73] Anthony Mascarenhas, *The Sunday Times* (London), 13 June 1971.

responsibility for the second partition lay in Islamabad. The two-nation theory which was 'formulated in the middle-class living rooms of Uttar Pradesh, was buried in the Bengali countryside'.[74]

Partition and religious nationalism in India and Pakistan

As well as creating ambiguous borderlands, which continue to challenge the nation- and state-building efforts of India and Pakistan, Partition also remains a powerful mainspring for religious nationalism in both countries. Since the 1980s, religious nationalism in South Asia has been substantially reinvented, but what continues to characterise it is the essentialisation of community and culture with projects of either political separatism or assimilation and integration. What Pandey calls the discourses of 'nationalisation of the subject'[75] by the religious right remain embedded, on the one hand, in everyday presence of partition that provides 'imagined dangers of future partitions'[76] (India), and on the other, as a permanent reminder of the dangers to communal sovereignty and national integrity (Pakistan). In these imaginings, Partition continues to foster historicised and essentialised communal constructions of the 'other' that have a strong resonance with powerful political constituencies as well as providing a permanent ideological resource to statecraft in both countries.

The persistence of religious nationalisms in India and Pakistan vitiated by Partition has certainly belied the expectations of many that because the new states were largely mono-religious, communalism would eventually 'wither away'. India's secularism seemed far more secure with a Muslim population of 12 per cent rather than the pre-Partition figure of nearly 30 per cent; and Pakistan as an overwhelmingly Muslim state appeared better equipped to manage the problem of minorities, religious or otherwise. However, as we have seen, state secularism in India was heavily tinged with majoritarian overtones, so much so that the post-1947 politically decapitated Muslim minority of India became a willing Congress votebank where political protection and communal rights were traded for *en-masse* support at the polls. While this arrangement provided political support to state secularism, it also eventually gave birth to the Hindu Right's charge of 'pseudo-secularism' which alleged that official state secularism merely pandered to religious minorities, especially Muslims.[77]

---

[74] Ali, *Can Pakistan Survive?*, p. 96.
[75] See Gyanendra Pandey, *Remembering Partition: Violence, Nationalism and History in India* (Cambridge University Press, 2001).
[76] Brass, *The Production*, p. 384.   [77] See Singh, *Ethnic Conflict*, chapter 1.

Likewise in Pakistan, notwithstanding in-built majoritarianism, the contestation between supporters of a state for Muslims and an Islamic state – against the backdrop of the failure of democracy – has become so entrenched that it has produced a praetorian-bureaucratic polity with Islam as a surrogate for effective legitimacy, resulting in wild oscillations between the modernist and conservative strands within the idea of Pakistan. Moreover, as a consequence of the geo-political developments since the Soviet intervention in Afghanistan (1979), it has also generated virulent strains of religious nationalism that have become the breeding grounds of global terrorism, with some of the seminaries of global terror (e.g. Deobandi) having their origins in the pre-Partition Pakistan movement.[78]

Of course the actual contexts in which the new religious nationalisms have emerged are remarkably different from the pre-colonial period. In India the growth of *Hindutva* forces led by the BJP, the RSS and the VHP since the early 1980s is generally attributed to the political demise of the Congress and the structural changes resulting from the processes of economic liberalisation and as a reaction against the political mobilisation of lower-caste parties, notably in north India.[79] Nevertheless, the moral panic created by the ethno-religious movements in India's peripheral states – Jammu and Kashmir, Punjab and the north-eastern states – contributed considerably to a crisis of national unity and governability that afflicted the Indian state in the 1980s and 1990s.[80] The *Hindutva* movement's campaign against 'minorityism' was given direct manifestation with the cultural 'remapping' of the country through *rath yatras* (national staged marches) through localities of Muslim strength. It reached its gory climax in the destruction of the Babri Masjid (mosque) in Ayodyha in December 1992, an event that was followed by almost 3,000 deaths in communal rioting between Hindus and Muslims throughout India. A more gruesome tragedy occurred in Gujarat in 2002 when anti-Muslim riots resulted in the deaths of 1,000 victims, mostly Muslim, and the displacement of over a further 100,000 as a result of organised violence in which the state BJP government was implicated.[81]

---

[78] See Oliver Roy, *Globalised Islam: The Search for a New Ummah* (London: Hurst, 2004); Haqqani, *Pakistan*; Gilles Kepel, *Jihad: The Trial of Political Islam* (London: I. B. Tauris, 2003). It must be generally acknowledged, however, that the Deobandis were apolitical during the colonial era and most leading Deobandi *ulama* were opposed to the demand for Pakistan.

[79] See Stuart Corbridge and John Harriss, *Reinventing India: Liberalisation, Hindu Nationalism and Popular Democracy* (Cambridge: Polity Press, 2000).

[80] See Atul Kholi, *India's Growing Crisis of Governability* (Cambridge University Press, 1990).

[81] Gurharpal Singh, 'State and Religious Diversity: Reflections on Post-1947 India', *Totalitarian Movements and Political Religions* 5:2 (Autumn 2004), p. 213.

The 're-imaging' of India in which minorities, particularly religious minorities, are designated as 'political Hindus',[82] has rekindled the argument that the Hindu Right has successfully re-invented the spectre of Partition as an omnipresent threat to the nation, while subtly advocating its undoing as the ultimate objective of a Hindu nation vivisected at birth. Certainly during the two BJP national governments between 1998 and 2004, the bellicosity shown in the managing of Indo-Pakistan relations was often highly suggestive of an agenda beyond containing Pakistan or its alleged support for terrorism in Jammu and Kashmir. Underlying the *Hindutva* project, it has been suggested, is perhaps a wider effort to 'wrongsize' India's borders by incorporating Pakistan.[83] While this drive has been necessarily checked, the association of Pakistan with terror and terrorist acts with Muslims has fed the encoded debates within *Hindutva* – and the wider public – that have accentuated the deep social chasms in the boundaries of communities of culture. For some analysts, these divisions are now more overtly manifest in the persistence of 'institutionalised riot systems' – the existence of political parties, an ideological context, and partisan state actors and institutions – that have in-built incentives to 'produce communal riots'. As such, it is argued, for militant Hindus these 'institutionalised riot systems' reconstruct in 'the very present the evidence of partition'. 'In every major town in northern India', Brass writes, 'there are ... symbols of that presence wherever there are large concentrations of Muslim populations. These "mini-Pakistanis" in turn are seen as the centres of riot production designed to intimidate Hindus and generate more and more partitions, more and more violence on the Hindu body.'[84]

Partition pathologies today are most evident in Hindu–Muslim communal relations in northern India, and more so during periods of heightened communal tension that nowadays tend to arise with conflict with Pakistan or acts of terrorism, or still, the aggressive politics of the Hindu Right. During these phases informed public opinion and the popular media are, more often than not, inclined to regress into the repertoire of Partition-style discourses that regularly allude to 'ethnic cleansing', 'riots', 'partition', 'communal massacres' 'political separatism', and more recently, 'political jihadism'.[85] Stereotypes drawn from the Partition-related

---

[82] Singh, *Ethnic Conflict*, p. 15.
[83] See Gurharpal Singh, 'Resizing and Reshaping the State: India from Partition to Present', in Brendan O'Leary, Ian S. Lustick and Thomas Callaghy (eds), *Rightsizing the State: The Politics of Moving Borders* (Oxford University Press, 2001), pp. 138–67.
[84] Brass, *The Production*, p. 384.
[85] See, for example, the coverage of 2002 riots in Gujarat, the post-Ayodhya killings in 1992, and the coverage of anti-Sikh riots in Delhi in 1984.

violence, along with portrayals of Muslim iconoclastic destruction of Hindu sacred space from the medieval period onwards have played a crucial role in the 'essentialisation' of the Indian Muslim 'other' as a sexually rapacious and violent aggressor. The persistence of these discourses suggests that in Indian politics today, partition still remains an unhealed wound which, under the appropriate conditions, has the potential to seriously infect the broader body politic. It marks, as Khilnani concludes, 'the moment of the Indian nation's origin through violent rupture with itself'. As such, it 'both defines and constantly suspects India's identity, dividing it between the responsibility to tolerate differences, and the dreams of a territory where all are compelled to worship in unison.'[86]

Partition also sits uncomfortably with Islamic writings in Pakistan, not least because of the secular leadership and nature of the Pakistan movement. Many of the leading religious parties had ambiguous relationships with the freedom struggle. It was only during the Zia-ul-Haq period of Islamisation that there was an attempt to portray the *ulama* as exerting a leading influence on the Pakistan struggle. More usually official histories have used Partition as a resource for anti-Hindu sentiment that has played well both with Pakistani nationalist opinion and Jamaat-i-Islami, and Partition-related violence has been linked with caricatures of Hindu treachery and a desire to destroy Muslim culture. These sentiments have been expressed most clearly in school textbooks sanctioned by the state that have produced a highly ideological version of recent modern history.

Today Pakistani religious nationalism has, in some measure, transmuted into global jihadism as the moderate and secular forces that have dominated state power since 1947 find themselves on the back foot in the backlash against the 'War on Terror'. This turn of events is largely the product of the 'insecurity state's' efforts to manage nationalist aspirations to its institutional interest. Thus the *jihadi* groups have been patronised by the Pakistan Army during the Afghan War and supplied with weapons and training by the ISI. After the Soviet defeat in Afghanistan, jihadist groups switched their attention to Indian-controlled Jammu and Kashmir. The insurgency there was a critical catalyst in reinventing religious nationalism in Pakistan by injecting a new religious zeal into a largely borderland issue.[87] However, taken together these developments provided a thread of continuity between the past and the present in which the politics of Muslim identity – traditionally centred around modernist,

---

[86] Khilnani, *The Idea of India*, p. 202.
[87] For a partisan but nonetheless an illuminating account of how these developments have been understood by contemporary Pakistani leadership, see Pervez Musharraf, *In the Line of Fire: A Memoir* (London: Simon and Schuster, 2006), chapter 26.

conservative and radical perspectives – have been gradually displaced by a virulent militant political Islam, though civilian administrations (1988–1999) and the military (post-1999 to 2008) have made strenuous efforts to establish some official distance from any formal association. Thus though the alliance between militant Islam and the military may have arisen from a desire to keep politicians at bay, it now provides the main justification for the 'parallel state' (the military) to be the 'defender of the communalist/separatist discourse and India-centred definition of Pakistan's self-perception'.[88] In short, India remains the principal 'other' of Pakistani religious nationalism today, a construction reinforced by perceptions of violence against subcontinental Muslims who are only too readily assumed to be victims of 'Hindu oppression'.

Conclusion

In this chapter we have attempted to highlight how the traumatic process of division of the Indian subcontinent in 1947 created new ethnic land-scapes in the hinterlands in India and Pakistan and troublesome border-lands that questioned the very essence of the nation- and state-building projects launched by the post-Independence elites in these two countries. Both developments, in their own ways, provided the momentum for the construction of highly centralised state formations that were distinguished by the domination of the state over society in order to ensure that Partition would, indeed, be the 'end of history'. However, despite these efforts, such objectives were only partially realised in India where successful democratisation has failed to provide a legitimate formula for the manage-ment of its troubled peripheral states. Equally in Pakistan the politics of control produced a second partition with the birth of Bangladesh as well as a deformed polity that is now structured around a praetorian-bureaucratic combine with a strong Islamist ideological tinge. But underpinning these developments in both countries have been deep reservoirs of religious nationalisms which, though significantly different from their predecessors that flowed to 1947, nonetheless share one important characteristic: they provide a contemporary presence to Partition as an idea as well as a lived experience. Partition in this sense is very much an ongoing process that defies closure as well as being easy prey to 'reinvention' and 'reconstruc-tion'. Beyond ethnic and religious nationalisms this ominous legacy is most evident in the enduring international rivalry between India and Pakistan, which forms the focus of our next chapter.

[88] Vali Nasr, 'National Identities and India–Pakistan Conflict', in T. V. Paul (ed.), *The India–Pakistan Conflict: An Enduring Rivalry* (Cambridge University Press, 2005), p. 186.

6   An enduring rivalry: India and Pakistan since 1947

In the summer of 2002, while global attention was fixed on the seventeenth staging of the football world cup in Japan and Korea, a more deadly game was unfolding in Kashmir. Following an attack on the Indian parliament in early December 2001 by Kashmir-based militants in Pakistan, the Indian government ordered a wholesale mobilisation of its forces in retaliation, for its own 'War on Terror' against Pakistani-sponsored groups. As the armies of the two nations confronted each other across the Radcliffe Line and the Line of Control (LOC), neither side denied the possibility that another war between these neighbours might turn nuclear with tens of millions of casualties. The rivalry between India and Pakistan which had begun at birth now threatened a global catastrophe which promised to make the Partition violence but a mere footnote.

Why had the India–Pakistan rivalry climaxed in a nuclear stand-off? What lay behind the failure to achieve peaceful Indo-Pakistan relations? Why had the intense differences between the Congress and the Muslim League in colonial India became translated into a permanent inter-state conflict? In what ways did Partition and its legacies contribute to structuring this competition?

In this chapter we examine the sources of this 'enduring conflict'[1] rooted in the competing conceptions of national identity, messy separation at birth, disputes over territory, especially Kashmir, and the emergence of post-1947 Pakistan as an 'insecurity state'. We also review how these factors intersected with broader regional and global processes in locking this rivalry, first, into the Cold War, and then, after 1989, into a new emerging post-Cold War regional order. The chapter concludes by reflecting on the current 'composite dialogue' between the two states and areas of cooperation over the last sixty years, which point to ways in which the two countries can escape the 'trap of history'.

---

[1] The conflict between India and Pakistan has been defined as an enduring rivalry, see T. V. Paul (ed.), *The India–Pakistan Conflict: An Enduring Rivalry* (Cambridge University Press, 2005).

Competing identities

Most official versions of the India–Pakistan rivalry often couch it in terms of primordial differences based on religion.[2] Post-1947 accounts of nation-building in Pakistan have drawn richly on the 'epic struggle' against 'overwhelming odds' against an indefatigable opponent (the Congress) that was determined to undermine the nascent state at every turn. At the same time, Indian versions of religious and communal violence regularly locate the source in the 'separatist' pursuit of Pakistan by the Muslim League which allegedly heightened religious differences and tore asunder the fabric of a diverse and plural society. These basic ideological differences between the Congress (for a secular, diverse and plural polity) and the Muslim League (for a separate, Islamic republic) have become the building blocks for the unbridgeable difference between the two establishments. Even after sixty years they continue to nourish irreconcilable discourses – notwithstanding the veracity of such claims.

Pakistani national identity has been constructed essentially in opposition to a perceived threat of Hindu majoritarianism and against India; and as a consequence, the Muslim League's minority nationalism subsequently developed strong overtones of real or imagined fears of Indian domination. Until recently, throughout the Pakistani establishment there was a pervasive belief that India remained unreconciled to Partition, and given the opportunity, would have readily dismembered Pakistan. President Ayub Khan once famously remarked to President Lyndon Johnson: 'I know you won't believe it but those Indians are going to gobble us up.'[3] Although this sense of insecurity has, at times, been overplayed, to extract funds and military hardware from the US, the massively asymmetrical relationship between India and Pakistan undoubtedly contributed to fuelling these fears as well as foregrounding Islam as the essential glue that could hold the disparate nation together. As we shall see below, Islamisation and the emergence of Pakistan as an 'insecurity state' were to be inextricably intertwined.

By contrast India's national identity construction has derided the exclusivist idea of Pakistan based on Islam. Emphasising secularism, pluralism and diversity, it has generally tended to portray the Pakistani state as 'feudal', 'obscurantist' and a 'theocratic' project which failed to capture the imagination of most South Asian Muslims. Yet despite these claims, Pakistan's *raison d'être* as a *religious state* continues to provide

[2] For examples, see J. N. Dixit, *India–Pakistan in War and Peace* (London: Routledge, 2002), p. 398.
[3] Quoted in Dennis Kux, *India–Pakistan Negotiations: Is Past Still a Prologue?* (Washington, DC: United States Institute for Peace, 2006), p. 17.

uncomfortable inspiration for other religious and ethnic groups in India; and as the struggle over Kashmir, Sikh and Naga separatism has demonstrated, the Indian national ideal has limited appeal in some of the peripheral regions where the exercise of democratic rule has been seriously qualified and where political secularism has been found wanting or is closely associated with Hindu majoritarianism.

In fact, behind the apparent clash of identities which are all too often portrayed as 'civilisational differences', are many uncomfortable truths. In Jammu and Kashmir, which is frequently described as the 'unfinished business of Partition', where both nations compete for control of the region, Pakistani claims based on Muslim self-determination overlook the competing demands of Hindus and Buddhists as well as the cross-cutting aspirations of some ethnic and tribal groups. Similarly, the birth of Bangladesh in 1971 highlighted the limited appeal of Islam as the basis of nation-formation: ethnicity proved to be a more enduring bond than religion.

If the limits of religious nationalism are all too obvious, similar short-comings are also apparent in the case of India's secular model which has struggled to provide inclusivity to religious minorities and Muslims in particular. Muslims remain overwhelmingly under-represented in the institutions of the state. This religious glass ceiling has also been accompanied by the relatively weak application of citizenship rights to India's peripheral regions where the religious minorities (Muslims, Sikhs, Christians) are concentrated. As was noted in chapter five, these regions have often been governed directly by the centre or have often been the sites of insurgency and counterinsurgency violence.

A messy separation

We have already seen in chapter two that the Partition of the subcontinent intensified the mistrust that had dogged the relations between the Congress and the Muslim League during the final decade of colonial rule. Unlike the 'velvet' divorce between the Czech Republic and Slovakia, the separation of Pakistan from India was a messy affair mired in acrimony, accusations of betrayal and lasting bitterness.[4] At the heart of this rancorous parting of the ways were disputes over assets and territory, but the daily resentments of millions of uprooted citizens whose lives had to be rebuilt afresh in new lands played a not insignificant part.

---

[4] This was rooted partly in the attitude that Pakistan was a seceding party, creating resentment in India and a sense of inferiority in Pakistan itself. This was, strictly speaking, incorrect: it was a partition rather than secession.

The Partition Council, which comprised Vallabhbhai Patel, Rajendra Prasad, Liaquat Ali Khan and Abdur Rab Nishtar, met in a soured atmosphere. This body along with its ten subcommittees was tasked to divide assets between India and Pakistan. These ranged from the sterling balances down to the lowliest inkstand which had to be itemised along with all government property. The division was generally along an 80:20 split between the two states-in-waiting. Disputes were referred to an Arbitration Tribunal. The bitterness and pathos surrounding the whole process is evidenced in memoirs and contemporary newspaper accounts and cartoons. Disputes over assets burnished the myth that India attempted to strangle Pakistan at birth and that its survival stemmed from the unity displayed in the face of adversity.

The subject of most intense dispute was the division of financial assets. In its process, 'both sides fought tooth and nail for every rupee of assets, the one anxious to deny, the other determined to secure'.[5] Pakistan as the seceding state was faced with the prospect of setting up an administration over territories that were devoid of any major industries or other sources of revenue generation. As such, Muslim League members of the Partition Committee fought hard to maximise their claims to the resources of united India. Their claim for a quarter of the cash balances of 4,000 million rupees, however, was whittled down to 200 million rupees, and after 15 August 1947, some of the balances were released only following a fast by Mahatma Gandhi. An additional 550 million rupees was made available as the final instalment. The division of non-cash balances – securities, debt, sterling balances, and material assets – was equally fraught. Whereas Pakistani representatives wanted 'joint control over the entire property belonging to the government of India', this claim was curtly dismissed by the Indian representatives as impractical, though there was some belated recognition that the former were entitled to some compensation for 'unique institutions which could not be duplicated'.[6] After protracted deliberations against the backdrop of fighting in Kashmir an agreement was reached in December 1947, according to which Pakistan's share of the final assets and liabilities was fixed at 17.5 per cent, but it secured only £147 million of the £1,160 million of the government of India's sterling balances. This settlement was reluctantly accepted by Pakistan, which remained convinced that apart from encouraging a flight of capital from the country, the government of India had deliberately prolonged the negotiations in order to undermine the new state at birth.

---

[5] Jalal, *The State of Martial Rule*, p. 33.   [6] Jalal, *The State of Martial Rule*, p. 35.

Equally bitter was the division of the Indian Army which had been the backbone of the colonial regime. British interests dictated that there should be a common defence agreement between India and Pakistan in order to ensure a degree of continuity. This proposal, however, was scuppered by Jinnah's decision to become the first governor general of Pakistan and the conflicts that ensued between the two countries. Pakistani advocates insisted on an independent army because without it the new state would 'collapse like a pack of cards'.[7] It was this consideration that led Liaquat Ali Khan and Jinnah to resolve 'that they would not take over the reins of government of Pakistan unless they had an Army on the spot, and under their control'.[8] This decision led to the setting-up of elaborate machinery which gradually devolved operational and administrative control to forces based in the territories that commanded India and Pakistan, though initially joint control was vested in the supreme commander General Claude Auchinleck. British and Indian serving officers were 'encouraged to opt for service in either state, thus ensuring a "successful reconstitution" with little or no break in continuity'.[9] The Indian army was divided on the ratio of 64:34 troops for India and Pakistan respectively but excluded the Gurkhas. The transfer of troops and equipment was overseen by a Joint Defence Council which was established on 15 August. It comprised the supreme commander, General Auchinleck, the defence ministers of India and Pakistan and the governor general of India, Lord Mountbatten, in his capacity as an independent chairman. Auchinleck stepped down as supreme commander in November 1947 following Indian complaints that he favoured Pakistani interests and an Inter-Dominion Committee completed his work. Although there had been an agreement that Pakistan would receive a third of the equipment and stores, the division of military assets did not go smoothly. Stores arrived late and damaged, if at all. Pakistan was at a disadvantage in that most equipment was located in India. The outbreak of hostilities in Kashmir, moreover, further hindered the division. Just over 23,000 of the 160,000 tons of ordnance allotted to Pakistan by the Joint Defence Council were actually delivered.[10]

Pakistan attempted to overcome the shortfall in military staff by the continued employment of British officers. Around 500 were employed in the army. The navy and the air force were even more dependent on British officers. Jinnah soon had to confront the stark reality of his independent army. When he ordered the army to advance into Kashmir, he was sternly

[7] Liaquat Ali Khan, quoted in Jalal, *The State of Martial Rule*, p. 38.
[8] Jalal, *The State of Martial Rule*, p. 38.   [9] Jalal, *The State of Martial Rule*, p. 39.
[10] Talbot, *Pakistan: A Modern History*, p. 99.

warned by Auchinleck of the 'incalculable consequences of any military action which could be construed as a violation of Indian territory'.[11] At this crucial juncture, as Pakistan faced internal turmoil, the exchange of populations in Punjab, Sindh and Bengal and conflict in Kashmir, its army was as much use to its leader as a 'tin soldier'.[12] Pakistan's response was to divert scarce resources to the 'political economy of defence' that rapidly expanded the Pakistan army from its modest beginnings, but at the cost of dependency on foreign aid and economic and social development.

That the Partition process from the Pakistani view appeared heavily stacked in India's favour was further underscored by the resentment created by the Radcliffe Award. The sense of bitterness at the lack of fair treatment is a crucial aspect of Pakistani historiography (see chapter one). The 'sketch map' controversy over the Ferozepore salient (see chapter two) lies at its heart. From the Muslim League's perspective, the Award had delivered strategically important Muslim-majority *tehsils* into Indian hands in the West. It thus left a bitter legacy of betrayal and unfairness – claims which were to find a rich vein in the nationalist discourses after 1947. It created, moreover, in the words of van Schendel, a state of 'territorial anxiety' fuelled by the inheritance of 'ill-defined nations and frayed territories',[13] an anxiety that was to find its permanent fixation in the struggle over Kashmir.

The Jammu and Kashmir dispute[14]

Once it became clear that power would be transferred to the governments of India and Pakistan only, Maharaja Hari Singh, the ruler of Jammu and Kashmir, was faced with the dilemma of determining the accession. Initially he signed a standstill agreement with Pakistan – indicating that the state would eventually opt for the new Muslim homeland – but as Hari Singh vacillated in confirming the formal accession in the months of September and October, the government of Pakistan organised a 'tribal rebellion' led by North West Frontier militias and irregular Pakistani troops.[15] These rebels threatened to capture Srinagar and make the accession a *fait accompli*. At this juncture Hari Singh acceded to India, accepting the condition

---

[11] Jalal, *The State of Martial Rule*, p. 44.   [12] Jalal, *The State of Martial Rule*, p. 42.

[13] William van Schendel, 'The Wagha Syndrome: Territorial Roots of Contemporary Violence in South Asia', in Amrita Basu and Sirupa Roy (eds), *Violence and Democracy in India* (London: Seagull, 2007), p. 44.

[14] For a good review of the literature on the Kashmir dispute and the post-1980s Kashmir crisis, see Ian Talbot, 'Foreword', in Sten Widmalm, *Kashmir in Comparative Perspective: Democracy and Violent Separatism in India* (Karachi: Oxford University Press, 2006), pp. vi–xiv.

[15] See P. Swami, *India, Pakistan and the Secret Jihad: The Covert War in Kashmir, 1947–2004* (New York: Routledge, 2007).

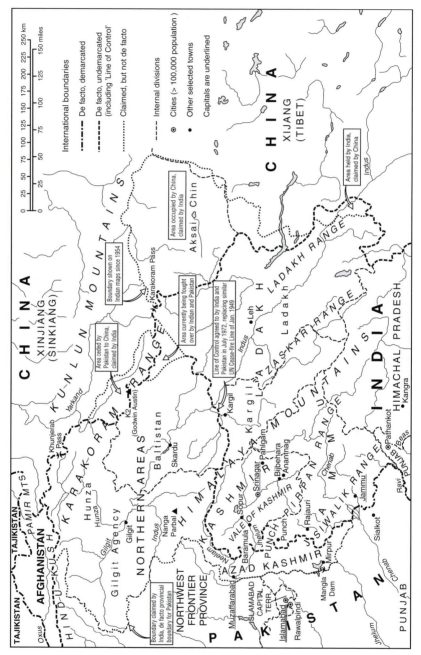

Map 5 Kashmir region

that the accession would have to be ratified by the people of the province. In return Indian troops were airlifted to the Kashmir valley and eventually thwarted and pushed back the advance of the 'tribal rebellion' to the contemporary LOC, then referred to as the Cease Fire Line (CFL). Although Nehru, at Mountbatten's bidding, referred the dispute to the United Nations in December 1947, and accepted a Security Council resolution that a plebiscite should be held to legitimise the accession to India, subject to the withdrawal of *all troops* in the province, hostilities between India and Pakistan in Jammu and Kashmir continued throughout 1948. They only formally ceased on 1 January 1949. The CFL marked the de facto division of the state between India and Pakistan: it was to be divided permanently, to become the 'oldest unresolved conflict before the United Nations' with the western territory (one third) under Pakistani occupation (and subsequently named 'Azad Kashmir', free Kashmir) and two thirds under Indian control, including the state capital Srinagar.

After 1947, Indian governance in Jammu and Kashmir rested on two foundations: first, the special status for the province within the Indian constitution guaranteed by Article 370 that restricted the central government's power to foreign affairs, defence, currency and communications, and, second, the popular appeal of the National Conference led by Abdullah. However Abdullah's aspirations for greater autonomy and self-rule were checked in the early 1950s by a rising tide of Hindu communalism which limited Nehru's scope for manoeuvre and 'marked the parting of the ways' as Abdullah was arrested and, subsequently, interned for almost two decades, while a pliant regional assembly in 1956 formally voted for a merger with India. Not unexpectedly, this was vigorously contested by Pakistan at the United Nations, but its efforts to get a Security Council resolution on the subject were vetoed by the Soviet Union. By then the Kashmir dispute had become thoroughly internationalised; more ominously, it became firmly set in the deep freeze of the Cold War.

Pakistan as an 'insecurity state'

In addition to Jammu and Kashmir the one factor that is regularly viewed as the principal cause of the India–Pakistan rivalry is the emergence of Pakistan from 1947 onwards as an 'insecurity state' that 'perceived itself not only small and disadvantaged but on the defensive against real and present threat, with its survival at stake'.[16] The immediate challenges of

---

[16] See Thomas Perry Thornton, 'Pakistan: Fifty Years of Insecurity', in Selig S. Harrison, Paul H. Kreisberg and Dennis Kux (eds), *India and Pakistan: The First Fifty Years* (Cambridge University Press, 1999), p. 171.

nation- and state-building were compounded by the arrival of several millions of refugees from India, a perilous economy and insecure borders threatened by a hostile neighbour. In this context the military and the bureaucracy emerged as the premier institutions that set the permanent template for the Pakistan polity in which democratic governance would always play second fiddle.

Pakistan's polity has been variously defined as a 'dyarchy' – resembling imperial governance in which governing institutions were separated from representative ones – or a form of 'praetorianism' that has institutionalised military predominance. Recent scholarship however has established that the institutional innovations in the formative years (1947–1954) created a form of path dependency that has subsequently been responsible for thwarted democratisation, military interventions and post-military withdrawal crises.[17] At the core of this development over time has been the emergence of the military as a 'parallel state' with distinctive institutional interests that have enabled it to repeatedly – some times creatively, at others fortuitously – reposition itself as the premier institution in the state. From the Cold War to the 'War on Terror', 'the military in Pakistan has shown a remarkable consistency in pursuing its institutional interests, regardless of the terms of debate'.[18] One reason why it has been so successful is its ability to link external threats to its own interests, and in the process, turn Pakistan into what some critics of militarism have often described as 'geo-political utility' or a 'neo-vassal state'.[19]

While British colonial officials had long recognised the potential value of the Pakistan areas as a base for policing the Middle East and the Soviet Union, it was only with the emergence of the Cold War that Pakistan was able to seize the new opportunities offered by alignment with the US to offset India's perceived threat. Pakistan's desire to become US's 'eastern anchor' was formalised when it joined the Southeast Asia Treaty Organisation (SEATO) in September 1954 and the Central Treaty Organisation (CENTO) in September 1956. These treaties were followed by US financial and military aid which significantly strengthened the military position vis-à-vis other state institutions as well as reinforcing the permanent 'insecurity state'. In fact it was during these critical years in the 1950s that features of the 'insecurity state' became apparent: institutionalised military predominance

---

[17] See Mazhar Aziz, *Military Control: The Parallel State* (London: Routledge, 2008); Jalal, *The State of Martial Rule*; Husain Haqqani, *Pakistan: Between Mosque and Military* (Washington, DC: Carnegie Endowment for International Peace, 2005).

[18] Aziz, *Military Control*, p. 24.

[19] The latter term is Imran Ali's. See 'Pakistan and the Continuing Dilemma of Inequality', unpublished paper presented at 'The Independence of India and Pakistan: Sixtieth Anniversary Reflections', University of Southampton, 17–20 July 2007.

over civilian structures, exclusive military control of security and foreign affairs, and dependence on a centralised bureaucracy which would serve as the 'steel frame'. Subsequently, the 'insecurity state' would become further entrenched in Pakistan's polity and society. In the following fifty years it would effectively marginalise democratic politics, assume supreme capacity in its ability to manufacture legitimacy – sometimes by deliberately sponsoring the mullah–military complex – and have its *raison d'être* as the permanent enmity with India (notwithstanding the Soviet invasion of Afghanistan or the 'War on Terror'). It would also seek to further strengthen its security with an alliance with communist China and the pursuit of a nuclear bomb. In short, the search for security by the Pakistani military would lead to deformed democratisation punctuated with cycles of militarisation and de-militarisation and a permanent institutional interest that thrived on geo-political conflicts in the South Asian region.[20]

The emergence of Pakistan as a military-dominated 'insecurity state' has had two long-term implications. First, like most such non-democratic states, it has been prone to adventurism and is, comparatively, an unsuitable candidate for promoting peace in the region.[21] Second, even when the Pakistani military has gone back to the barracks, it has remained – and remains – the dominant player in defining the nature of civilianised governance. It is this consideration which has led some to argue that democratic consolidation in Pakistan will remain heavily circumscribed precisely because it is a prerequisite for the dismantling of the 'insecurity state'. At a time when Pakistan is witness to another transition from military to civilian rule (February–March 2008), it is appropriate to remember that Pakistan's history suggests that 'a transition from military rule to an elected government … is likely to produce weak civilian governments due to the presence of a strongly institutionalised military'.[22]

Jammu and Kashmir, Cold War and the India–Pakistan conflict up to 1972

By the late 1950s the basis of the inter-state rivalry between India and Pakistan had been firmly established. On the one hand, Pakistan's quest for security had driven it willingly into the US-led Cold War camp which

---

[20] See Ayesha Siddiqa, *Military Inc.: Inside Pakistan's Military Economy* (London: Pluto, 2007).

[21] See in particular Daniel S. Geller, 'The India–Pakistan Rivalry: Prospects for War, Prospects for Peace', in Paul (ed.), *The India–Pakistan Conflict*, pp. 80–102.

[22] Aziz, *Military Control*, p. 7.

provided the necessary protection against Indian aggression, and also an umbrella from which to test India's resolve in Jammu and Kashmir. The military coup by General Ayub Khan in 1958, moreover, further consolidated the 'insecurity state' that would postpone effective civilian control of the state until after 1971. On the other hand, India's increasing proximity to the Soviet Union after 1953 and leadership of the non-aligned movement made it extremely hostile to Pakistan's design of bringing the Cold War to South Asia. Indeed as early as 1954, Nehru had warned Mohammed Ali Bogra, the Pakistani prime minister, that Pakistan's membership of SEATO – in exchange for military assistance that could be used against India – would qualitatively alter India's stand on Kashmir. It appears that this factor further strengthened Indian resolve to integrate the region within the Indian Union.

However before Pakistan could test its new found strength, India was engaged in a short border war with communist China (1962) in which it suffered serious reversals on its north-west and the eastern border. Although during this conflict Pakistan remained neutral, subsequently it became party to US pressure on India to negotiate a final settlement to the Kashmir dispute. Six rounds of talks were held between the two countries and US representatives between 1962 and 1963 but they failed to provide a decisive breakthrough. During these talks Pakistan established formal links with China and signed a border agreement.

In the aftermath of the India–China war, which was accompanied by heavy Indian rearmament, Pakistani leadership was of the opinion that there was only a small window of opportunity to secure a military solution to the Kashmir dispute. As India planned further measures to integrate Jammu and Kashmir, Pakistan attempted to exploit the regional discontent in the province by launching 'Operation Gibraltar' (1965), a military advance in the Vale of Kashmir. India responded by opening a second front on the plains of Punjab that threatened the heartland around Lahore. The hostilities lasted only fifteen days and the Soviet Union acted as an honest broker in sponsoring a cease fire. The status quo ante bellum was restored, but it made only a passing reference to Kashmir in the 'context of the desirability of reducing tensions'.[23]

The next major conflict between the two countries occurred in the struggle for Bangladesh's independence in December 1971 – one of the most complex episodes in the Cold War, involving the US, USSR and China.[24] The background to this conflict has been discussed in chapter five and was essentially *internal* in that it arose from the gross political

---

[23] Kux, *India–Pakistan Negotiations*, p. 32.
[24] For an Indian account of the conflict, see Dixit, *India–Pakistan*, pp. 169–237.

mismanagement of East Pakistan which had been governed after 1947 as an internal colony by the western Pakistani regimes. Mrs Indira Gandhi, the Indian prime minister, decided to intervene in East Pakistan mainly because of the exodus of almost 10 million refugees to West Bengal following a military crackdown by the Pakistan army against Bengali nationalists. In a conflict that lasted just twelve days, the Indians captured 93,000 Pakistani prisoners of war in East Pakistan and some territory on the western front. Bangladesh was liberated but it had taken the Indian army to secure its independence.

The break-up of Pakistan in 1971 was followed by the withdrawal of the military from Pakistan politics and the installation of a civilian leadership under Zulfikar Ali Bhutto, a former foreign minister under Ayub Khan who had floated the Pakistan People's Party (which had won a majority in West Pakistan in the general elections of 1970 but had no presence in East Pakistan). In negotiating a peace deal with India, Bhutto was only too conscious of Pakistan's military weakness, while Mrs Indira Gandhi sought to secure a deal that would recognise India's hegemonic position in the region. The Simla Agreement (1972), signed in the former colonial summer capital that had been host to many Congress–Muslim League parleys, eventually produced a fudged compromise. India secured agreement that the two countries 'would settle their differences by peaceful means and through bilateral negations'. The CFL that had divided the two armies was to be converted into the LOC. Pakistani prisoners detained in India were only to be released with the consent of Bangladesh. Bhutto's firm stand against Gandhi ensured that the final text of the agreement acknowledged that the periodic summits and discussions between representatives of both countries would aim to establish 'a durable peace and normal relations ... including a final settlement of Jammu and Kashmir'.[25]

In retrospect the Simla Agreement marked a major turning point in the India–Pakistan rivalry. While India succeeded, at least on paper, in making bilateralism the operative norm in India–Pakistan relations, for Pakistan the loss of East Pakistan reignited the anxieties which dated back to 1947 about India's real intent. Thus began the search for a new 'equaliser' that would correct this imbalance as well as provide renewed legitimacy to the national idea that had been severely dented by Bangladesh's independence. Over the next two decades this search would lead to a fatal combination: Islam, the military and the nuclear bomb. Equally, in India the inexorable rise of Mrs Gandhi would

[25] Quoted in Kux, *India–Pakistan Negotiations*, p. 37.

eventually culminate in the destruction of the historic Congress Party and the spectacular growth of the Hindu Right.

India–Pakistan rivalry in a nuclear age

Bhutto's challenge after 1971 was not only to build a democratic Pakistan, but also to fashion a new foreign policy that would address Pakistan's weaknesses. Both the US and China had failed to provide direct support to the beleaguered Pakistan troops in East Pakistan; at best they limited their intervention to diplomatic manoeuvres. In the aftermath, Bhutto increasingly turned his attention to the Islamic world in order to forge a new vision for Pakistan. The Organisation of the Islamic Conference was hosted in Lahore (1974), and following the hike in oil prices after 1973, Pakistani professionals and workers provided essential manpower for the massive infrastructure projects in the Middle East – an involvement that led to large remittances to the Pakistan economy over the decades. These links were also strengthened by the successful testing of an atomic device by India (1974), an event which prompted Bhutto to commit Pakistan to construction of a nuclear bomb, repeating his comments made almost a decade earlier, that Pakistan would do so 'even if it meant eating grass'. Under the direction of Abdul Qadeer Khan, in the subsequent decades Pakistan's clandestine development of a nuclear device would lead to the establishment of complex networks across the Islamic and communist worlds.[26] By the mid-1980s there was a general perception that Pakistan had the capacity to build a nuclear device. The nature of this network was only fully revealed in 2004 when it became apparent that Khan was at the centre of a nuclear-proliferation programme that involved Pakistan, Libya, Iran and North Korea.

Bhutto's ability to carry through his reform programme was severely compromised by his turn to populism. In a brief period he succeeded in alienating both the left and right forces within Pakistan. Even his slogan of 'Islamic Socialism' proved wanting as he desperately attempted to rig the March 1977 elections. In the aftermath the army under General Zia-ul-Haq took control. The general promised to 'restore democracy within 100 days'; he stayed in office for almost eleven years.

Pakistan's second period of military rule (1977–1988) overlapped with the second Cold War which began with the Soviet invasion of Afghanistan in December 1979. Once again it became a frontline state, commanding Washington's attention and resources. From the early 1980s onwards,

---

[26] See G. Corera, *Shopping for Bombs: Nuclear Proliferation, Global Insecurity and the Rise and Fall of the A. Q. Khan Network* (Victoria: Scribe, 2006).

Pakistan secured $7 billion in economic and military aid,[27] enabling General Zia to further consolidate the 'insecurity state' by marginalising political forces, fighting the West's war against communism, and appeasing Islamists. The latter's accommodation within the regime was made possible by the efforts both to build legitimacy through a programme of Islamisation of the state and the encouragement of a *jihadi* culture – a militant Islamic struggle in Afghanistan (funded by US and Saudi Arabia) and the promotion of para-military groups in Pakistan against political opponents. This policy had a devastating impact in the province of Sindh and the city of Karachi (see chapter five) and was to leave a lasting legacy. Even the second phase of democratisation (1988–1999) was unable to reverse the Islamisation of the state, as weak governments competed with each other for the Islamic vote, while the military maintained control of defence and foreign policy. Indeed, in the post-Soviet withdrawal from Afghanistan and the collapse of the Soviet Union (1991), the military through its Inter-Services Intelligence agency (ISI) was able to successfully establish the Taliban regime in Afghanistan (1996) and engage some of the *jihadis* in the militancy that had broken out in Kashmir from the late 1980s onwards.

Islamisation in Pakistan had its parallel in India in the rise of the Hindu Right in the 1980s.[28] Like Bhutto, Mrs Gandhi also became a victim of political populism when she first succeeded to the helm of the Congress Party and then destroyed it through a process of de-institutionalisation – making her the focus of power. This process culminated in the Emergency (1975–1977) which suspended the constitution, and following her return to power in 1980, was marked by a lurch to the right in which Hinduism was seen as the new legitimising ideology for the Congress. In this about-turn, Mrs Gandhi and the Congress severed the traditional relationship with the minorities, making the Muslims, and, to some extent, the lower-caste groups, the new opponents. The entry of the Indian army into the Golden Temple (1984), the Sikhs' holiest shrine, marked the decline of Congress's traditional relationship with India's minorities. Mrs Gandhi was to pay the price with her life.[29]

Despite his youthful promise, Rajiv Gandhi continued with the disastrous policies of his mother. In Punjab, these polices further alienated the Sikhs, leading to a militancy that lasted almost a decade and cost nearly

---

[27] Thornton, 'Pakistan', p. 179.
[28] Iftikhar H. Malik, *Jihad, Hindutva and the Taliban: South Asia at the Crossroads* (Karachi: Oxford University Press, 2005).
[29] For the background to the Punjab crisis, see Gurharpal Singh, *Ethnic Conflict in India: A Case-Study of Punjab* (Basingstoke: Macmillan, 2000).

25,000 lives. In Jammu and Kashmir, he condoned the systematic rigging of elections in 1987 that triggered the insurgency that claimed 60,000 lives. Above all, he re-opened the case over the disputed mosque in Ayodhya (1986) which provided the basis for mobilisation by the Hindu Right – the Bharatiya Janata Party (BJP) and its associated organisations. From a party with six MPs in the national parliament in 1984, the BJP was catapulted to national governing party in 1998 (in coalition with minor parties). *Hindutva* (promotion of Hindu values) was no longer a marginal force: the destruction of the Ayodhya mosque (1992) by Hindu militants symbolised the emergence of a 'new India', one which was defined by its aggressive communalism against Muslims and other minorities.[30]

Heightened religious mobilisation in both countries in the 1980s and 1990s added a new dimension to the India–Pakistan rivalry. It coincided with the rise of militancy in Kashmir from 1987, and almost brought the two countries to the brink of a nuclear exchange in 1990.[31] It also deeply embittered relations following the anti-Muslim riots that broke out throughout India (1992–1993) after the destruction of the Ayodhya mosque by Hindu militants. India regularly accused Pakistan of sponsoring terrorism in Jammu and Kashmir, Punjab and the north-eastern states. Pakistan in turn often pointed an accusing finger at Indian intervention in Karachi and Sindh, while exploiting the new human rights agenda to highlight Indian atrocities in Jammu and Kashmir. These bitter exchanges were conducted against mounting global concern about nuclear 'rogue states' in a post-Cold War world. US efforts to rein in India and Pakistan into the Nuclear Proliferation Treaty (NPT) and the Comprehensive Test Ban Treaty (CTBT), proved fruitless as first India demonstrated its nuclear capability in May 1998, and then, a week later, Pakistan followed with its own tests.[32] The logic of Partition had ended in nuclearisation: henceforth the fate of the two nations could no longer be separate.

In the aftermath of the nuclear tests, both countries faced intense international pressure to begin a dialogue to resolve outstanding differences. In February 1999, the Indian prime minister, Atal Bihari Vajpayee, travelled by bus to Lahore, where he was greeted by his counterpart, Nawaz Sharif. In a meeting resonant with symbolism the two leaders agreed to begin a 'composite dialogue' 'about all issues, including

---

[30] Thomas Blum Hansen, *The Saffron Wave: Democracy and Hindu Nationalism in Modern India* (New Delhi: Oxford University Press, 2001).

[31] See Devin Hagerty, 'Nuclear Deterrence in South Asia: The 1990 Indo-Pakistani Crisis', *International Security* 20:3 (1995/6), pp. 79–114.

[32] See Hilary Synnott, *The Causes and Consequences of South Asia's Nuclear Tests*, Adelphi Papers 332 (Oxford University Press, 1999).

Kashmir, and to initiate a series of nuclear-related discussions and confidence-building measures'.[33]

However, the ink on the Lahore Declaration was hardly dry before India and Pakistan were embroiled in a new conflict in Kashmir.[34] During the winter months, the Pakistan army in the high peaks of the Kargil sector had succeeded in building bunkers across the LOC. When in spring the Indians discovered these incursions, which could potentially cut off the road to Leh, India launched an assault on these positions. Pakistan maintained the fiction that the intruders were 'Kashmiri freedom fighters', but India won the international argument by mobilising support against Pakistan which included open opposition to the course of Pakistani policy by the US and China. Internationally isolated, Prime Minister Nawaz Sharif had to accept a humiliating withdrawal of 'Kashmiri militants' across the LOC that was demanded by President Bill Clinton. This retreat also sealed Nawaz Sharif's fate. In October 1999 he was overthrown in a military coup that brought General Pervez Musharraf to power and introduced the third phase of military rule in Pakistan.[35]

Perhaps the most serious confrontation between India and Pakistan occurred in 2001–2002 (noted above) when, following a terrorist attack on the Indian parliament by militants trained in Pakistan, the Indian government ordered a full-scale mobilisation of its land, air and sea forces. Despite General Musharraf's statements that he would curtail the flow of militants into Kashmir in response to Indian mobilisation, in May 2002 the militants struck an Indian army camp in Kashmir killing children, women and army personnel. In response, Vajpayee made a sabre-rattling tour of the province and urged the field troops to prepare for a 'decisive battle'.

India's war rhetoric gained further momentum with widespread suggestions of a 'clinical strike' against militants' camps in Pakistani-administered Kashmir. Musharraf replied to these threats by testing missiles capable of delivering nuclear weapons deep into Indian territory. He also reaffirmed that in the event of an Indian attack he would not rule out the use of nuclear weapons. By the end of May it appeared that India and Pakistan were sleepwalking into a nuclear exchange that threatened to wipe out most of northern India and Pakistan with a minimum level of casualties estimated at 25 million.

---

[33] Kux, *India–Pakistan Negotiations*, p. 41.

[34] Paradoxically, the possession of nuclear weapons by India and Pakistan has made localised conflicts more likely; see Michael Krepon, *The Stability–Instability Paradox* (Washington, DC: Stimson Centre, 2004), at www.stimson.org/pub.cfm?id=370.

[35] For an insider account of these developments, see Strobe Talbott, *Engaging India: Diplomacy, Democracy and the Bomb* (Washington, DC: Brookings Institute, 2004).

In the event, the two states were brought back from the brink by the strong-arm tactics employed by the US. The campaign against the 'War on Terror' in east Afghanistan, the need to keep the Pakistan regime on board, and to assuage Indian anger – all led to intense US and international diplomatic pressure on Musharraf to relent in his support for Kashmiri militants operating from Pakistan. It now appears that an informal understanding was reached between the US and Pakistan in which Musharraf agreed to control the infiltration of militants across the LOC in return for a promise that the US would lead a diplomatic initiative on Kashmir. India also agreed to de-escalate the military build-up once it was able to test Musharraf's assurance that militant infiltration would be controlled. One notable feature of the crisis was indirect diplomacy: warnings to western citizens to leave India and Pakistan had a profound psychological impact on informed public opinion in both countries, leading to calls, from leading businessmen in particular, to reflect seriously on the economic implications of the war rhetoric.[36]

From the nuclear brink to a composite dialogue

The road from India–Pakistan confrontation to dialogue was built not only by US pressure but also by the attempts on the life of General Musharraf by Afghan and Kashmiri militants. This led to the serious reappraisal within Pakistan of the militant–military nexus that had spawned the *jihadi* culture. In February 2004, after the South Asian Association for Regional Cooperation (SAARC) meeting, the two countries restarted the 'composite dialogue' agreed at the Lahore summit. This process was to include eight distinct 'baskets' that ranged from minor territorial disputes (e.g. barrage over the Jhelum river and Sir Creek) to significant issues such as the Siachin Glacier, economic and commercial ties, and Kashmir. Since then several full rounds have been held, with the relations between the two countries improving further as result of 'cricket diplomacy', the opening of a bus services across the LOC in Kashmir, and the deepening of cultural and economic ties that have led to the flourishing of trade across the Wagha border in Punjab. Opportunities for economic cooperation, moreover, have further expanded with the rapid growth rate of the Indian economy and a Pakistani willingness to act as conduit for an Iran–India land gas line for India's growing energy needs. Overall, these initiatives have created a new sense of confidence, a belief that the peace

---

[36] Gurharpal Singh, 'On the Nuclear Precipice: India, Pakistan and the Kashmir Crisis', *OpenDemocracy* (6 August 2002), www.opendemocracy.net/conflict-india_pakistan/article_194.jsp.

process is now 'irreversible' – a sentiment that is regularly embedded in joint statements – and reflect new realities in which post-1947 borders cannot be 'erased' but can be made 'irrelevant'.

While the 'composite dialogue' since 2004 has undoubtedly contributed to lowering the tension between the two neighbours, it remains to be seen whether it can lead to a breakthrough on major issues such as Kashmir. Musharraf has made it clear that Kashmir is a 'core issue' while other differences are 'just aberrations, minor differences of opinion which can be resolved'.[37] Progress has been remarkably slow, with India rejecting Pakistani proposals for joint control of the valley, while the Pakistan side suspects that India is content to allow talks and negotiations to continue without making substantive concessions. There is a likelihood that the 'composite dialogue', like other peace processes – Northern Ireland and Israel and Palestine – will be punctuated by serious setbacks. As analysts have frequently cautioned, the asymmetrical nature of the rivalry between India and Pakistan has condemned the two countries 'to live in a situation resembling a permanent Cuban missile crisis'.[38] When this is placed in the context of the general pattern of enduring rivalries in modern history, the outcome of the India–Pakistan case is even more unpromising. As Geller concludes, 'The origins of this rivalry, its intensity of violence, the failure of both mediation and conflict management, and its persistence all point towards future confrontations.'[39] In short, it appears that India and Pakistan could remain 'trapped in history'.

One further reason why such confrontations are likely is the persistence of Pakistan as an 'insecurity state' dominated by the army. Democracies rarely, if at all, go to war.[40] However, the weak process of democratisation in Pakistan has created a structural imbalance between the military and other state and civil institutions. This imbalance, as we have seen, arose from the Pakistani elite's perception of insecurity at the state's birth; it continues now as the *raison d'être* of an institutionalised military predominance over a quasi-democratic polity. Long-term peace-building between India and Pakistan will, therefore, also require thoroughgoing democratisation in Pakistan with a substantially reduced role in politics for the armed forces. Current developments, on the other hand, suggest

---

[37] Quoted in Victoria Schofield, *Kashmir in Conflict: India, Pakistan and the Unending War* (London: I. B. Taurus, 2003), p. 222.
[38] Mario E. Carranza, 'Avoiding a Nuclear Catastrophe: Nuclear Arms Control after the 2002 India–Pakistan Crisis', *International Politics* 40:3 (2003), pp. 313–14.
[39] Geller, 'The India–Pakistan rivalry', p. 81.
[40] The one example that is cited is the Kargil conflict between India and Pakistan in 1999. Given that the conflict was initiated by the Pakistan army, it is doubtful whether the Pakistan regime under Nawaz Sharif can be classified as democratic, let alone liberal democratic.

that this is highly improbable, and that in the medium term the Taliban insurgency in Afghanistan and Pakistan will continue to consolidate the Pakistani army's role in the 'insecurity state', while it is only the fear of two-front war (in Afghanistan and Kashmir) that has led Pakistan to pursue a policy of *détente* with India.

Reasons for hope

Whatever the underlying causes of Pakistan's engagement in the 'composite dialogue', there are several reasons for suggesting that the two nations might escape from the 'trap of history' which has imprisoned them since August 1947. The geo-political divisions during the Cold War, which reinforced the India–Pakistan rivalry, no longer hold sway. Pakistan's foreign policy remains closely tied to the US, and though this relationship has waxed (1950s, 1980s and after 2001) and waned (1970s and 1990s), it remains the US's sheet 'anchor' in this region. Since the late 1990s, however, India has begun to emerge as a potential strategic partner for the US. Its economic growth, trading relations with the US, and competition with China have all contributed to a new approach by both nations that has recently been best reflected in the nuclear energy deal between the two governments; and though this increasing proximity may well be a long-term strategy by the US of 'engaging India' in a greater regional role, from an Indian perspective it has helped to moderate Pakistani adventurism (1999 and 2001–2002). In sum, the US interests lie in moderating, not exacerbating differences between India and Pakistan.

At the same time, alternative policy options for a more aggressive posture by Pakistan against India are seriously limited. The 'War on Terror' in Afghanistan and within Pakistan has left it exposed on two fronts. China, Pakistan's traditional ally, like the US, has acted as a moderating force and is also engaged in its own rapprochement with India. The support of the Islamic bloc, moreover, is firmly with the 'moderate camp' – though given the instability in Pakistan and Afghanistan the possibility of Pakistan becoming a member of a 'rogue' nuclear Islamic club (Iran, Syria) cannot be completely overlooked. Despite these forebodings, the general consensus is that external developments have helped to moderate more extreme policy options available to India and Pakistan in managing their rivalry.

Notwithstanding the sharp ideological differences between the two countries, they also possess substantial experience in working together. In the immediate aftermath of Partition, for instance, cooperation between administrators in West and East Punjab hastened the process of resettlement through the exchange of revenue records. There were also,

as we have seen in earlier chapters, a number of Inter-Dominion conferences which discussed such issues as evacuee property and the recovery
of abducted women. Perhaps the most notable example of such cooperation is the Indus Waters Treaty (1960) which marked the final agreement
on the vexed issue of sharing of river waters in Punjab. Among the
reasons cited for the treaty's success were the willingness of India and
Pakistan to 'address the issue as a technical problem', the World Bank's
creative thinking, and the international community's 'general financial
support'.[41] The way the negotiations were conducted and the commitment of the two sides to agree to a solution provided by a third party
contributed immeasurably to the final outcome.[42] Although it is perhaps
over-optimistic to see the treaty as a successful model for conflict resolution, the treaty-making process holds invaluable lessons for future India
and Pakistan negotiations.[43]

The prospect of deepening economic ties between India and Pakistan
also holds out the promise of greater economic integration in the region
and could also be the driver of political change. Since Partition, much of
the trade between the two countries has been routed through the Gulf
countries, fuelling the growth of Sheikhdoms such as Dubai. The beginning of the 'composite dialogue' in 2004 coincided with implementation
by the South Asian Association for Regional Cooperation (SAARC) of the
South Asian Free Trade Area (SAFTA) agreement.[44] As a result direct
trade between the two countries has witnessed rapid growth from us$300
million in 2003/4 to $1 billion in 2006/7.[45] There are some projections
that this figure could rise to $10 billion by the end of the decade, with
tremendous potential for growth in the future. Businessmen and politicians have spoken optimistically about reconnecting the region for global
trade through historic land routes while exploiting new and emerging
opportunities where the comparative cost advantage would benefit both
nations. Pakistan's readiness, for example, to meet the increasing energy
demand in India by facilitating the overland gas pipeline from Iran demonstrates a new flexibility as well as the potential to earn significant
revenue from this joint venture. Similarly, the widening of trade has also
revived regional economies. The impact of the new flow of goods and
people across the Radcliffe Line at Wagha has been palpable, with the city
of Amritsar enjoying renewed importance as a trading and religious

[41] Kux, *India–Pakistan Negotiations*, p. 24.   [42] Kux, *India–Pakistan Negotiations*, p. 24.
[43] See, R. K. Arora, *The Indus Water Treaty Regime* (New Delhi: Mohit Publications, 2007).
[44] Bibek Debroy, *The South Asia Free Trade Agreement (SAFTA); With a Focus on India–Pakistan Trade* (New Delhi: PHDCCI, 2006).
[45] See Nisha Taneja, 'India–Pakistan Trade', Working paper no.182. ICRIER (June 2006), www.icrier.org/pdf/WP182.pdf and *Tribune* (Chandigarh), 28 March 2006.

centre. Both Lahore and Amritsar have major international airports which could also provide the gateway for diasporic Punjabis to exploit new opportunities for investment in their homelands – a constituency that is increasingly being courted by regional politicians who seek new sources of funding for internal investment.

The Musharraf regime might well have decided to commercially engage with India not only to support economic reconstruction in Pakistan but also to ensure that Pakistan maintains some leverage on India's economic growth in the future and retains some capacity to be a permanent thorn in India's side. Given the example of China's ability to neutralise the Tibet issue in recent years, this outlook might also reflect the fears that India might well pocket the economic concessions arising from better trade relations but remain reluctant to change the status quo in Kashmir. Nonetheless it is reasonable to assume that greater economic integration will also bring greater economic dependence, and as the role of the business lobby in both countries demonstrated during the crisis of 2001–2002, it might also generate new priorities that require resolving existing disputes.

Finally, since the mid-1980s the India–Pakistan rivalry has produced a notable grassroots lobby through 'people-to-people contact' that has promoted better relations between the two 'distant neighbours'.[46] Started as an initiative of professionals, over the years the people-to-people contact programmes have grown to include NGOs, professional organisations and schools. These contacts have increased remarkably in the period since 2004 with some official encouragement in fields of culture, academia, media entertainment and sport. Although some unnecessary regulations are still in force, visas for travel to both countries have been significantly eased as the logic of economic integration suggests that it will gradually be accompanied by greater flows of people. People-to-people contacts from below have provided a major boost to confidence-building measures in both countries. For example, among other factors, it was the people-to-people contacts after the terrorist bombing of trains in Mumbai in July 2006 that enabled the 'composite dialogue' to remain on track.

Conclusion

After Independence the historic rivalry between the Congress and the Muslim League became transformed into a bitter inter-state 'enduring conflict'. This outcome was largely unanticipated by Jinnah or Nehru who

---

[46] See Ranabir Samaddar and Helmut Reifeld (eds), *Peace as Process: Reconciliation and Conflict Resolution in South Asia* (New Delhi: Manohar, 2001).

had hoped that the two dominions would eventually develop fraternal relations enabling them to overcome the initial hostility of separation and division. However the unexpected mass transfers of population and the armed conflict over Jammu and Kashmir created the bases of an 'enduring conflict'. This rivalry has served to reinforce the ideological foundations of the two states, making the resolution of the Jammu and Kashmir dispute intractable. It was also intensified by Pakistan's induction into the Cold War, and has contributed significantly to the emergence of Pakistan as an 'insecurity state' that is dominated by the army that perpetually distorts democratisation. Likewise in India, the rivalry continues to reinforce the politics of the Hindu Right while requiring the authoritarian management of peripheral regions such as Jammu and Kashmir, Punjab and the north-east.

In one respect, the unresolved dispute over Jammu and Kashmir highlights that the nation- and state-building in both India and Pakistan has failed in erasing the 'third option', preferred by those who did not share the Congress's or Muslim League's visions of nationalism, nor desired to accede to the two dominions of India and Pakistan and wanted to exercise their right of self-determination – an option that was foreclosed by Britain. It also highlights the limitations of highly centralised nation- and state-building projects in the two countries after 1947 where the region continues to be the key critical political and social unit. Nuclearisation notwithstanding, contemporary developments suggest that the long-term trends in South Asia point towards the future pre-eminence of the regions. If these trends do, indeed, take hold, then they are also likely to call into question further the legitimacy of the Partition itself. It remains to be seen whether in the medium term the Partition will be interpreted as an aberration or a turning point. At least, almost sixty years after the event both India and Pakistan are beginning to think about escaping from the 'trap of history' that it constructed.

Conclusion

This volume has examined the causes, consequences and contestations surrounding the 1947 division of the Indian subcontinent. It has been set against the conventional Punjab-centric understandings and the tendency to see Partition as an event which marked a closure in August 1947, without significant longer-term consequences. The events in Punjab were dramatic and tragic, but they do not encapsulate the entire story. Indeed, they also largely overlook the long-term legacies of Partition that still continue to influence individual and community lives and relations between the two successor states of the British Raj, a fact most evident in the diplomatic relations between the nuclear-armed 'distant neighbours' and their opposite understandings of Partition itself. In this sense, historically at least, the consequences of the division of 1947 remain part of the long transition to normalcy by India and Pakistan.[1]

Naturally, official nationalisms in both countries have sought to appropriate the event in their own terms. In Pakistan it is played down in preference to the historical construction of national origins of the Muslim community. In India, in contrast, the emphasis has traditionally been on Independence with undertones of national loss. The violence which surrounded the division of India is similarly understood in diametrically opposed ways: either as a singular event or as merely an especially bloody chapter in a longer history of Hindu and Muslim conflict.

Until the 1980s it was the creative writers who provided the more searching reflections on the human and political consequences of the 1947 division. Qurrat ul Ain Haider's novel, *River of Fire*,[2] for instance, painted Partition on the vast canvas of Indian history and reflected on the questions which still dominate understandings of its causes: Were the

---

[1] For a recent example which underpins the reading of Partition as a drawn-out process, see Vazira Fazila-Yacoobali Zamindar, *The Long Partition and the Making of Modern South Asia: Refugees, Boundaries, Histories* (New York: Columbia University Press, 2007).

[2] Qurrat ul Ain Haider, *River of Fire*, translated from the original Urdu by the author (Karachi: Oxford University Press, 1999).

events of 1947 an inevitable destiny for Indian Muslims? Or were they, in some sense, an aberration which disrupted the longer-term flows of Indian history?

Answers to such crucial questions have always been troubling. Almost all interpretations of Partition, as we have shown, are shot through with some degree of political intent. A major thrust of recent scholarship on the subject has been to rescue history from politics, whether these are the politics of national, religious or ethnic ideology. These people-centred accounts have added immeasurably to our understanding of the human tragedy of the events that unfolded before and after 1947 as well as opening new departures for research where the human experience is fore-grounded, deconstructed and contextualised. As we have seen, these accounts have enriched the reading of the tragic events which flowed from August 1947 and have provided a necessary corrective to state-centric and high politics perspectives that have dominated the Partition historiography.

Nevertheless these accounts, invaluable though they are, also carry the risks of their own biases and silences. This turn in academic scholarship has been accompanied by fragmentary and sometimes disparate discourses which inhibit a broader appreciation of the complexities of causation and the comparative insights that can be derived from such analysis.[3] In short, these perspectives 'self-consciously evade the perspective of the state' and in doing so 'miss the point of what Partition was about';[4] namely, as a conflict for state power by competing nationalisms.

As such Partition also cannot be merely understood as 'the parting gift' of British rule in India who, it must be recognised, remained 'reluctant partitionists' right until the end.[5] Its background was rooted in a Muslim-rights discourse which intersected with increasing democratisation from the 1920s onwards as representative governments emerged in the provinces and more and more power was devolved to them, most notably after the Government of India Act (1935) that created the template for a united, federal India of the provinces. The demand for a separate state was the culmination of a search for a guarantee where earlier measures

---

[3] The work of Vazira Zamindar is a notable exception. It utilises both oral and documentary sources to examine the human experiences of migration and the state's management of this. She also reflects on the parallels between the subcontinent's legislation on evacuee property and that of the Israeli state with respect to the Palestinian Arabs. Zamindar, *The Long Partition*, pp. 130–1.

[4] Sunil Khilnani, *The Idea of India* (New Delhi: Penguin, 1998), p. 202.

[5] For a recent, popular Indian nationalist restatement of British design, see Narendra Singh Sarila, *The Shadow of the Great Game: The Untold Story of India's Partition* (London: Constable and Robinson, 2005).

such as separate electorates had been found wanting and were cruelly exposed by the experience of Congress provincial rule from 1937–1939. It is unlikely that the division would have occurred without this critical development, the British attempts to counterbalance the non-cooperating Congress during the Second World War, and above all, the political leadership of the Muslim League by Jinnah. But then the choices made by the Congress leadership from 1945 to 1947 were also to prove critical, if not fatal. The decolonisation timetable imposed by Mountbatten from March 1947 also limited these options against the backdrop of rising flames of communal violence.

It is important to remember that the Pakistan movement was led by the Muslim secular elite drawn primarily from the minority areas of population and the *ulama* remained largely aloof from the struggle. Islamic symbols were used as the campaign reached its climax to galvanise support in the future Pakistan heartland, especially during the provincial elections in February 1946. The hitherto largely constitutional campaign provoked a wave of violence which swept across north India when 'Direct Action' was launched by the Muslim League in Calcutta in August 1946. The Punjab at first remained immune because of its power-sharing Unionist ministry. Direct action in the province along with the British announcement that they would leave India by June 1948 led to the resignation of Khizr Tiwana and the unfolding of an immense human tragedy. The Congress and the British administration reluctantly saw Partition as an alternative to civil war. In return the Hindus and Sikhs of Punjab and Bengal demanded the division of their provinces as their price for evacuating the Pakistan areas. Partition was thus not foisted on reluctant Indian political leaders but in large measure willed into existence by them. As Nehru was to acknowledge in 1960, 'The truth is that we were tired men .... We saw the fires burning in Punjab and heard everyday of killings. The plan for partition offered us a way out and we took it.'[6]

Remarkably, despite the local population movements and preparations for violence across north India during the final year of British rule, officials and politicians alike were taken aback by the magnitude of the transfer of populations that occurred in the immediate aftermath of Independence. Subsequently, myths of the refugee experience and of the state response were constructed around events in the Punjab. The post-Independence states emphasised their role in the rehabilitation process by highlighting the heroic and improvised efforts to feed, clothe, house and find work for the millions of displaced citizens. As we have seen in chapter four, such accounts

---

[6] Quoted in Ranabir Samaddar, *The Politics of Dialogue: Living under the Geopolitical Histories of War and Peace* (Aldershot: Ashgate, 2004), p. 24.

were often at variance with experience of the refugees who had to fend for themselves. The whole resettlement experience was far more complicated and drawn out than the state accounts would suggest, and they have largely effaced the prejudicial impact of evacuee property laws on north Indian Muslims.[7] Official accounts in fact disguised immense regional variations in patterns of refugee settlement and their differing experience by class, caste, gender and linguistic group. Population flows continued in Bengal throughout the 1950s and beyond and clearly the refugees from East Bengal were probably the Partition's chief victims – a fact which has received little recognition outside of the province.

Paradoxically, the Muslim League, which had campaigned for provincial autonomy as a safeguard for Muslim rights in a united India, reversed this stance once Pakistan was realised. The perceived threat from India lay behind this sudden *volte face*. Democratic consolidation, already put at risk by weak institutions and a threatening geo-political environment, was further undermined. Nation- and state-building after 1947 was to be constructed on the edifice that denied pluralism, regionalism and ethnic diversity with devastating results for relations between the centre and ethnic minorities. The Bengalis were not only geographically distant but had to endure the marginalisation of their language and culture in an Urdu-dominated national life. Uneven economic development and exclusion from the army and the bureaucracy compounded the situation, turning East Pakistan (Bengal) into a colony of West Pakistan. The emergence of Bangladesh in 1971 following civil war and Indian military intervention was thus not the inevitable inheritance of Partition; it was mainly the product of a flawed nation- and state-building enterprise shaped by it. With the creation of Bangladesh, the political architecture in the east put in place by Radcliffe lay in ruins. It had lasted less than a quarter of a century.

The subcontinent has changed dramatically in other ways during the six decades since Independence. Both India and Pakistan are more populous, prosperous and powerful than might have been imagined in 1947. Both countries possess nuclear weapons – the ultimate symbol of the contemporary sovereign nation-state. India since economic liberalisation in 1991 is rapidly emerging as an economic powerhouse that might rival China in the dash for growth in the early twenty-first century. While questions may be raised concerning the environmental and even political sustainability of the Indian 'economic miracle' of the past decade, its

[7] Zamindar, *The Long Partition*, pp. 134–49.

achievements are visible in the rise of a consumerist middle class which uneasily shares power in shifting coalitions with representatives of the backward castes and the Dalits who have been empowered by state-reservation policies and democratic participation.[8] The Pakistan middle class, in contrast, is much smaller, and is overshadowed by the power of the feudal elite who, along with the mainstream representatives of the *ulama*, form the civilian component of the army-dominated political establishment. The increased Islamisation in Pakistan society and polity from 1971 onwards has resulted in the unfolding of developments that have, arguably, led to 9/11 and the current 'War on Terror'.[9] It remains to be seen whether in retrospect 1971 or 1991 will be considered more significant landmarks in the modern history of the subcontinent than 1947.

This volume has argued that the legacy of Partition still looms over contemporary India and Pakistan. The relations between the neighbours are anchored in the understandings of 1947 and the uses to which they have been put in the cause of state- and nation-building. In India, as we have seen, the emergence of a centralised secular state in response to 1947 led to the framing of political movements based on religion in terms of communalism, and thereby facilitated the rise of *Hindutva* from the 1980s onwards. Similarly, in Pakistan, the idea of a state for Muslims has been strongly challenged by powerful constituencies that demand its logical fulfilment – an Islamic state.

Indian and Pakistani policies towards ethno-linguistic and regional demands in the peripheral regions, moreover, illustrate the contemporary presence of these troublesome Partition legacies. At best they have sown deep distrust; at worst, they have spilled over into quasi-genocidal state violence since 1947 (Bengal, Jammu and Kashmir, Punjab, Sindh). Both states' inability to manage these regions reflects an underlying unease about the failure to convert the 1947 division into an enduring settlement. It is also an uncomfortable reminder of the continued persistence of the 'third way'. In Jammu and Kashmir and Punjab (India), Sindh, Azad Kashmir and the north-eastern states (India), important remnants of ethno-regional nationalist movements, remain unreconciled to the 1947 settlement and continue to harbour self-determination aspirations beneath the surface calm of 'normalcy'. And though secular, long-term trends towards regionalisation are evidently in their favour, the potential

[8] See Christophe Jaffrelot, *India's Silent Revolution: The Rise of the Lower Castes* (London: Hurst, 2003); *The BSP in Uttar Pradesh: Party of the Dalits or of the Bahujans – or catch-all-party?* Occasional paper No. 2 (Cambridge: Centre of South Asian Studies, 2005).
[9] Sarila argues that the roots of 9/11 lie in the Partition, *The Shadow of the Great Game*, p. 11.

danger that these movements hold for the very idea of modern India and Pakistan is likely to ensure that their aspirations will remain largely frustrated.

Finally, it is now increasingly recognised that partitions provide a blunt instrument for managing ethno-religious conflict. India's division, along with that of Ireland, Palestine and Cyprus, belong to a rare category of twentieth-century partitions that actually qualify to be coded as such – in contrast to the recent revival of the concept in the post-Cold War era.[10] Such divisions have proved to be much more violent than their designers anticipated; and in the case of India and Pakistan the late colonial political conflict between the Congress and the Muslim League has been transformed into an inter-state rivalry between two nuclear-armed nations. It remains a great 'if' of history whether the Partition could have been avoided. Certainly there is plenty of evidence that both the Congress and Muslim League leadership were aware of some of the methods of political engineering – such as power-sharing, special rights, federalism – that have worked successfully in contemporary multi-religious, multi-ethnic and multi-linguistic societies.[11] The real unbridgeable gulf appears to have been between the latent confederalism of the Lahore Resolution in 1940 and in Jinnah's acceptance of the Cabinet Mission proposals, on the one hand, and Congress's determination to pursue a centralised, united India, even at the cost of vivisection of its Muslim-majority territories, on the other.

Comparative evidence also suggests that partitions are not easily reversed.[12] External partitions, as in India, imposed along 'fundamental lines of hatred' among proto-nationalist religious communities provide a very high threshold for reversibility, though this threshold might be reduced by geo-political factors or secular trends such as changes in demography. Current developments between India and Pakistan suggest that the two nations are beginning to look beyond the trap of history that Partition has constructed. As SARRC begins to resurrect some of the political and economic framework of the Cabinet Mission, while the two nations edge towards a permanent solution to the Jammu and Kashmir dispute, the borders between them might not be erased, but could become less relevant. What happens in the next decade will be crucial in determining whether Partition was a turning point or periodic episode in the modern history of South Asia.

---

[10] O'Leary, 'Analysing Partition', pp. 1–23.
[11] See I. Talbot, 'Back to the Future? The Punjab Unionist Model of Consociational Democracy for Contemporary India and Pakistan', *International Journal of Punjab Studies* 3, 1 (January–June 1996), pp. 65–75.
[12] See O'Leary, 'Analysing Partition'.

Select bibliography

Ahmad, Shahid, 'Dilhi ki Bipta', in M. Shirin (ed.), *Zulmat-e-Neem Roze*, Karachi: no pub., 1990

Ahmed, Akbar S., *Jinnah, Pakistan and Islamic Identity: The Search for Saladin*, London: Routledge, 1997

Ahmed, Imtiaz, 'Political Economy of Communalism in Contemporary India', *Economic and Political Weekly* 19, 23 (1984), pp. 903–6

Ahmed, Ishtiaq, *State, Nation and Ethnicity in Contemporary South Asia*, London: Pinter, 1996

Aiyar, S., 'August Anarchy: The Partition Massacres in Punjab, 1947', *South Asia* 18 (1995), pp. 13–36

Alam, J., and S. Sharma, 'Remembering Partition', *Seminar* 461 (January 1998), pp. 71–4

Alavi, Hamza, 'Pakistan and Islam: Ethnicity and Ideology', in Fred Halliday and Hamza Alavi (eds), *State and Ideology in the Middle East and Pakistan*, New York: Monthly Review Press, 1987, pp. 64–111

Albiruni, A. H., *Makers of Pakistan and Modern Muslim India*, Lahore: Muhammad Ashraf, 1950

Ali, Chaudhri Muhammad, *The Emergence of Pakistan*, New York: Columbia University Press, 1967

Ali, Imran, 'Pakistan and the Continuing Dilemma of Inequality', unpublished paper presented at the conference on 'The Independence of India and Pakistan: Sixtieth Anniversary Reflections', University of Southampton, 17–20 July 2007

Ali, S. Mahmud, *The Fearful State: Power, People and Internal Wars in South Asia*, London: Zed Books, 1993

Ali, Tariq, *Can Pakistan Survive? The Death of a State*, Harmondsworth: Penguin, 1983

Amnesty International, *India: Torture, Rape and Death in Custody*, London: Amnesty International, 1992

Anand, Som, *Lahore: Portrait of a Lost City*, Lahore: Vanguard Books, 1998

Ansari, Sarah, *Life after Partition: Migration, Community and Strife in Sindh 1947–1962*, Karachi: Oxford University Press, 2005

Sufi Saints and State Power: The Pirs of Sind, 1843–1947, Cambridge University Press, 1992

Arora, R. K., *The Indus Water Treaty Regime*, New Delhi: Mohit Publications, 2007

Ashton, S. R., *British Policy towards the Indian States 1905–1939*, London: Curzon, 1982

Austin, Granville, *The Indian Constitution: Cornerstone of a Nation*, Oxford: Clarendon Press, 1966

Aziz, Mazhar, *Military Control: The Parallel State*, London: Routledge, 2008
'The Parallel State: Understanding Military Control in Pakistan', PhD dissertation, University of Nottingham, 2006

Bagchi, Jasodhara, and Subhoranjan Dasgupta, *The Trauma and Triumph: Gender and Partition in East Bengal*, Kolkata: Stree, 2003

Bahadur, Lal, *Struggle for Pakistan: Tragedy of the Triumph of Muslim Communalism in India, 1906–1947*, New Delhi: Sterling, 1988

Balagopal, K., 'Kashmir: Self-determination, Communal and Democratic Rights', *Economic and Political Weekly* (2 November 1997), pp. 2916–21

Baldwin, Shauna Singh, *What the Body Remembers*, London: Black Swan, 2001

Ballard, Roger, '*Panth, Kismet Dharma te Qaum*: Continuity and Change in Four Dimensions of Punjabi Religion', in Pritam Singh and Shinder Singh Thandi (eds.), *Globalisation and the Region: Explorations in Punjabi Identity*, Coventry: Association of Punjab Studies, pp. 7–38

Bandyopadhyay, Sekhar, 'Freedom and Its Enemies: The Politics of Transition in West Bengal, 1947–1949', *South Asia* n.s., 29, 1 (April 2006), pp. 43–68

Bartov, O. and P. Mack (eds), *In God's Name: Genocide and Religion in the Twentieth Century*, New York: Berghahn Books, 2001

Batabyal, Rakesh, *Communalism in Bengal: From Famines to Noakhali 1943–7*, New Delhi: Sage, 2005

Bayley, C. A., 'The Pre-History of "Communalism"? Religious Conflict in India 1700–1860', *Modern Asian Studies* 19, 1 (1993), pp. 3–43

Bhalla, Alok, *Stories about the Partition of India*, New Delhi: Indus, 1994

Bhattacharyya, H., 'Post-Partition Refugees and the Communists: A Comparative Study of West Bengal and Tripura', in Ian Talbot and Gurharpal Singh (eds), *Region and Partition: Bengal, Punjab and the Partition of the Subcontinent*, Karachi: Oxford University Press, 2000, pp. 325–46

Bose, Sugata, 'A Doubtful Inheritance: The Partition of Bengal in 1947', in D. A. Low (ed.), *The Political Inheritance of Pakistan*, London: Macmillan, 1991, pp. 130–43

Brass, P. R., 'Elite Groups, Symbol Manipulation and Ethnic Identity among the Muslims of South Asia', in David Taylor and Malcolm Yapp (eds), *Political Identity in South Asia*, London: Curzon Press, 1979, pp. 35–77
Ethnicity and Nationalism: Theory and Comparison, New Delhi: Sage, 1991
'India: Democratic Progress and Problems', in Selig S. Harrison, Paul H. Kreisberg and Dennis Kux (eds), *India and Pakistan: The First Fifty Years*, Cambridge University Press, 1999, pp. 23–44
Language, Religion and Politics in North India, Cambridge University Press, 1974
'The Partition of India and Retributive Genocide in the Punjab 1946–47: Means, Methods and Purposes', *Journal of Genocide Research* 5, 1 (2003), pp. 71–101
The Production of Hindu–Muslim Violence in Contemporary India, Seattle, WA: University of Washington, Press, 2003

The Theft of an Idol: Text and Context in the Representation of Collective Violence, Princeton University Press, 1997

'Victims, Heroes and Martyrs: Partition and the Problem of Memorialisation in Contemporary Sikh History', *Sikh Formations* 2, 1 (January 2006), pp. 17–31

Brown, Judith M., *Nehru. A Political Life*, New Haven, CT: Yale University Press, 2003

Burke, S. M., and Salim Al-Din Qureshi, *Quaid-i-Azam Mohammad Ali Jinnah: His Personality and His Politics*, Karachi: Oxford University Press, 1997

Butalia, Urvashi, 'Muslims and Hindus, Men and Women: Communal Stereotypes and the Partition of India', in T. Sarkar and U. Butalia (eds), *Women and the Hindu Right: A Collection of Essays*, New Delhi: Kali for Women, 1995, pp. 58–82

The Other Side of Silence. Voices from the Partition of India, New Delhi: Penguin, 1998

Campbell-Johnson, A., *Mission with Mountbatten*, London: Hamilton, 1985

Carranza, Mario, 'Avoiding a Nuclear Catastrophe: Nuclear Arms Control after the 2002 India–Pakistan Crisis', *International Politics* 40, 3 (2003), pp. 313–39

Chakrabarty, Bidyut (ed.), *Communal Identity in India: Its Construction and Articulation in the Twentieth Century*, New Delhi: Oxford University Press, 2003

Chakrabarti, Prafulla, *The Marginal Men: The Refugees and the Left Political Syndrome in West Bengal*, Kalyani: Lumiere Books, 1990

Chakravarty, Tapati, 'The Paradox of a Fleeting Presence: Partition and Bengali Literature', in S. Settar and Indira B. Gupta (eds), *Pangs of Partition: The Human Dimension*, vol. 2, New Delhi: Manohar, 2002, pp. 261–83

Chandra, Bipan, *Communalism in Modern India*, New Delhi: Viking, 1984

India's Struggle for Independence, Harmondsworth: Penguin, 1989

Chatterjee, N., 'The East Bengal Refugees. A Lesson in Survival', in Sukanta Chaudhuri, *Calcutta. The Living City*, vol. 2*: The Present and the Future*, New Delhi: Oxford University Press, 1999, pp. 70–8

Chatterji, Joya, *Bengal Divided. Hindu Communalism, and Partition 1932–1947*, Cambridge University Press, 1994

'Of Graveyards and Ghettos: Muslims in Partitioned West Bengal, 1947–1967', in Mushirul Hasan and Asim Roy (eds), *Living Together Separately: Cultural India in History and Politics*, New Delhi: Oxford University Press, 2005, pp. 222–50

'Right or Charity? The Debate over Relief and Rehabilitation in West Bengal in 1947–50', in Suvir Kaul (ed.), *The Politics of Memory: The Aftermath of the Division of India*, New Delhi: Permanent Black, 2001, pp. 74–110

The Spoils of Partition: Bengal and India, 1947–1967, Cambridge University Press, 2007

Chattopadhyay, Jayanti, 'Representing the Holocaust: The Partition in Two Bengali Plays', in S. Settar and Indira B. Gupta (eds), *Pangs of Partition: The Human Dimension*, vol. 2, New Delhi: Manohar, 2002, 301–13

Chaudhuri, Pranati, *Refugees in West Bengal. A Study of the Growth and Distribution of Refugee Settlements within the CMD*. Occasional Paper No. 55, Calcutta: Centre for Studies in Social Sciences, March 1983

Chester, Lucy, *On the Edge: Borders, Territory and Conflict in South Asia*, Manchester University Press, 2008

Chimni, B. S., 'The Geo-politics of Refugee Studies: A View from the South', *Journal of Refugee Studies* 11, 4, (1998), pp. 350–74

Cohen, S. P., 'State Building in Pakistan', in A. Banuaziz and M. Weiner (eds), *The State, Religion and Ethnic Politics: Pakistan, Iran and Afghanistan*, Lahore: Vanguard Books, 1987

Copland, Ian, 'The Master and the Maharajas: The Sikh Princes and the East Punjab Massacres of 1947', *Modern Asian Studies* 36, 3 (2002), pp. 657–704

Corbridge, Stuart, and John Harriss, *Reinventing India: Liberalisation, Hindu Nationalism and Popular Democracy*, Cambridge: Polity Press, 2000

Corera, Gordon, *Shopping for Bombs: Nuclear Proliferation, Global Insecurity and the Rise and Fall of the A. Q. Khan Network*, Victoria: Scribe, 2006

Damodaran, Vinita, *Broken Promises. Popular Protest, Indian Nationalism and the Congress Party in Bihar 1935–1946*, New Delhi: Oxford University Press, 1992

Darwin, John, *Britain and Decolonisation: The Retreat from Empire in the Post-war World*, Basingstoke: Macmillan, 1988

Das, Samir Kumar, 'Refugee Crisis. Responses of the Government of West Bengal', in Pradip Kumar Bose (ed.), *Refugees in West Bengal. Institutional Practices and Contested Identities*, Calcutta: Mahanirban Calcutta Research Group, 2000, pp. 7–48

Das, Suranjan, *Communal Riots in Bengal, 1905–1947*, New Delhi: Oxford University Press, 1991

Das, Veena, *Life and Words: Violence and the Descent into the Ordinary*, Berkeley, CA: University of California Press, 2007

and Ashis Nandy, 'Violence, Victimhood and Language of Silence', in Veena Das (ed.), *The Word and the World: Fantasy, Symbol, and Record*, New Delhi: Sage, 1986, pp. 177–90

Dasgupta, Anindita, 'Denial and Resistance: Sylheti Partition Refugees in Assam', *Contemporary South Asia* 10, 3 (2001), pp. 343–60

Dasgupta, J. B., *Jammu and Kashmir*, The Hague: Martinus Nijhoff, 1968

Datta, V. N., 'Amritsar: When Riots Shattered a Heritage', *The Sunday Tribune* (Chandigarh), 26 April 1998

'Interpreting Partition', in Amrik Singh (ed.), *The Partition in Retrospect*, New Delhi: Anamika, 2000, pp. 274–87

'Punjabi Refugees and Urban Development of Greater Delhi', in R. E. Frykenberg (ed.), *Delhi through the Ages: Essay on Urban History, Culture, and Society*, Delhi: Oxford University Press, 1986

De, S. L., and A. K. Bhattacharjee, *The Refugee Settlement in Sunderbans, West Bengal: A Socio-economic Survey*, Calcutta: no pub., 1972

Debroy, Bibek, *The South Asia Free Trade Agreement (SAFTA): With a Focus on India–Pakistan Trade*, New Delhi: PHDCCI, 2006

Dewey, Clive, 'The Rural Roots of Pakistani Militarism', in D. A. Low (ed.), *The Political Inheritance of Pakistan*, Basingstoke: Macmillan, 1991, pp. 255–83

Diwan, Chief Khalsa, *Amritsar. Happenings of 1947 Atrocities and Brief Notes*, Amritsar: n.d. (translated from Punjabi)

Dixit, J. N., *India–Pakistan in War and Peace*, London: Routledge, 2002

'Kashmir: The Contemporary Geo-political Implications for India and Regional Stability', paper presented at the School of Oriental and African Studies, London, 8 April 1994, unpublished, pp. 1–10.

Durrani, F. K., *The Meaning of Pakistan*, Lahore: Muhammad Ashraf, 1944

Fraser, Thomas G., *Partition in Ireland, India and Palestine. Theory and Practice*, London: Macmillan, 1984

French, Patrick, *Liberty or Death: India's Journey to Independence and Division*, London: Flamingo, 1998

Fukuyama, Francis, *The End of History and the Last Man*, Harmondsworth: Penguin, 1992

Gallagher, John, Gordon Johnson, Anil Seal, (eds), *Locality, Province and Nation: Essays on Indian Politics, 1870–1914*, Cambridge University Press, 1973

Geller, Daniel S., 'The India–Pakistan Rivalry: Prospects for War, Prospects for Peace', in T. V. Paul (ed.), *The India–Pakistan Conflict: An Enduring Rivalry*, Cambridge University Press, 2005, pp. 80–102

Ghosh, Papiya, *Partition and the South Asian Diaspora: Extending the Subcontinent*, London: Routledge, 2007

'Partition's Biharis', *Comparative Studies of South Asia, Africa and the Middle East* 17, 2 (1997), pp. 21–35

Gilmartin, David, *Empire and Islam. Punjab and the Making of Pakistan*, Berkeley, CA: California University Press, 1988

Goswami, Omkar, 'Calcutta's Economy 1918–1970: The Fall from Grace', in Sukanta Chaudhuri, *Calcutta. The Living City*, vol. 2: *The Present and the Future*, New Delhi: Oxford University Press, 1999, pp. 88–97

Government of India, *Millions on the Move: The Aftermath of Partition*, New Delhi: Ministry of Information, 1948

Government of West Punjab, *Note on the Sikh Plan*, Lahore: Government Printing Press, West Punjab, 1948

RSSS in Punjab, Lahore: Government Printing Press, West Punjab, 1948

The Sikhs in Action, Lahore: Government Printing Press, West Punjab, 1948

Gupta, A. K. (ed.), *Myth and Reality: The Struggle for Freedom in India 1945–47*, New Delhi: Manohar, 1987

Gupta, Dipankar, *The Context of Ethnicity: Sikh Identity in a Comparative Perspective*, Delhi: Oxford University Press, 1997

'The Indian Diaspora of 1947: The Political and Ethnic Consequences of the Partition with Special Reference to Delhi', in K. N. Panikkar (ed.), *Communalism in India. History, Politics and Culture*, New Delhi: Manohar, 1991, pp. 80–108

and Romila Thaper, 'Who Are the Guilty? Punishment and Confidence Building in Gujarat', *The Hindu* (Chennai) 2 April 2002

Gupta, S., *India Redefines its Role*, Oxford University Press, 1995

Hagerty, Devin, 'Nuclear Deterrence in South Asia: The 1990 Indo-Pakistani Crisis', *International Security* 20, 3 (1995/6), pp. 79–114

Hansen, Anders Bjorn, *Partition and Genocide. Manifestation of Violence in Punjab 1937–1947*, New Delhi: India Research Press, 2002

Haqqani, Husain, *Pakistan: Between Mosque and Military*, Washington, DC: Carnegie Endowment for International Peace, 2005

Harun-or-Rashid, *The Foreshadowing of Bangladesh: Bengal Muslim League and Muslim Politics, 1936–1947*, Dhaka: Asiatic Society of Bangladesh, 1987

Hasan, Mushirul (ed.), *India Partitioned. The Other Face of Freedom*, 2 vols, New Delhi: Lotus, 1995

(ed.), *India's Partition: Process, Strategy and Mobilization*, Delhi: Oxford University Press, 1994

(ed.), *Inventing Boundaries. Gender, Politics and the Partition of India*, New Delhi: Oxford University Press, 2000

Legacy of a Divided Nation. India's Muslims since Independence, New Delhi: Oxford University Press, 1997

A Man of Conscience: M. A. Ansari, the Congress and the Raj, Delhi: Manohar, 1987

Hassan, Mashkur, *Azaadhie ke Charaagh*, 3rd edn, Lahore: no pub., 1986.

Hitchens, C., 'The Perils of Partition', *Atlantic Monthly* (March 2003), pp. 99–107

Hodson, H. V., *The Great Divide: Britain–India–Pakistan*, London: Hutchinson, 1969

Horowitz, Donald L., *The Deadly Ethnic Riot*, Berkeley, CA: University of California Press, 2001

Howarth, T. B., *Prospect and Reality: Great Britain, 1945–1955*, London: Collins, 1985

Hutchins, F. G., *India's Revolution: Gandhi and the Quit India Movement*, Cambridge, MA: Harvard University Press, 1973

Jaffrelot, C., *The BSP in Uttar Pradesh: Party of the Dalits of the Bahujans- or catch-all- party?* Occasional Paper no. 2 , Cambridge: Centre of South Asian Studies, 2005

'The Hindu Nationalist Movement in Delhi. From 'Locals' to Refugees and towards Peripheral Groups?', in V. Dupont, E. Tarlo and D. Vidal (eds), *Delhi. Urban Space and Human Destinies*, New Delhi: Manohar, 2000, pp. 181–203

India's Silent Revolution: The Rise of the Lower Castes, London: Hurst, 2003

Jain, Girilal, *The Hindu Phenomenon*, New Delhi: UBSPD, 1994

Jalal, A., *Democracy and Authoritarianism in South Asia*, Cambridge University Press, 1995

'Nation, Reason and Religion. Punjab's Role in the Partition of India', *Economic and Political Weekly* (8 August 1998), pp. 2183–90

'Secularists, Subalterns and the Stigma of "Communalism". Partition Historiography Revisited', *Modern Asian Studies* 30, 3 (1996), pp. 681–9

The Sole Spokesman. Jinnah, the Muslim League and the Demand for Pakistan, Cambridge University Press, 1985

The State of Martial Rule: The Origins of Pakistan's Political Economy of Defence, Cambridge University Press, 1990

Jansson, Erland, *India, Pakistan or Pakhtunistan? The Nationalist Movements in the North-West Frontier Province, 1937–47*, Uppsala: Acta Universitas Upsaliensis, 1981

Jeffrey, Robin, *India's Newspaper Revolution: Capitalism, Politics and the Indian-language Press, 1977–97*, London: C. Hurst, 2000

What's Happening to India? Punjab, Ethnic Conflict, Mrs Gandhi's Death and the Test for Federalism, Basingstoke: Macmillan, 1986

Kabir, Humayn, *Muslim Politics, 1906–1942*, Calcutta: Gupta, Rahman, Gupta, 1943

Kamra, A. J., *The Prolonged Partition and Its Pogroms: Testimonies on Violence against Hindus in East Bengal 1946–64*, New Delhi: Voice of India, 2000

Kaul, S. (ed.), *The Partitions of Memory. The Afterlife of the Division of the Subcontinent*, New Delhi: Permanent Black, 2001

Kaur, Ravinder, 'Narratives of Settlement. Past, Present and Politics among Punjabi Migrants in Delhi', unpublished 2004 Ph.D. thesis, Roskilde University Centre, Denmark

Since 1947: Partition Narratives among Punjabi Migrants of Delhi, New Delhi: Oxford University Press, 2007

Kennedy, C. H., *Bureaucracy in Pakistan*, Karachi: Oxford University Press, 1987

Kepel, Gilles, *Jihad: The Trial of Political Islam*, London: I. B. Tauris, 2003

Khairi, Saeed R., *Jinnah Reinterpreted: The Journey from Indian Nationalism to Muslim Statehood*, Karachi: Oxford University Press, 1995

Khan, Nighat Said, 'Identity, Violence and Women: A Reflection on the Partition of India, 1947', in Nighat Said Khan, Rubina Saigol and Afiya Shehrbano Zia, *Locating the Self: Perceptions on Women and Multiple Identities*, Lahore: ASR Publications, 1994, pp. 157–71

Khan, Saleem Ullah, *The Journey to Pakistan. A Documentation on Refugees of 1947*, Islamabad: National Documentation Centre, 1993

Khan, Yasmin, *The Great Partition. The Making of India and Pakistan*, New Haven, CT, and London: Yale University Press, 2007

Khawaja, Iftikhar, *Jab Amritsar jal raha tha*, 9th edn, Lahore: no pub., 1995

Khilnani, Sunil, *The Idea of India*, London: Hamish Hamilton, 1997

Kholi, Atul, *India's Growing Crisis of Governability*, Cambridge University Press, 1990

Khosla, Gopal Das, *Memory's Gay Chariot: An Autobiography*, New Delhi: Allied Publishers, 1995

Stern Reckoning. A Survey of Events Leading up to and Following the Partition of India, New Delhi: Oxford University Press, 1989; new edn 1995

Kinnvall, Catrina, 'Nationalism, Religion and the Search for Chosen Traumas: Comparing Sikh and Hindu Identity Construction', *Ethnicities* 2, 1 (March 2002), pp. 79–106

Krepon, Michael, *The Stability–Instability Paradox*, Washington, DC: Stimson Centre, 2004

Kudaisya, Gyanesh, 'Divided Landscapes, Fragmented Identities. East Bengal Refugees and their Rehabilitation in India, 1947–79', in D. A. Low and Howard Brasted (eds), *Freedom, Trauma, Continuities: Northern India and Independence*, New Delhi: Sage, 1998, pp. 105–33

Kux, Dennis, *India–Pakistan Negotiations: Is Past Still a Prologue?*, Washington, DC: United States Institute for Peace, 2006

Louis, Wm Roger, *The British Empire in the Middle East 1945–51 Arab Nationalism, the United States and Postwar Imperialism*, Oxford: Clarendon, 1984

Low, D. A., and Howard Brasted (eds), *Freedom, Trauma, Continuities. Northern India and Independence*, New Delhi: Sage, 1998

Luthra, K. L., *Impact of Partition on Industries in Border Districts of East Punjab*, Board of Economic Inquiry 1, Ludhiana: East Punjab Printers, 1949

Mahajan, S. 'Congress and the Partition of Provinces', in Amrik Singh (ed.), *The Partition in Retrospect*, New Delhi: Animika Publishers, 2000, pp. 222–46

Independence and Partition: The Erosion of Colonial Power in India, New Delhi: Sage, 2000

Major, Andrew, 'The Chief Sufferes: Abduction of Women during the Partition of Punjab', in D. A. Low and Howard Brasted (eds), *Freedom, Trauma, Continuities: Northern India and Independence*, New Delhi: Sage, 1998, pp. 57–72

Malik, Hafeez, *Moslem Nationalism in India and Pakistan*, Washington, DC: Public Affairs Press, 1963

Malik, Iftikhar H., *Jihad, Hindutva and the Taliban: South Asia at the Crossroads*, Karachi: Oxford University Press, 2005

Maniruzzaman, T., *The Bangladesh Revolution and Its Aftermath*, Dhaka: Bangladesh Books International, 1980

Mansergh, Nicholas, E. W. R. Lumby and Penderel Moon (eds), *Constitutional Relations Between Britain and India: The Transfer of Power 1942–7*, 12 vols., London: HMSO, 1970–83, vol. 1: *The Cripps Mission, Jan. – April 1942*, 1970

vol. 2: *'Quit India', 30 April – 21 Sept. 1942*, London: HMSO, 1971

vol. 3: *Reassertion of Authority, Gandhi's Fast and the Succession to the Viceroyalty, 21 Sept. 1942 – 12 June 1943*, London: HMSO, 1971

vol. 4: *The Bengal Famine and the New Viceroyalty, 15 June 1943 – 31 Aug. 1944*, London: HMSO, 1973

vol. 6: *The Post-war Phase: New Moves by the Labour Government, 1 Aug. 1945 – 22 March 1946*, London: HMSO, 1976

Mansergh, Nicholas, and Penderel Moon (eds), *The Simla Conference, Background and Proceedings, 1 Sept. 1944 – 28 July 1945*, vol. 5, London: HMSO, 1974

(eds) *The Cabinet Mission, 23 March – 29 June 1946*, vol. 7, London: HMSO, 1977

The Interim Government, 3 July – 1 Nov. 1946, vol. 8, London: HMSO, 1979

The Fixing of a Time Limit, 4 Nov. 1946 – 22 March 1947, vol. 9, London: HMSO, 1980

The Mountbatten Viceroyalty, Formulation of a Plan, 22 March – 30 May 1947, vol. 10, London: HMSO, 1981

The Mountbatten Viceroyalty, Announcement and Reception of the 3 June Plan, 31 May – 7 July 1947, vol. 11, London: HMSO, 1982

The Mountbatten Viceroyalty: Princes, Partition and Independence, 8 July – 15 Aug. 1947, vol. 12, London: HMSO, 1983

Maxwell, Neville, *India, Nagas and the North-east*, London: Minority Rights Group, 1980

Mayaram, Shail, 'Speech, Silence and the Making of Partition Violence in Mewat', in Shahid Amin and Dipesh Chakrabarty (eds), *Subaltern Studies IX Writings on South Asian History and Society*, New Delhi: Oxford University Press, 1996, pp. 126–65

Mehrotra, S. R., 'The Congress and the Partition of India', in C. H. Philips and M. D. Wainwright (eds), *The Partition of India*, London: George Allen and Unwin, 1970

Mehta, Asoka, Achut Patwardhan, *The Communal Triangle in India*, Allahabad: Kitabistan, 1942

Mehta, Uday Singh, 'The Gujarat Genocide: A Sociological Appraisal', in Asghar Ali Engineer (ed.), *The Gujarat Carnage*, New Delhi: Longman, 2003, pp. 186–97

'The Making of the Indian Constitution and Comparative Experience', paper presented to a workshop on 'The Indian Constitution after Fifty Years', School of Oriental and African Studies, London, 24 November 2000, pp. 1–16

Menon, Ritu, and Kamla Bhasin, *Borders and Boundaries. Women in India's Partition*, New Brunswick, NJ: Rutgers University Press, 1998

Minault, G., *The Khilafat Movement: Religious Symbolism and Political Mobilisation in India*, New York: Columbia University Press, 1982

Mitra, Subrata K., 'The Morality of Communal Politics: Paul Brass, Hindu–Muslim Conflict and the Indian State', *India Review* 2, 4 (October 2003), pp. 15–30

Momen, Humaira, *Muslim Politics in Bengal: A Study of the Krishak Praja Party and the Elections of 1937*, Dacca: Sunny House, 1972

Moon, Penderel, *Divide and Quit. An Eyewitness Account of the Partition of India*, New Delhi: Oxford University Press, 1998

Moore, R. J., *Churchill, Cripps and India, 1939–1945*, Oxford: Clarendon Press, 1979

The Crisis of Indian Unity, 1917–1940, Oxford University Press, 1974

Endgames of Empire: Studies of Britain's Indian Problem, New Delhi: Oxford University Press, 1988

Escape from Empire. The Attlee Government and the Indian Problem, Oxford University Press, 1982

Morgan, Kenneth O., *Labour in Power 1945–1951*, Oxford: Clarendon, 1984

Musharraf, Pervez, *In the Line of Fire: A Memoir*, London: Simon and Schuster, 2006

Nanda, B. R., 'The Tragedy and Triumph of Mahatma Gandhi', in Amrik Singh (ed.), *The Partition in Retrospect*, New Delhi: Anamika Publications, 2000, pp. 48–60

Nandy, Ashis, *At the Edge of Psychology: Essays in Politics and Culture*, Delhi: Oxford University Press, 1980

The Intimate Enemy: Loss and Recovery of Self under Colonialism, Delhi: Oxford University Press, 1983

Nasr, Vali, 'National Identities and India–Pakistan Conflict', in T. V. Paul (ed.), *The India–Pakistan Conflict: An Enduring Rivalry*, Cambridge University Press, 2005

Nayer, Baldev Raj, *Minority Politics in Punjab*, Princeton University Press, 1966

Nevile, Pran, *Lahore: A Sentimental Journey*, New Delhi: Allied Publishers, 1993

O'Leary, B., 'Analysing Partition: Definition, Classification and Explanation', *Political Geography* 26, 8 (2007), pp. 886–908

Page, David, *Prelude to Partition: The Indian Muslims and the Imperial System of Control, 1920–1932*, Cambridge University Press, 1985

Pandey, Gyanendra, 'Citizenship and Difference: The Muslim Question in India', in Mushirul Hasan and Nariaki Nakazato (eds), *The Unfinished Agenda: Nation Building in South Asia*, New Delhi: Manohar, 2001, pp. 101–29

The Construction of Communalism in North India, Delhi: Oxford University Press, 1990
'In Defence of a Fragment. Writing about Hindu–Muslim Riots in India today', *Economic and Political Weekly* 26 nos. 11–12 (March 1991), pp. 559–72
Remembering Partition. Violence, Nationalism and History in India, Cambridge University Press, 2001
Panikkar, K. N., 'The Agony of Gujarat', in Asghar Ali Engineer (ed.), *The Gujarat Carnage*, New Delhi: Longman, 2003, pp. 24–47
Parekh, Bhikhu, 'Ethnocentricity of the Nationalist Discourse', *Nations and Nationalism* 1, 1 (1995), pp. 25–52
Patel, S., 'On the Discourse of Communalism', in T. V. Sathyamurthy (ed.), *Nation, Religion, Caste, Gender and Culture in Contemporary India*, vol. 3, Delhi: Oxford University Press, 1999, pp. 145–79
Paul, T. V. (ed.), *The India–Pakistan Conflict: An Enduring Rivalry*, Cambridge University Press, 2005
Potter, D. C., 'Manpower Shortages and the End of Colonialism: The Case of the Indian Civil Service', *Modern Asian Studies* 7 (1973), pp. 47–73
Prasad, Bimal, 'Jawaharlal Nehru and Partition', in Amrik Singh (ed.), *The Partition in Retrospect*, New Delhi: Animika Publishers, 2000, pp. 24–77
Prasad, Rajendra, *India Divided*, 3rd edn, Bombay: Hind Kitabs, 1947
Pritam, Amrita, *The Skeleton*, translated by Khushwant Singh, London: Oriental UP, 1987
Qureshi, Ishtiaq Hussain, *The Muslim Community of the Indo-Pakistan Subcontinent (610–1947): A Brief Historical Analysis*, 2nd edn, Karachi: Ma'aref, 1977
Rahman, Md. Habibur, 'Bhasa Andalan (Language Movement) and the Beginning of the Break-up of Pakistan', *Indo-British Review* 17 (1989), pp. 175–91
Rahman, S., *Why Pakistan?* Lahore: Islamic Book Service, 1946
Rahman, Tariq, *Language, Politics in Pakistan*, Karachi: Oxford University Press, 1996
Rai, S. M., *Partition of Punjab*, Bombay: Asia Publishing House, 1965
Punjab since Partition, Delhi: Durga Publications, 1986
Randhawa, M. S., *Out of the Ashes. An Account of the Rehabilitation of Refugees from West Pakistan in Rural Areas of East Punjab*, Chandigarh: Public Relations Department, Punjab, 1954
Rashid, Harun-or, *The Foreshadowing of Bangladesh. Bengal Muslim League and Muslim Politics 1936–1947*, Dhaka: Asiatic Society of Bangladesh, 1987
Raychaudhuri, Tapan, 'Shadows of the Swastika: Historical Perspectives on the Politics of Hindu Communalism', *Modern Asian Studies* 34, 2 (May 2000), pp. 259–79
Rizvi, Gowher, *Linlithgow and India: A Study of British Policy and the Political Impasse in India, 1936–1943*, London: Royal Historical Society, 1978
Roberts, Andrew, *Eminent Churchillians*, London: Weidenfeld and Nicolson, 1994
Robinson, Francis, 'Islam and Muslim Separatism', in David Taylor and Malcolm Yapp (eds), *Political Identity in South Asia*, London: Curzon Press, 1979, pp. 78–112
Separatism among Indian Muslims: The Politics of the United Provinces' Muslims 1860–1923, Cambridge University Press, 1974

Roy, Asim, 'The High Politics of India's Partition. The Revisionist Perspective', in Mushirul Hasan (ed.), *India's Partition: Process, Strategy and Mobilization*, Delhi: Oxford University Press, 1993, pp. 101–31

Roy, O., *Globalised Islam: The Search for a New Ummah*, London: C. Hurst, 2004

Roy, Tathagata, *My People Uprooted: A Saga of Hindus of East Bengal*, Kolkata: Ratna Prakashan, 2001

Samad, Yunas, *A Nation in Turmoil: Nationalism and Ethnicity in Pakistan, 1937–1958*, New Delhi: Sage, 1995

'Pakistan from Minority Rights to Majoritarianism', in Gyanendra Pandey and Yunas Samad, *Fault Lines of Nationhood, Cross-Border Talks*, New Delhi: Lotus, 2007, pp. 67–138

'Pakistan or Punjabistan: Crisis of National Identity', in Gurharpal Singh and Ian Talbot (eds), *Punjabi Identity: Continuity and Change*, New Delhi: Manohar, 1996, pp. 61–87

Samaddar, Ranabir, *The Politics of Dialogue: Living under the Geopolitical Histories of War and Peace*, Aldershot: Ashgate, 2004

and Helmut Reifeld, *Peace as Process: Reconciliation and Conflict Resolution in South Asia*, New Delhi: Manohar, 2001

Sambanis, N., 'Partition as a Solution to Ethnic War: An Empirical Critique of the Theoretical Literature', *World Politics* 52 (2000), pp. 437–83

Sanyal, Jhuma, *Making of a New Space: Refugees in West Bengal*, Kolkata: Ratna Prakashan, 2003

Sarila, Narendra Singh, *The Shadow of the Great Game: The Untold Story of India's Partition*, New Delhi: HarperCollins, 2005

Sarkar, Sumit, *Modern India 1885–1947*, Delhi: Macmillan, 1985

Sathyamurthy, T. V., 'The State of Debate on Indian Nationalism', 25th Millennium Anniversary paper (unpublished), October 1996, pp. 1–30.

Sayeed, Khalid bin, *Pakistan: The Formative Phase 1857–1948*, Oxford University Press, 1968

Schendel, Willem van, *The Bengal Borderland: Beyond State and Nation in South Asia*, London: Anthem Press, 2005

'The Wagha Syndrome: Territorial Roots of Contemporary Violence in South Asia', in Amrita Basu and Sirupa Roy (eds), *Violence and Democracy in India*, London: Seagull, 2007

Schofield, Victoria, *Kashmir in Conflict: India, Pakistan and the Unending War*, London: I. B. Taurus, 2003

(ed.), *Old Roads, New Highways: Fifty Years of Pakistan*, Karachi: Oxford University Press, 1997

Seetal, Sohan Singh, *Punjab da Ujaarha (Tragedy of Punjab)*, n.p.: Mattar Sher Singh Kharan Singh, 1948

Sen, Shila, *Muslim Politics in Bengal 1937–47*, New Delhi: Impex India, 1976

Settar, S., and Indira B. Gupta, *Pangs of Partition*, 2 vols, New Delhi: Manohar, 2002

Shaikh, Farzana, *Community and Consensus in Islam: Muslim Representation in Colonial India, 1860–1947*, Cambridge University Press, 1989

Sherwani, Latif Ahmed, *The Partition of India and Mountbatten*, Karachi: Council for Pakistan Studies, 1968

Shibutani, Tamotsu, and Kian M. Kwan, *Ethnic Stratification: A Comparative Approach*, New York: Macmillan, 1965

Shirin, M., *Zulmat-e-Neem Roze*, Karachi: no pub., 1990

Shorie, Arun, Jay Dubashi, Ram Swarup and Sita Ram Goel, *Hindu Temples: What Happened to Them (A Preliminary Survey)*, New Delhi: Voice of India, 1990

Siddiqa, Ayesha, *Military Inc.: Inside Pakistan's Military Economy*, London: Pluto, 2007

Singh, Anita Inder, *The Origins of the Partition of India, 1936–1947*, New Delhi: Oxford University Press, 1987

Singh, Darbara, *The Punjab Tragedy 1947*, Amritsar: Steno House Agency, 1949

Singh, Giani Partap, *Pakistani Ghallughara*, Ludhiana: Lahore Bookshop, 1948

Singh, Gopal, 'The Transfer of Power and the Sikh Question', *Indo-British Review* 17 (1989), pp. 52–62

Singh, Gurharpal, 'Beyond Punjabi Romanticism', *Seminar* 513 (November 2006), pp. 17–21

  Ethnic Conflict in India: A Case-Study of Punjab, Basingstoke: Palgrave, 2000

  'The Indo-Pakistan Summit: Hope for Kashmir?', *OpenDemocracy* (16 February 2004), www.opendemocracy.net/conflict-india_pakistan/article_1738.jsp.

  'On the Nuclear Precipice: India, Pakistan and the Kashmir Crisis', *OpenDemocracy*, (6 August 2002), www.opendemocracy.net/conflict-india_pakistan/article_194.jsp.

  'The Partition of India in a Comparative Perspective: A Long Term View', in Ian Talbot and Gurharpal Singh (eds), *Region and Partition: Bengal, Punjab and the Partition of the Subcontinent*, Karachi: Oxford University Press, 1999, pp. 95–116

  'Re-examining Centre–State Relations in India since 1947', inaugural lecture, 15 May 2000, University of Hull, unpublished, pp. 1–34

  'Resizing and Reshaping the State: Indian from Partition to Present', in Brendan O'Leary, Ian S. Lustick and Thomas Callaghy (eds), *Rightsizing the State: The Politics of Moving Borders*, Oxford University Press, 2001, pp. 138–67

  'State and Religious Diversity: Reflections on Post-1947 India', *Totalitarian Movements and Political Religions*, 5, 2 (Autumn 2004), pp. 205–25

Singh, Khushdeva, *Love Is Stronger than Hate. A Remembrance of 1947*, Patiala: Guru Nanak Mission, 1973

Singh, Khushwant, 'Last Days in Lahore. From the Brittle Security of an Elite Rooftop, a View of a City Burning', *Outlook* (Delhi) 28 May 1997

Singh, Kirpal, *The Partition of the Punjab*, Patiala: Punjabi University, 1989

Singh, Rajendra, *The Military Evacuation Organisation 1947–8*, New Delhi: Government of India Press, 1962

Singh, Trilok, *Land Resettlement Manual for Displaced Persons in Punjab and PEPSU*, Simla: Controller of Printing and Stationery, 1951

Sipe, K. P., 'Karachi's Refugee Crisis: The Political, Economic and Social Consequences of Partition Related Migration', unpublished Ph.D. thesis, Duke University, 1976

Smith, A. D., *Chosen People: Sacred Sources of National Identity*, Oxford University Press, 2000

The Ethnic Revival in the Modern World, Cambridge University Press, 1981

Swami, P., *India, Pakistan and the Secret Jihad: The Covert War in Kashmir, 1947–2004*, New York: Routledge, 2007

Synnott, Hilary, *The Causes and Consequences of South Asia's Nuclear Test*, Aldephi Papers 332, Oxford University Press, 1999

Taj-ul-Islam, Hashmi, 'Peasant Nationalism and the Politics of Partition: The Class-Communal Symbiosis in East Bengal, 1940–7', in Ian Talbot and Gurharpal Singh (eds), *Region and Partition: Bengal, Punjab and the Partition of the Subcontinent*, Karachi: Oxford University Press, 2000, pp. 1–41

Talbot, Ian, 'Back to the Future? The Punjab Unionist Model of Consociational Democracy for Contemporary India and Pakistan', *International Journal of Punjab Studies* 3, 1 (January–June 1996), pp. 65–75

  Divided Cities. Partition and Its Aftermath in Lahore and Amritsar 1947–1957, Karachi: Oxford University Press, 2006

  Freedom's Cry. The Popular Dimension in the Pakistan Movement and Partition Experience in North-West India, Karachi: Oxford University Press, 1996

  India and Pakistan, London: Arnold, 2000

  Khizr Tiwana the Punjab Unionist Party and the Partition of India: The Subcontinent Divided: A New Beginning, Karachi: Oxford University Press, 2002

  Pakistan. A Modern History, London: Hurst, 1998

  Punjab and the Raj, 1849–1947, Delhi: Manohar, 1988

  'The 1947 Violence in Punjab', in Ian Talbot (ed.), *The Deadly Embrace: Religion, Politics and Violence in India and Pakistan, 1947–2002*, Karachi: Oxford University Press, 2007 pp. 1–15

Talbot, Ian, and Gurharpal Singh (eds), *Region and Partition. Bengal, Punjab and the Partition of the Subcontinent*, Karachi: Oxford University Press, 2000

Talbot, Ian (ed.), and Darshan Singh Tatla, *Epicentre of Violence. Partition Voices and Memories from Amritsar*, Delhi: Permanent Black, 2006

Talbott, Strobe, *Engaging India: Diplomacy, Democracy and the Bomb*, Washington, DC: Brookings Institute, 2004

Talib, G. S. (compiler), *Muslim League Attack on Sikhs and Hindus in the Punjab, 1947*, Allahabad Shiromani Gurdwara Parbandhak Committee: Law Journal Press, 1950

Tan, T. Y., 'Prelude to Partition: Sikh Responses to the Demand for Pakistan 1940–47', *International Journal of Punjab Studies*, 1, 2 (October 1996), pp. 167–95

  and Gyanesh Kudaisya, *The Aftermath of Partition in South Asia*, London: Routledge, 2000

Tanwar, Raghuvendra, *Reporting the Partition of Punjab. Press, Public and Other Opinions*, New Delhi: Manohar, 2006

Taylor, David, and Malcolm Yapp (eds), *Political Identity in South Asia*, London: Curzon Press, 1979

Thandi, Shinder Singh, 'Counterinsurgency and Political Violence in Punjab', in Gurharpal Singh and Ian Talbot (eds), *Punjabi Identity: Continuity and Change*, New Delhi: Manohar, 1996

Thornton, T. P., 'Pakistan: Fifty Years of Insecurity', in Selig S. Harrison, Paul H. Kreisberg and Dennis Kux (eds), *India and Pakistan: The First Fifty Years*, Cambridge University Press, 1999

Tomlinson, B. R., *The Political Economy of the Raj, 1914–47: The Economics of Decolonisation in India*, London: Macmillan, 1979

Tuker, Francis, *While Memory Serves: The Last Two Years of British Rule in India*, London: Cassell, 1950

Turner, John, *Filming History: The Memoirs of John Turner Newsreel Cameraman*, London: British Universities Film and Video Council, 2001

Varshney, A., *Ethnic Conflict and Civic Life. Hindus and Muslims in India*, New Haven, CT: Yale University Press, 2002

Virdee, P., 'Partition and Locality: Case Studies of the Impact of Partition and Its Aftermath in the Punjab Region, 1947–61', unpublished Ph.D. thesis, Coventry University, 2005

Vohra, Sahdev, *Lahore, Loved, Lost and Thereafter*, Delhi: Indus Publishers' Distributors, 2004

Wallimann, I., and M. N. Dobkowski (eds), *Genocide and the Modern Age. Etiology and Case Studies of Mass Death*, New York: Greenwood, 1987

Widmalm, Sten, *Kashmir in Comparative Perspective: Democracy and Violent Separatism in India*, Karachi: Oxford University Press, 2006

Wolpert, S., *Shameful Flight. The Last Years of the British Empire in India*, New York: Oxford University Press, 2006

Zafar, Rukhsana (compiler), *Disturbances in the Punjab 1947*, Islamabad: National Documentation Centre, 1995

Zamindar, Vazira Fazila-Yacoobali, *The Long Partition and the Making of Modern South Asia: Refugees, Boundaries, Histories*, New York: Columbia University Press, 2007

Ziegler, P., *Mountbatten: The Official Biography*, London: Collins, 1985

Zins, Max Jean, 'The Vivisection of India: The Political Usage of Carnage in the Era of Citizen-Massacres', in Mushirul Hasan and Nariaki Nakazato (eds), *The Unfinished Agenda: Nation-Building in South Asia*, New Delhi: Manohar, 2001, pp. 49–79

Index